Law and the Brontës

Also by Ian Ward

LAW AND LITERATURE: Possibilities and Perspectives

SHAKESPEARE AND THE LAW

A STATE OF MIND? The English Constitution and the Popular Imagination

THE ENGLISH CONSTITUTION: Myths and Realities

LAW, TEXT, TERROR

Law and the Brontës

Ian Ward
Professor of Law, Newcastle University, UK

© Ian Ward 2012

All rights reserved. No reproduction, copy or transmission of this publication may be made without written permission.

No portion of this publication may be reproduced, copied or transmitted save with written permission or in accordance with the provisions of the Copyright, Designs and Patents Act 1988, or under the terms of any licence permitting limited copying issued by the Copyright Licensing Agency, Saffron House, 6–10 Kirby Street, London EC1N 8TS.

Any person who does any unauthorized act in relation to this publication may be liable to criminal prosecution and civil claims for damages.

The author has asserted his right to be identified as the author of this work in accordance with the Copyright, Designs and Patents Act 1988.

First published 2012 by
PALGRAVE MACMILLAN

Palgrave Macmillan in the UK is an imprint of Macmillan Publishers Limited, registered in England, company number 785998, of Houndmills, Basingstoke, Hampshire RG21 6XS.

Palgrave Macmillan in the US is a division of St Martin's Press LLC, 175 Fifth Avenue, New York, NY 10010.

Palgrave Macmillan is the global academic imprint of the above companies and has companies and representatives throughout the world.

Palgrave® and Macmillan® are registered trademarks in the United States, the United Kingdom, Europe and other countries.

ISBN 978–0–230–25147–2

This book is printed on paper suitable for recycling and made from fully managed and sustained forest sources. Logging, pulping and manufacturing processes are expected to conform to the environmental regulations of the country of origin.

A catalogue record for this book is available from the British Library.

A catalog record for this book is available from the Library of Congress.

10 9 8 7 6 5 4 3 2 1
21 20 19 18 17 16 15 14 13 12

Printed and bound in the United States of America

Contents

Acknowledgements   vi

Introduction: The Brontë Cases   1
1   *Huntingdon v Huntingdon*   25
2   Heathcliff's Case   48
3   The Rochester Wives   71
4   The State and Shirley Keeldar   96
Conclusion: The Trials of Lucy Snowe   122

Notes   145
Bibliography   175
Index   191

Acknowledgements

As is so often the case, I owe debts of gratitude to many colleagues, friends and family, all of whom have helped in different ways to make the writing of *Law and the Brontës* such a rewarding experience. On a more formal note I should first express my thanks to various editors and publishers for permission to republish material that previously appeared in their journals. A version of Chapter 1 first appeared in volume 49 of *Criticism*, and is republished with kind permission of the Wesleyan University Press. An earlier version of Chapter 3 was first published in volume 2 of *Law and Humanities*. Thanks are due to Paul Raffield and Richard Hart for permission to republish. And finally, to Heinz Antor for permission to reproduce material in Chapter 4 which was first published in volume 19 of *Anglistik*. During the last couple of years I have presented a series of papers on various aspects of law and the Brontës; to the Newcastle University Political Philosophy group; to an AIDEL symposium at the University of Verona; and at the Centre for Advanced Studies at the Ludwig Maximilians University in Munich, where I was very kindly invited to assume a visiting fellowship in the summer of 2010. I learned much on each occasion, and my thanks to all who attended and offered advice. The greatest debt, however, is owed to my family, to Clare, to Ross and to Freya; for their patience, their support and for the love they bring.

Introduction: The Brontë Cases

In August 1838 John Stuart Mill published an essay simply entitled 'Bentham' in the *London and Westminster Review*. As perhaps the leading contemporary utilitarian, his choice of subject was in no way surprising. Bentham, he declared at the outset, was one of 'two great seminal minds of England' in his 'age'. He was the 'great subversive', the first to 'speak disrespectfully' of the British constitution. For this he was to be praised. The same should be said of his organisational capacity. Having 'found the philosophy of law a chaos', Mill advised, Bentham had 'left it a science'. He expelled 'mysticism' and made the law make sense (Mill, 1987, pp. 132–4, 158, 162). But there was also a problem with Bentham. He was emotionally 'inadequate':

> In many of the most natural and strongest feelings of human nature he had no sympathy; from many of its graver experiences he was altogether cut off; and the faculty by which one mind understands a mind different from oneself, and throws itself into feelings of that other mind, was denied him by his deficiency of Imagination.
>
> (Mill, 1987, p. 148)

Bentham's failings were evident, finally, in his dislike of poets. Mill, by way of contrast, liked poets. He particularly liked Wordsworth, and also Coleridge.[1] Nineteenth months after publishing his essay on Bentham, Mill published a companion piece, again in the *London and Westminster Review*. It was entitled, just as simply, 'Coleridge'. Coleridge was the second of the 'great seminal minds' of his 'age'.

Compared to Bentham, he 'saw so much farther into the complexities of the human intellect and feelings' (Mill, 1987, p. 178). Much of the essay, in truth, addressed Coleridge's later writings on the established Church. Mill's anti-clerical tenor opened into a broader defence of utility against the metaphysics of theology, and by implication natural law and justice. On such matters of politics and political economy Coleridge was an 'arrant driveller' (Mill, 1987, p. 217). But he did at least understand how the human mind worked, and how its heart beat. Each and 'every Englishman', Mill concluded, 'of the present day is by implication either a Benthamite or a Coleridgean'; but not, by further implication, both (Mill, 1987, p. 180).

Mill's essays on Bentham and Coleridge have assumed a modest position in his prodigious canon. But they reveal much, most obviously about mid-Victorian perceptions of the relation and apparent dislocation of legal and literary thought. The tone is very obviously one of regret. Lawyers might be able to interpret statutes, to articulate, even resolve, legal disputes. But in terms of justice understood as an aesthetic and emotional experience they were deficient. Poets, conversely, whilst they might be able to compensate for the latter, could not be trusted to govern. Not for Mill the pleasing image of the poet as 'unacknowledged legislator'. The realms of sense and sensibility, like those of science and art, reason and revelation, took the form of polarities. If there was to be accommodation, Mill implied, it would not come in the form of some kind of Carlylean super-hero. It would come through the education of humanity, and the liberation of the mind.

Eight years after Mill published 'Bentham', Currer, Ellis and Acton Bell published a collection of *Poems*. One of the poems, entitled 'To Imagination', engaged precisely the same polarity:

> Reason, indeed, may oft complain
>   For Nature's sad reality,
> And tell the suffering heart how vain
>   Its cherished dreams must always be;
> And Truth may rudely trample down
>   The flowers of Fancy, newly-blown
>
> But, thou art ever there, to bring
>   The hovering vision back, and breathe

> New glories o'er the blighted spring,
>   And call a lovelier Life from Death,
> And whisper, with a voice divine,
>   Of real worlds, as bright as thine.
>
> (Brontë, 1992, pp. 19–20)

'To Imagination' was written, of course, by Emily Brontë. But the sentiment was not hers alone. A year later, in response to G.H. Lewes's review of *Jane Eyre*, sister Charlotte refuted the insinuation that she had strayed too 'far from the ground of experience' by invoking precisely the same idea. The 'imagination is a strong, restless faculty', she replied, unrepentant, 'which claims to be heard and exercised' (Gaskell, 1997, p. 255).[2] The faculty of reason is never secure from the claims of imagination; and nor should it be.

We will revisit the sentiments written into Emily poem and Charlotte's riposte time and again in the chapters that follow. We will do so because this book is about this schism, and more particularly still, how it has continued to define the mutual relation, in varying degrees distant and detached, between the disciplines of literature, history and jurisprudence. For whilst Mill might have hoped, maybe with some justification, for a closing of the gap between the Benthamites and the Coleridgeans, the evolution of jurisprudence over the last century and half tells a rather different story. Lawyers and poets have by and large continued to inhabit separate intellectual spheres. In recent years, however, as we shall see, there has been a movement within the academy to somehow cut across these margins, to persuade the Benthamites to think a bit more about literature, and to convince the Coleridgeans that the kind of things the Benthamites prefer to do might have a poetic resonance. It is with this elusive prospect in mind that the following chapters will unfold. A closer focus will be provided by a particular concentration on literature and law in mid-nineteenth-century England, in what is commonly – if sometimes controversially – termed the Victorian age.

A still sharper focus is provided by a close concentration on one set of texts, the novels of the Brontë sisters. At first glance it does not appear that the Brontë sisters had much to say about law. Occasional allusions to questions of law and justice can be discerned on the surface of their novels. But there is not that much direct discussion of legal issues, certainly not in comparison with contemporary canons of 'law and literature', such as *Bleak House* or *Pickwick Papers* or *Mary Barton*. But look below the surface, and the picture is rather different. At first glance, then, it is tempting to suppose that the Brontë sisters had rather more in common with Coleridge than Bentham. But there again, as we shall see, the picture is not really so clear. The supposition that 'every' man was either a Benthamite or a Coleridgean was intended to be arresting. We are left to contemplate whether the same should be expected of every woman.

The strategies of law and literature

One of the defining features of legal scholarship in recent decades has been a growing enthusiasm for crossing disciplinary boundaries. 'Law and' movements abound. Eschewing in the main an inherited disposition towards the doctrinal and the formal, lawyers are increasingly prepared to embrace the insights of economics, history, sociology, literature and so on (Leff, 1978). This latter species of interdisciplinarity has recently morphed into a potentially broader, if slightly vaguer, 'law and humanities' movement (Baron, 1999, pp. 1071–3; Petch, 2007, pp. 376, 380). Despite the prospective loss of disciplinary precision, this transmutation is an important concession to the fact that 'law and literature' is a potentially limiting endeavour (Seaton, 1999). The investigation of the relation between the disciplines of law and literature cannot, except in the most abstract of forms, be readily detached from considerations of history, culture, society, gender and so on. Once one boundary is crossed, it becomes increasingly obvious that crossing some more is neither too difficult nor too dangerous. In fact it is rather exciting.

Advocates of law and literature/humanities scholarship, particularly those who come from within the legal academy, commonly identify three particular conceptual virtues, and a rather more prosaic one. The latter addresses the more parochial issue of legal pedagogy. It is often remarked that the peculiarity of 'law and literature' is that it is far more concerned with what happens in the classroom than what happens in the courtroom. There is an engaging quality to literature which the law, it is equally often observed, seems to lack. Otherwise sustained by a rigorous diet of 'facts, facts, facts', law students, it is time and again reported, find exposure to literature both liberating and stimulating (Gemmette, 1989; Dunlop, 1991; Ward, 1993; Turner, 1995).

As to the first conceptual virtue, it is commonly argued that an engagement with literature and literary theory informs the lawyer as to the necessarily textual and aesthetic nature of their enterprise. Writing in 1983, Robert Cover proclaimed that 'No set of legal institutions or prescriptions exists apart from the narratives that locate it and give it meaning' (Cover, 1983, p. 4). 'All law', as Kieran Dolin has more recently affirmed, 'is inevitably a matter of language' (Dolin, 2007, p. 2).[3] This can come as a particular shock to the doctrinal lawyer, who had otherwise supposed that law is only about reading statutes and second-guessing how judges might decide cases. The fact that law might be a textual expression opens up collateral concerns alternately exciting and terrifying to lawyers of varying disposition. It means, for one, that a legal text is interpretable, perhaps even infinitely so.[4] It insinuates the possibility that the better lawyer might be the lawyer who has spent a little less time reading cases, and a little more time reading Coleridge.

A second conceptual virtue is the capacity for literature to reinvest an otherwise dormant ethical sensitivity. We will soon encounter some of the defining jurisprudential debates of the nineteenth century between the natural lawyers and the positivists; debates that not only shaped contemporary perceptions of the relation between law and justice, but which have also shaped modern perceptions. The ultimate triumph of the positivists, consolidated through much of the twentieth century, saw a significant marginalisation of ethics in legal scholarship. Here the fashioning of what Richard Weisberg terms 'poethical' jurisprudence represents a credible 'strategy' for the reinvestment of ethics in the law (Weisberg, 1992). Martha Nussbaum has made the same case for a consciously 'poetic' jurisprudence written in terms not of statutes and cases, but of 'imagination, inclusion, sympathy and voice' (Nussbaum, 1995, pp. 118–19).[5] Nussbaum's recommendation gestures towards a collateral virtue; that literature not only invites deeper ethical consideration of legal issues, but also their necessarily political complement. The line between what is supposedly ethical but is in practice intensely political is not a sharp one; as a generation of feminist lawyers have repeatedly affirmed.

The third conceptual virtue is more obviously historical. It suggests that our present comprehension of law is founded on its past experiences. If we want to know today how the criminal law deals with domestic abuse, we need to know how that law was shaped, as a matter of history as well as culture and indeed language. Domestic abuse is merely an example, of course; but it is one to which we shall return frequently in subsequent chapters. Another is marriage.[6] The Brontës wrote a great deal about both, and in so doing, it can be argued, did much to shape contemporary and indeed later attitudes. Literature, in this way, serves to provide a vital supplementary jurisprudential chronicle; taking advantage of what George Eliot termed its 'rare, precious quality of truthfulness' (Eliot, 2008, p. 177). It is certainly true that the most convincing law and literature scholarship is that which evidences a deeper awareness of historical context. There is, moreover, an immediate resonance here with strategies advocated by literary historicists such as Louis Montrose, Stephen Greenblatt and most recently James Chandler. In its simplest form, following Montrose's arresting injunction, such a methodology is concerned with 'the historicity of texts and the textuality of history' (Montrose, 1989, p. 20). It is also concerned with the constitutive role of different audiences in 'negotiating' and 'fashioning' meaning (Greenblatt, 1988, pp. 1–20). In this way a text has no existence outside of its own ever-changing historical narrative; a point reinforced by Chandler in his extended study of Shelley's sonnet 'England in 1819' (Chandler, 1998, pp. xv, 4–6).

In this sense *Law and the Brontës* is unapologetically historicist. It engages with what Lisa Surridge terms the 'cultural moment' (Surridge, 2005, p. 4). It is concerned with moments of writing and moments of reception. We will examine the particular lures of authorial fetish in due course. The Brontë 'myth' is perhaps second only to the Shakespeare 'myth'. The historicist, of course, is peculiarly sensitive to the attendant hazards of meta-histories. Lawyers like cases. The common law prides itself upon being created by cases. The idea that broad principles might be extrapolated from particular cases holds no fear. The literary historicist, however, is rather more troubled by the tendency to presume too much of the supposedly 'exemplary' case (Chandler, 1998, pp. 39–40). There is in the idea of the case an inherent conceptual as well as terminological ambiguity, and we must remain sensitive to it. History pretends to be fixed. Historicity demurs.

Finally, it must be admitted that much of what has gone before appears to be rather skewed. I write as a member of the legal academy. The 'law and literature' movement has been nurtured, in the main, from within this academy (Petch, 2007, p. 362). Its commonly stated virtues tend to focus on how best to educate and sensitize law students, and this apparent insularity has attracted critical commentary from within and without the legal academy (Peters, 2005). To some degree such a prejudice is to be expected. Everyone writes from somewhere. But that is no reason for either complacency or insularity. As Margot Finn has recently argued, the case for literature scholars and students knowing rather more about the law is just as strong (Finn, 2002, p. 134).[7] Moreover, even if terminological opacity often seems to reinforce disciplinary particularity, literary and legal scholars are engaged in the same essential debates between those who prefer to focus on the integrity of texts and those who are persuaded that any text is constituted by its cultural and historical context.

The continuation of such disciplinary scepticism benefits no one.[8] Speaking to the particular lack of literary and legal engagement in the Victorian period, Finn deploys the metaphor of disciplinary ships passing in the night (Finn, 2002). Stephen Petch has more recently echoed the same measure of puzzlement and regret (Petch, 2007). This is peculiarly perverse for at least two reasons: first in the context of what Cora Kaplan terms our particular 'fascination with things Victorian', and second because any study of Victorian England is, as Michael Wolff observed, necessarily interdisciplinary (Kaplan, 2007, pp. 2–3; Wolff, 1964, pp. 59–60). Dickens is, of course, the exception; a towering figure in both the grander canon of English literature and the narrower canons of nineteenth-century literature and narrative jurisprudence. Dickens assumes a central position in Kieran Dolin's study of the relation between literature and contemporary debates regarding legal reform (Dolin, 1999, pp. 71–96). But otherwise, occasional essays on Austen or Browning or Melville aside, it is true that the nineteenth century is relatively under-represented in the 'law and literature' canon.[9] The Brontës, moreover, as we shall see, remain pretty much untouched.[10] The simple answer, or at least the answer most commonly assumed, is that the presence of law in nineteenth-century literature is rare. This may be so. But that does not preclude us looking for a narrative jurisprudence that might lie a little deeper beneath the surface.

Below the surface

At the beginning of her popular domestic manual, *Women of England*, published in 1838, Sarah Stickney Ellis advised that 'there is an appropriate sphere for women to move in, from which those of the middle class of England seldom deviate very widely'. This 'sphere', she added, 'has duties and occupations of its own, from which no woman can shrink without culpability and disgrace' (Ingham, 2006, p. 128).[11] Chief amongst these, as Coventry Patmore confirmed in his iconic poem, 'The Angel in the House', is the woman's duty to 'please' her husband (Dolin, 2007, p. 121). Women were intended to stay home, raise children and bake.[12] The 'nation's moral worth', as Ellis reiterated in *Women of England*, depended on women 'keeping' precisely these responsibilities (Newton, 1985, p. 3). Men occupied a very different sphere, as Sarah Lewis confirmed in her pointedly entitled *Women's Mission*:

> Let men enjoy in peace and triumph the intellectual kingdom which is theirs, and which, doubtless, was intended for them; let us participate in its privileges without desiring to share its domination. The moral world is ours – ours by position; ours by qualification, ours by the very indication of God himself.
> (Sarah Lewis quoted in Tosh, 1999, p. 47)

The thought that God preferred women to stay at home and refrain from thinking too much was not uncommon. Scripture masked prejudice. The 'household hearth', as Ellis confirmed in another of her many manuals *The Young Lady's Reader*, possessed an 'inviolable sanctity' (Chase and Levenson, 2000, p. 64). So did morality, and poetic whimsy. Ruskin alluded to the 'sweet orderings' of nature, an aspersion which segued readily with attendant notions of a distinctly female 'cult of sensibility' (Gilbert and Gubar, 2000, p. 24). Others, such as Frances Power Cobbe, ridiculed the whimsy:

> Themis, when she presides at the domestic hearth, doffs her wig and allows herself to be swayed by poetical, not to say, romantic considerations. We are rarely allowed in debating it to examine accurately the theory of conjugal justice. We are called upon rather to contemplate the beautiful ideal of absolute union of heart, life and purse which the law has provided for and which it alone deigns to recognise.
> (Cobbe quoted in Hamilton, 1995, pp. 112–13)

Even so, the home and the institution of marriage mattered to Victorians with an intensity that we might today find peculiar. As lawyer, judge and writer Fitzjames Stephen[13] observed, the mid-Victorians made 'domestic happiness' the 'object of idolatry'; so much so that John Bull might so relish his 'comfort' that he would 'lose the power and the wish to live for other than fireside purposes' (Chase and Levenson, 2000, pp. 215–16).[14]

Whilst many women eagerly read the countless manuals presented by the likes of Ellis and Lewis, and just as eagerly subscribed to the attendant cults of 'separate spheres' and sensibility, by the middle of the century others were contemplating dissent. Ideas seeded by the likes of Mary Wollstonecraft or Mary Hays a generation earlier had begun to take root, finding further expression in the writings of Harriet Martineau, Mona Caird and Frances Power Cobbe; ideas not just about political or suffrage rights, but about rights to education, reforms to associated areas of matrimonial and property law, about the place of women within and without the family home (Hamilton, 2001). A nascent feminist 'consciousness' could be discerned, at the centre of which can be located attendant debates regarding female, and indeed male, sexuality.[15] As the century progressed an identifiable 'woman question' became the subject of intense interest, so much so that Cobbe would later observe, with a neat irony, that 'of all theories concerning women, none is more curious than the theory that it is needful to make a theory about them'.[16]

Modern contemplation of this 'question' is very often set alongside a rather broader debate about literature and social reform in mid-nineteenth-century England.[17] Here again it was the thought that the present order was not necessarily a natural order, that maybe the will of God, if such existed, might not be so readily comprehended, that exercised the educated Victorian mind. It drove Carlyle's rage, Ruskin's melancholia and Newman's resignation.[18] Borrowing from Carlyle, this is commonly termed the 'condition of England' debate, and has perhaps inevitably nurtured its own particular literary canon; much of which, following the lead of Raymond Williams has tended to move closely around the industrial context of mid-Victorian literature (Williams, 1963; Gilmour, 1993, pp. 1–16). We will consider this latter movement in greater detail in Chapter 4 in the context of Charlotte Brontë's almost incidental contribution, *Shirley*. Charlotte's principal concern, as we shall see, is really with the fate of the established Church. But larger fears attached to what Friedrich Engels termed the 'spirit of resistance' that haunted the broader literary consciousness of mid-nineteenth-century England (Ingham, 1996, p. 15).

The 'woman question' also assumes a necessary if elusive textual resonance, one principally concerned with the excavation of the female voice. The novel, and the female novelist, have jointly emerged as a principal site of feminist nineteenth-century literary criticism (Kaplan, 2007, pp. 38–40).[19] As Sandra Gilbert and Susan Gubar famously argued, in the matter not just of detecting individual voices but of tracing female conversation the value of the literary and epistolary text is patent.[20] The same argument is pressed by Kate Flint, who concludes that it was in the 'practice of reading' that women first began to imagine a 'sense of selfhood' (Flint, 1993, p. 330). Dramatic technological and commercial advances, allied with improved literacy rates, meant that more and more women were reading more and more novels.[21] Writing over a century ago, Margaret Oliphant noted the role that novels such as *Shirley* or *Jane Eyre* played in nurturing an emergent female state of 'mind' (Allott, 1974, p. 390).[22] Josephine Butler attested to the same, noting that the 'conspiracy of silence' that hitherto had shrouded female discourse 'forced us to create a literature of our own' (Hamilton, 1995, p. 9). In correspondence George Eliot anticipated precisely this, observing that we are 'imitative beings'. 'We cannot', she added, 'help being modified by the ideas that pass through out minds' (Flint, 2001, p. 18). It was, of course, precisely this that troubled so many male contemporaries. Women readers, W.R. Greg advised, are 'always impressionable', their 'feelings' too 'easily aroused' (Flint, 1993, p. 4). The importance of guided reading was strongly pressed. Stickney Ellis published *The Young Ladies' Reader* for this very purpose.[23] Medical science offered little reassurance. Reading the wrong kind of novel, it was advised, could lead to hysteria and any number of allied addictive and neurological pathologies. Metaphors of morbidity could be found scattered across literary and scientific reviews. Novel reading, the *Medical Critic* advised, satisfied a 'morbid craving for excitement' (Flint, 1993, p. 55). Ruskin agreed, averring that the 'best romance becomes dangerous' when it excites 'a morbid thirst' (Flint, 2001, p. 26).[24] And to many it seemed that a conspicuous number of such romances, including it might be said those of the Brontë sisters, aspired to do just that.

The idea that women read, and wrote, in certain ways has retained its influence in modern literary criticism. According to Nancy Armstrong, much of the fiction written by women was 'private' and intended to engage matters of 'sensibility' (Armstrong, 1987, pp. 28–9). The belief that women read in certain ways reinforced the assumption that women could only read and indeed write about certain things.[25] In his essay 'Currer Bell', published in 1857, E.S. Dallas suggested that women were peculiarly suited to writing about related matters of 'personal discourse and familiar narrative' (Showalter, 1977, p. 82). It is certainly true that this 'private fiction' tended to focus more urgently on associated matters of family, femininity and sexuality; the 'master-narrative' of the genre, as Ruth Perry terms it (Perry, 2004, pp. 7, 187). Such reflections, as we shall see, lie at the heart of each novel the Brontë sisters wrote.

And their readers, like those of Gaskell and Eliot and so many other writers, female and male, seemed to be especially keen to read about one particular institution, and one particular experience: that of marriage. As the century progressed associated debates regarding the merits and demerits of alternative ideas of marriage, consanguineous and companionate, became the subject of increasingly intense reflection; a process which was nurtured in considerable part by a literature which championed romantic affinity. There are lots of Brontë marriages, most of which clearly presume this reflective engagement. Some of these marriages, as we shall see, are happy. Many are not. It might be speculated that in presenting marriage in such terms the Brontës were casting a darker insinuation, one that presumed that their readers were as likely to identify with marital failure as with marital contentment. And in the background, and just occasionally the foreground, of each is the spectre of a legal regime that assumed that averting matrimonial failure depended less on promoting happiness than it did on securing patriarchal and institutional authority. We will revisit this regime shortly.

Of course it would be a mistake to assume that the emergent discourses of female sexuality and consciousness were necessarily supposed to challenge the established order.[26] Conduct books were clearly intended to nurture domestic conformity. Even novel reading, Ellis's *Reader* advised, if properly guided could promote the 'intercourse of friendship, and the communion of "mutual minds"' (Flint, 1993, pp. 101–3). But it is still true that this emergent female consciousness was as much shaped by adversity. Addressing the particular experience of spousal violence in mid-nineteenth-century England, Lisa

Surridge has recently argued that novels such as Anne Brontë's *The Tenant of Wildfell Hall* can be read as narratives of 'active resistance' to a culture of embedded jurisprudential misogyny. In this sense they can be interpreted as providing a form of 'public regulation' of private violence in a context where the common law appeared singularly reluctant to intrude (Surridge, 2005, pp. 4, 9–10, 86). Mary Poovey has reached the same conclusion, arguing that such novels transformed the female reader, and writer, 'from silent sufferer of private wrongs into an articulate spokesperson in the public sphere'. In doing so, these same narratives served to 'collapse the boundary between the private sphere, where injustices go unchecked, and the public domain, where laws are made and enforced by men' (Poovey, 1989, pp. 64–5, 81–2). Images of violence and constraint pervade the critical literature in pretty much the same way as they do the novels themselves. As a complement to their image of the madwoman in the attic, Gilbert and Gubar employed the metaphor of the 'sentence' as a 'weapon in a kind of metaphorical warfare' (Gilbert and Gubar, 2000, p. 52).

The same is true of associated metaphors of sublimation and subversion. Patricia Ingham presents the Brontë novels as 'subversive' critiques of mid-Victorian idylls of domesticity (Ingham, 1996, p. 30). Constance Harsh cites *Shirley* as an exemplar of precisely the same (Harsh, 1994, p. 30). John Sutherland comments on the 'modestly submerged' situation of the female Victorian novelist (Sutherland, 2006, p. 167). Patricia Meyer Spacks traces the 'subterranean challenge' presented in the female novel of the period (Spacks, 1975, p. 317). Perhaps the most striking allusion is found in Elaine Showalter's observation that the female writer sees more deeply below the surface of the text, so that the 'orthodox plot recedes, and another plot, hitherto submerged in the anonymity of the background stands out in bold relief like a thumbprint' (Showalter, 1975, p. 435). Adopting a similarly visual species of metaphor, Nancy Armstrong singles out the Brontës for their peculiar determination to 'represent' the 'unseen desires of women' (Armstrong, 1987, pp. 192, 195).

Neither the insight nor the metaphor are new. Writing towards the end of the nineteenth century, Margaret Oliphant adopted a subterranean metaphor suggesting that novels such as those written by the Brontës reveal what lies 'beneath the surface of life', giving hope to 'every woman' who had 'dropped out of sight' (Allott, 1974, pp. 390–1). Oliphant was acutely aware of the hazards concomitant to such a strategy. Sometimes just too much might be brought to public view. Dickens was altogether less troubled, his narrator in *Dombey and Son*, famously appealing for 'a good spirit who would take the house-tops off', so as to 'show a Christian people what dark shapes issue from amidst their homes' (Dickens, 2002, p. 702).[27] Whether or not properly benevolent, *Law and the Brontës* is written in this critical spirit. It seeks to excavate a subterranean literary jurisprudence through a close examination of one set of texts which enjoy an obvious if sometimes perplexing relation.[28] It is, ultimately, a study of various kinds of interconnected exclusions, literary and legal. It is about a set of novels that lie outside the presumptive canon of law and literature. It is about a textually inscribed jurisprudence that is evasive, obscure even. And it is about one category of people who, for reasons of gender alone, were denied legal personality and cast, in effect, outside the common law of England.

Inlaws and outlaws

Whilst the law likes to see itself as a reassuring presence, a constant in a sea of social and cultural change, few generations have been immune from debates about the efficacy of particular laws, about the possible injustices that law might be promoting, about the need perhaps for change and reform. It is true today, and it was true a century and a half ago. It has been suggested that the mid-nineteenth century marks the 'historical moment' at which a distinct feminist legal 'discourse', aligned with incipient movements for legal reform, including perhaps most obviously Brougham's Law Amendment Society founded in 1844, first took shape (Drakopoulou, 2007, pp. 331, 334–5). It is an arresting thought. But what shape did this discourse take? And what, more particularly, were the debates that concerned those who read the novels of the Brontës? We will take a look at the likely composition of the contemporary Brontë readership in due course. But for now we can broadly assume it to be middle-class, educated and reasonably well informed, perhaps weighted more towards the female. How prominent was the law in their lives and, more particularly perhaps, their consciousnesses?

At the more esoteric level, the mid-Victorian jurist spent his time engaged in a somewhat parochial variant of the 'condition of England' debate.[29] From within utilitarianism sprang legal positivism, the shape of which could be discerned in Jeremy Bentham's *Principles of Morals and Legislation* but which finds its definitive statement in his pupil John Austin's *Province of Jurisprudence Determined* published in 1832, the first sentence of which confirmed that laws 'properly so called, are commands' (Austin, 1995, p. 10). If law is properly enacted and enforceable it is valid. Natural law, the ready alternative, was swept aside. There were protests, of course, from the likes of Fitzjames Stephens. But the prospective mood was positivist, looking forward rather than back, championing liberty and utility over conservation and paternalism.[30] On a broader intellectual canvas it found famous expression in John Stuart Mill's *On Liberty*. However, the year 1832 is, of course, rather better known for the passage of the 'great' Reform Act. The 1832 Act was just one, admittedly the most famous, of a series of significant reforms in public and local governance. The Catholic Emancipation Act had passed just three years earlier, and the New Poor Law Act passed just two years later, to be followed a year after by the Municipal Corporations Act.

The extent to which the Brontës registered the significance of this statutory shift from paternal to utilitarian and regulatory forms of governance is uncertain. They were not jurists. They probably never read Austin. Political debate, Charlotte opined in correspondence, was too 'factious' (Gaskell, 1997, p. 379).[31] Nevertheless they were certainly cognisant of issues such as Catholic emancipation and reform of the franchise, and when they wrote about women in mid-Victorian England they wrote about matters of politics and law.[32] The distinction between the public and private is cherished by jurists, particularly those who subscribe to the kind of positivism recommended by Austin. But, as many nineteenth-century feminists knew, it is also a fabricated distinction. Private lives are shaped by public policy, whether in conformity or in rebellion (Shanley, 1989, pp. 10–16; Gordon and Nair, 2003, pp. 107–9, 202, 229–30; Chandler, 1998, pp. 238, 260). The myriad instances of human misery and familial dysfunction found in the novels of the Brontës cannot be readily detached from disquiet at the broader 'condition' of England and its public governance.

The 'question of women', as a species of this broader anxiety, was shaped by the law. Not exclusively of course. But the way in which the law defined, and very often excluded, women was critical in this shaping. And here again one institution, the same institution – marriage – mattered far more than any other. Of course, some chose to remain outside marriage, either as spinsters or as partners in some kind of extra-marital relationship; an unambiguously 'unnatural and anomalous arrangement' as a disapproving Margaret Oliphant termed it (Hamilton, 1995, p. 213). The apparent determination of the 1753 Clandestine Marriage Act to tighten state regulation of marriages has convinced some historians, concerned particularly by the apparent popularity of *per verba* contracts, to project a preceding state of widespread confusion and nonconformity.[33] Alongside runs the complementary assumption that the Act reinforced a 'patrician' view of matrimonial law (Probert, 2009, p. 3; Perry, 2004, pp. 35, 277–8). The countervailing idea that the Act merely confirmed existing social practice, pressed more recently by Rebecca Probert, does not detract from the importance of the Act as a statement of political intent (Probert, 2009, pp. 5–6, 236–7, 340–3).[34] Nonconformity may have been infrequent. But it was to be discouraged all the same.[35] As Lord Lyndhurst remarked, women who chose not to marry in conformity with the 1753 Act or who then chose to separate were deemed, in effect, to reside in a 'state of outlawry' (Holcombe, 1983, p. 101). It was perhaps unsurprising therefore that the vast majority chose not to. It was Lyndhurst's 1835 Marriage Act which was supposed to provide comparable clarity with regard to the vexed issue of prohibited degrees of intra-familial marriage. As we shall see in Chapter 2, incest troubled the Victorian jurist, not just for physiological or even scriptural reasons, but for reasons rooted in property and probate law. Lyndhurst's Act was not, however, as we shall also see, much use, and the case for a specific Deceased Wife's Sister Act continued on into the 1850s. In the main, marriage in line with the provisions of Hardwicke's Act and the spirit of Lyndhurst's, in short as preferred by the established Church, was the expectation.[36]

And by and large it was the hope too. Certainly no Brontë heroine hoped for anything other, even if Queen Victoria herself might have confided in private correspondence with one of her daughters, that marriage was 'such a lottery after all, and for a poor woman a very doubtful happiness' (Hager, 2010, p. 1). Bronte novels do not move round the fate of poor women, and the Brontë sisters certainly did not write for them. Regardless of its attendant hazards, marriage is presented as a desirable state; one that it was the duty of the law and the Church to promote and support. Affinity did not of course stop the sisters contemplating what made for a good marriage. Indeed it lent the contemplation a certain urgency. Novels such as *Jane Eyre* and *Shirley* can be read as commentaries on the various merits of 'companionate', even romantic, marriages. But the institution of marriage remained firmly embedded in sacrament, and in law; and neither the priest nor the common lawyer was to be distracted by simple concerns of the heart. Marriage was far too serious a matter for that, as Blackstone famously confirmed in his *Commentaries*. And the law, according to Blackstone at least, was clear. On marriage a woman became subsumed in the legal person of her husband:

> In marriage the husband and wife are one person in law: that is, the very being or legal existence of the woman is suspended during the marriage, or at least is incorporated and consolidated into that of the husband: under whose wing, protection and cover, she performs everything ... For this reason, a man cannot grant any thing to his wife, or enter in to covenant with her: for the grant would be to suppose her separate existence; and to covenant with her, would be only to covenant with himself.
>
> (Blackstone, 1828, p. 130)

This was the common law doctrine of coverture, the jurisprudential complement to a cultural prejudice which preferred to see the married woman as the 'angel of the house'.[37] And even though it was subject to the concerted criticism of early feminists such as Cobbe and Caird, it was not about to change. The interest of the law in the private lives of English men and women did not diminish during the nineteenth century, and nor was it inclined to favour a 'narrative' of emancipation (Wright, 2004, pp. 305–15).

It was unsurprising that so many critics should so frequently allude to marriage as a form of slavery – domestic, sexual and economic. The metaphor was repeatedly deployed by Mill in his *The Subjection of Women*, writing of the wife as the 'actual bond-servant of her husband: no less so, as far as legal obligation goes, than slaves commonly so-called'. 'There are', he concluded, alluding to recent emancipation statutes, 'no legal slaves, except the mistress of every house' (Mill, 1988, pp. 32, 86). Rather more poetically, but no less notoriously, Mona Caird made comparison between the state of marriage and the Mongolian market-place 'with its iron cage, wherein women are held in bondage, suffering moral starvation, while the thoughtless gather round to taunt and to insult their lingering misery' (Hamilton, 1995, p. 279). We will take a closer look at the nature of marriage in each of the chapters to come. We will see that the cause of matrimonial law reform emerged as a centrepiece of nascent mid-Victorian feminist writing. And it took time, as we will also see. As late as 1886, Chief Justice Coleridge was moved to remark that across much of Victorian society a wife was still 'regarded as some kind of inferior dog or horse' (Wiener, 2004, p. 161).

A primary concern for many within marriage was how to get out of it. Divorce was notoriously difficult prior to the 1857 Matrimonial Causes Act which established a distinct Divorce Court, and not that much easier after.[38] The only other remote possibility of divorce being private parliamentary statute, the practical solution prior to 1857 was separation. It was anyway the preferred solution, even after 1857, for those who were troubled by the possibility of public speculation. Whilst the common law did not recognise separation, or indeed any contracts or deeds of separation, ecclesiastical courts continued to grant decrees *a mensa et thoro* or *a vinculo*. The former meant literally a divorce from 'bed and board', and could be granted on the grounds of adultery, sodomy or cruelty; it also prevented either party remarrying. The second was rather more complex, and could again be granted on the grounds of adultery, or mental incompetence, sexual impotence or fraud. In this instance it could lead to a more complete break, leaving either party free to marry again. But such a decree could only be attained following the prior grant of a decree *a mensa*, and a successfully prosecuted civil action for 'criminal conversation'. Failing the latter, common law courts would refuse to recognise any common law authority in a separation decree. The difficulty of extracting oneself from an unhappy marriage was the first of what Danaya Wright terms the 'traditional triad' of concerns that faced married women in nineteenth-century England (Wright, 2004, p. 222).

The second was economic dependency. Property law, it is often thought, is about the relation between people and estate. It is not. Property is about the relation between different people who have interests in property. The problem for the mid-Victorian married woman was that she had no such interest because the law denied her difference; a point fully appreciated by Lord Brougham in presenting a petition to Parliament in support of a prospective divorce law in 1856. The 'absolute' financial authority of the husband, and the inevitable 'pecuniary dependence' of the wife, Brougham declared, was one of those 'manifold evils occasioned by the present law' (Chedzoy, 1982, p. 248). It was a view commonly supported by nineteenth-century feminist campaigners for reform of matrimonial law. Cobbe wrote her iconic *Criminals, Idiots, Women and Minors* a decade later in support of an attempt to further reform the law with 'respect to the Property of Married Women' (Hamilton, 1995, p. 111). Harriet Taylor Mill coined a familiar metaphor, rooting the real cause of marital 'slavery' in the principle that any property brought to a marriage, and any subsequently acquired, belonged to the husband.[39] Writing towards the end of the century, Mona Caird still felt the need to press the case for greater 'economical independence' as the 'first condition of free marriage' (Hamilton, 1995, p. 283).

Not only did a woman's property pass to a husband on marriage, it stayed with him in the event of any subsequent separation. Decrees *a mensa* confirmed continuing control of property in the husband. Decrees *a vinculo* could, conversely, lead to a declaration ending the husband's control of his wife's separate estate. We will revisit the uncertain legal status of separate estates, where a wife's property was held in a settlement trust for her 'use', in the next chapter. In principal, as a species of settlement trust, separate estates were intended to provide reassurance to fathers that estate that passed with a daughter on marriage might be secured by entail against potentially dissolute spouses.[40] Given that the principal purpose of a strict settlement was to reinforce the cultural jurisprudence of primogeniture, by concentrating the passage of estates through the male line, the fact that separate estates were not written to somehow liberate women should come as no surprise (Perry, 2004, pp. 38–50). Chancery could, at its discretion, recognise these 'interests' in 'use' provided the applicant came to equity 'with clean hands' and had 'good cause' to seek its protection.[41] In all, however, the financial situation of a married or separated woman was precarious indeed; a fact which, as we shall see, was well appreciated by each of the Brontë sisters.

The third and equally troubling concern was child custody. Here again, when we take a closer look at the breakdown of the Huntingdon marriage in *The Tenant of Wildfell Hall*, we will encounter a very pointed commentary on the iniquities of contemporary custody law, much of which moves around the celebrated contemporary case of Caroline Norton. As it stood in the late 1840s, child custody provisions were still written in deference to the same principle of coverture (Wright, 2002, p. 180). Children were deemed to be the property of the father, regardless of whether he was separated from the mother. As we shall see, Chancery courts occasionally exercised a historical jurisdiction to protect children from abusive fathers. But the exercise of equitable wardship was entirely discretionary and wholly inconsistent. And in the first decades of the nineteenth century, the courts of Chancery had anyway shown themselves to be peculiarly disinclined to intervene (O'Halloran, 1999, pp. 11–13, 24–5; Shanley, 1989, pp. 133–5). The 1839 Infant Custody Act, the first in a series which would over the century eventually ameliorate the rigours of the common law, had sought to give equitable principles some statutory authority, allowing mothers to petition Chancery for custody of children under seven, and for periodic rights thereafter. But, aside from the obvious substantive limitations, being a matter of Chancery jurisdiction any remedy was purely discretionary and thus also entirely unreliable.

Of course, the jurisprudential subjugation of married women was just as readily celebrated as regretted in mid-nineteenth-century England. Many an Honourable Member applauded its virtues in many a parliamentary debate. Others matters of jurisprudence – incest and illegitimacy, adultery and domestic violence among them – were consigned to darker imaginations. Images of husbands beating wives, rather like those of fornicating siblings, did not fit the imagined idyll of the blessed Victorian family, and outside occasional literary depictions, were only rarely encountered at least until 1857.[42] Thereafter, as reported cases before the Divorce Court confirmed, it became painfully clear that 'aggravated' adultery and 'wife-torture', as Frances Power Cobbe evocatively termed it, were experienced as much by daughters of the genteel middle classes as by inebriated working-class wives. Barbara Leckie has recently argued that reported proceedings of the new court represented a kind of 'legal confession' (Leckie, 1999, p. 67).[43] 'Who could have imagined' such 'brutality', Cobbe asked of her readers? (Hamilton, 1995, p. 82).[44] The readers of Brontë novels probably could, certainly those, as we shall see, who had encountered *The Tenant of Wildfell Hall* or *Wuthering Heights*.[45] Lots of middle-class Victorian husbands, real or fictive, it seemed, liked to beat their wives. Such a propensity, it has been argued, 'stood at the vortex' of a whole range of debates which were concerned with the apparent breakdown of the marriage idyll (Surridge, 2005, p. 6). Here, of course, the jurisprudential discourse lies a little more deeply embedded.

The Brontë cases

The term 'case', as we have already noted, has a certain ambiguity. Common law is made up of cases, from which larger doctrines and principles might be drawn. Lawyers are entirely comfortable with the particular. Literary scholars, particularly literary historicists, are nothing like so reconciled. They worry that there is no sure connection between the particular case and the grander theory, that the particular case is as likely to represent an 'anomaly' in any 'normative scheme' (Chandler, 1998, pp. 207–8). We must tread the margins here, respecting the particular without allowing it to debilitate our ambition. We have already reflected on two aspects of the context within which the Brontës wrote; the 'question of women' and contemporary debates on women and legal reform. But there is also a further, perhaps more immediate, context. The Brontës enjoy, or perhaps endure, their own very particular literary reputation.

Much of this criticism moves around the extent to which the Brontës might be seen as feminist. The idea that their novels raise female voices tends to nurture this view. But it is not quite the same thing. Those voices raised by the Brontës may not be representative of mid-nineteenth-century women, even middle-class ones. It may well be that the search for a representative voice is anyway illusory. The suspicion that the Church Tory inflection in Charlotte's voice in particular might give the Brontë canon a peculiarly conservative moral and political tone has often been noted (Gaskell, 1997, pp. 70, 80–8; Barker, 2001, pp. 177–9, 241, 265–6, 416; Ingham, 2006, pp. 38–41; Miller, 2001, p. 30). It is certainly true that Charlotte had very little sympathy for contemporary feminist writings, particularly those by women who, she surmised, 'longed for power and had never felt affection' (Gaskell, 1997, pp. 368–9).[46] It may be that the determination to eschew more obviously political and, by inference, jurisprudential commentary in the Brontë novels is a testament to precisely this conservative inclination.

Striving somehow to elevate Charlotte above the fury of modern feminist debate, Virginia Woolf famously cast the romantic image of the three sisters sat in the parlour of Haworth Parsonage, possessed of 'solitary visions over distant fields' (Woolf, 1998, p. 91); conjuring collateral images of gendered as well as cultural and political isolation alongside a compensatory metaphysical genius.[47] It has lost little of its strength through ensuing generations. Thousands come to pay homage at the same parsonage each year.[48] It is not, of course, accidental homage. The novels, particularly *Jane Eyre* and *Wuthering Heights*, regularly top lists of 'most popular' or 'most read', especially amongst women. But the sheer force of this success and this succour has generated its own peculiar critical context. Lucasta Miller refers to it as the Brontë 'myth', born more immediately in the persuasive poetics of Elizabeth Gaskell's *Life of Charlotte Bronte*, published just two years after its subject's death in 1855, but originally conceived in Charlotte's own carefully managed self-fashioning in the persons of Jane Eyre and Lucy Snowe.[49] We will revisit the particular fashioning of Lucy Snowe alongside Gaskell's *Life* in the final chapter. But it is interesting in passing to note that Oliphant praised Gaskell's testament precisely because it – and by implication its subject – seemed to be written 'for every woman dropped out of sight'; a metaphor which revisits, albeit at a slight tangent, the associated images of life 'below the surface' (Miller, 2001, p. 91).

In spinning the first threads of the myth, Gaskell was seeking to refine further the relation of author and audience.[50] She was, most obviously, trying to sanctify, to reassure potential readers of a Brontë novel that it can be trusted. And who were these prospective readers? In some sense the nature of the Brontë audience, predominantly middle-class and female, might seem to be rather obvious.[51] It is also rather simplistic. As we have already noted, technological and commercial innovation during the early decades of the nineteenth century promoted an 'explosion in reading', which fashioned, and was fashioned by, a number of emergent 'communities' of readers (St Clair, 2007, pp. 11–13, 114–20).[52] And it is limiting too. Whilst G.H. Lewes famously welcomed a new kind of fiction which invited the female reader to contemplate the 'woman's view of life, woman's experience', later critics have understandably worried that such a presumption also imports a debilitating pejorative (Foster, 1985, pp. 2–3; Armstrong, 1987, pp. 7–8). In a sense this is the sinister aspect of the critical assumption that such literature facilitated the raising of female voices.[53] It is certainly true that the evolving nature of the nineteenth-century audience was as much a concern to contemporaries as it has remained a matter of fascination to modern critics.[54]

There were more journals, more books, and perhaps most troubling of all, they were all more readily available. The prospect of a generation of young men, and worse still young women, let loose to roam about Mudie's Circulating Library and other such vehicles, certainly registered with many critics; not least those who, as we shall see, on reviewing the novels of the Brontë sisters chose to articulate their dismay. As briefly noted above, it was popularly surmised by medical and literary critics alike that reading could be addictive, and that young women were peculiarly susceptible to having their heads turned. To many, the portrayal of events found in novels such as *Wuthering Heights* or *The Tenant of Wildfell Hall* or *Villette* was little short of pornographic. It was for this reason, as we shall see in Chapter 5, that the case for specific legislation designed to regulate their reading was so strongly pressed; pressure that eventually resulted in the notorious 1857 Obscene Publications Act. Proposing this legislation Lord Campbell felt moved to observe that 'indecent books' were 'more deadly than prussic acid, strychnine or arsenic' (Leckie, 1999, p. 36). Even those who advised the virtue of reading to educate the mind, even the sensibility, agreed that it was best if that education was closely regulated. With the notable exception of the elder Catherine Earnshaw, Brontë heroines tend to like reading, just as their creators, it might be rejoined, relished the chance of educating their readers.

The recognition that the Brontës are a peculiar 'case' does not prevent us contemplating the extent to which they might, nonetheless, be exemplary. Elizabeth Deeds Ermarth, for example, sees the Brontës at the rearguard of a providential 'aesthetic' struggling against the oncoming industrial age (Ermarth, 1997, pp. 3–7, 96–7). Paradoxically, of course, the Brontë 'myth' feeds on this possibility, that the three sisters who wrote such extraordinarily powerful novels were just ordinary middle-class West Yorkshire girls living in an ordinary rather drab little West Yorkshire village. They were of course middle-class girls, and they were brought up without a mother; factors which both tend to exercise Brontë scholars. But again that hardly made them unusual. Neither does it diminish their suitability as a prospective 'case' in literary or jurisprudential historicism.[55] The same can be said of their regional focus.[56] By and large the Brontë novels are about women of a certain class who lived in a particular 'moment'. Temporality further limits the case. It has been argued, for example, that the 1840s was a peculiar decade in nineteenth-century literature; peculiar not least for its presentation of a species of assertive female protagonist who would later vanish from the literary landscape. But again, everyone writes from somewhere and at some time. It does not diminish the value of the text in suggesting broader trends or perceptions, jurisprudential or otherwise. But it does remind us that we need to remain sensitive to context, to the relation between the general and the particular.

Half a century ago, Michael Wolff suggested that in their attempt to address the myriad challenges of Enlightenment the Victorians were the first 'moderns' (Wolff, 1964, p. 61). It is a vaunting supposition, open to all the challenges that such sweeping statements attract. And it begs a critical question: What does being a Victorian mean anyway?[57] Certainly, as Mary Poovey has emphasised, it is difficult to presume any constant sense of cultural identity (Poovey, 1989, p. 4). At the same time, however, it is also an exciting supposition. It certainly reinforces the 'case' for reading Victorian literature in order to access not just a better understanding of what Victorians thought and how they perceived themselves, but also to clarify what and how we think today.[58] The resonances are various. It makes the case, as Sandra Gilbert and Susan Gubar stressed, for locating the 'vital origins' of modern feminism in the Victorian period (Gilbert and Gubar, 2000, p. xxxii). And the case is no less compelling in matters of feminist jurisprudence or family law history. It is, for our purposes, a guiding supposition. And it is not just that the Victorian experience might have continued resonance. It is every bit as true that the Victorian novel, as John Sutherland has commented, 'is still with us and thriving' (Sutherland, 2006, p. xxiii). We in the twenty-first century do not live in a cocoon. Our perception of ourselves today is shaped in considerable part by our fascinated comprehension of how our immediate predecessors lived; a fascination sharpened by a genre of literary fiction the popularity of which remains perhaps unparalleled.

The chapters that follow proceed in broad deference to the relatively compressed publication chronology of the Brontë canon. There is certainly a common tone to the first three novels that we will encounter, in turn *The Tenant of Wildfell Hall*, *Wuthering Heights* and *Jane Eyre*. Given that the latter was published first in October 1847, to be followed by *Wuthering Heights* three months later and then the *Tenant* in June 1848, the order might seem a little perverse. But the evidence of compositional and conceptual coincidence diminishes any potential chronological incoherence. Across each hangs a mood of pervasive violence; one that, of necessity, shapes the jurisprudence that can be discerned, however dimly, beneath the surface. Domestic abuse, marital and familial dysfunction, the crisis of masculinity, the potential collapse of estates and the issue of child custody; the homes that Emily, Anne and Charlotte chose to depict in these three novels are clearly far from happy. The 'idolatry' depicted in these homes owes far more to the tradition of Gothic horror than it does to the idylls of domestic bliss cherished by the likes of Stickney Ellis or Coventry Patmore (Chaplin, 2007, pp. 1–9, 12–14, 52).

The final two chapters concentrate on Charlotte's two later novels, *Shirley* and *Villette*. Here it might seem that the law is particularly conspicuous by its absence. Yet, if domestic relations in *Shirley* seem to be more benign, the presentation of issues of public governance gestures towards a greater concern. In engaging the larger 'condition of England' question, Charlotte is compelled to cross the treacherous divide between the public and the private; itself a potentially subversive gesture. And the England she describes as beset by religious discord and the apparent demise of Tory traditions of local governance presents a distinctly uncertain prospect. It is perhaps for this reason that Charlotte returned, with a peculiar intensity, to matters of private testament in her final novel; and to matters of particular jurisprudential intensity too (Kaplan, 2007, pp. 17, 21–2). In its interrogation of related aspects of sexuality, its cultural and textual regulation, the defining themes of *Villette* have an immediate resonance with a range of pivotal debates in modern feminist legal thought. If the novels of 1846–48 present a collective indictment of an old order characterised by violence, corruption and decay, *Shirley* and *Villette* contemplate a present with which the only remaining sister was clearly uncomfortable and a future that offered little in the way of reassurance.

Read together, the five Brontë 'cases' provide a fascinating chronicle, and an indictment of an England in which the role and effectiveness of law, public and private, was a matter of ongoing concern. The jurisprudence, as we shall see, might remain essentially subterranean. But anyone who read a Brontë novel in mid-nineteenth-century England, like anyone who reads one today, cannot deny the presence either of the law or of the concern which likewise hovered beneath and just occasionally broke through the surface of the text.

1
Huntingdon v Huntingdon

Of course it never happened: *Huntingdon v Huntingdon*. That is the issue. Helen Huntington was unhappily married, subject to various forms of spousal abuse. But the law offered no respite. Instead, it left her with a choice: put up with it, or run away. It was not an uncommon dilemma in mid-nineteenth-century England. It was, however, an uncommon subject for public discourse, and it was an even more uncommon subject for literary commentary. It was also the subject of *The Tenant of Wildfell Hall*. And the furtive tenant, hiding from her husband and from the law was Helen Huntingdon.

Modern critics have been keen to praise Anne Brontë's novel, identifying a significant 'voice' in mid-nineteenth-century women's literature (Gordon, 1984, pp. 719–25, 731–4, 739; Langland, 1989, pp. 119, 134–5, 143; Westcott, 2001, pp. 213–14; Morse, 2001, pp. 106–8; Jacobs, 1986, pp. 204–5; Carnell, 1998, pp. 9–12). Contemporaries, as we shall see, were far less inclined to praise (Wright, 2002, pp. 244–5).[1] In its stark portrayal of a dysfunctional, abusive marriage, the *Tenant* shattered the pretences of marital harmony so cherished by the age. It displayed, in harrowing detail, the reality of marriage for many Victorian women; and not just any women, but middle-class bourgeois women, the kind of women who could, indeed, be expected to read a Brontë novel. In this it resonated, not just with personal experience, but with all the 'hideous revelations' that Frances Power Cobbe identified in the published reports of the new Divorce Court (Hamilton, 1995, pp. 81–2).

The author's intent, moreover, was made very clear, as the Preface to the second edition confirmed:

> My object in writing the following pages was not simply to amuse the Reader, neither was it to gratify my own taste, nor yet to ingratiate myself with the Press and the Public: I wished to tell the truth, for truth always conveys its own moral to those who are able to receive it.
>
> (4)

And she continued, referring to some of the more notorious scenes to follow:

> I know such characters do exist, and if I have warned one rash youth from the following in their steps, or prevented one thoughtless girl from falling into the very natural error of my heroine, the book has not been written in vain.
>
> (4)

The Tenant of Wildfell Hall can be read, as its author intended, as a strategic literary intervention in an emergent, and increasingly vociferous, debate regarding a range of jurisprudential issues which attached to the 'question' of women in the England of the late 1840s, most obviously those of spousal abuse, matrimonial property and child custody.[2] Whilst eschewing too brusque an engagement, this intent remained apparent:

> Let it not be imagined, however, that I consider myself competent to reform the errors and abuses of society, but only that I would fain contribute my humble quota towards so good an aim, and if I can gain the public ear at all, I would rather whisper a few wholesome truths therein than much soft nonsense ... and when I feel it my duty to speak an unpalatable truth, with the help of God, I *will* speak it, though it be to the prejudice of my name and to the detriment of my reader's immediate pleasure as well as my own.
>
> (4)

The Tenant of Wildfell Hall was written with the same aspiration that fired George Eliot's composition of *Adam Bede*: to reveal that 'rare precious quality of truthfulness' (Eliot, 2008, p. 117). It was not, conversely, intended to be another of those 'silly novels' so eagerly devoured by silly young women; such as the flighty Annabella Wilmot who, when not seducing men like Arthur Huntingdon, preferred to pass her extensive leisure time devouring the latest 'new novel' (270). *The Tenant*, instead, was written to challenge a range of associated pejoratives of immediate concern to generations of wives and mothers, and husbands and fathers. We have already explored the cultural and theological root of these pejoratives, finding their expression in the associated myths of 'separate spheres' and the 'angel in the house'. We have also noted the jurisprudential root that sustained what Mary Wollstonecraft evocatively termed the 'Divine Right of Husbands' (Hamilton, 1995, p. 83). It was not that women did not crave a happy marriage and a happy home. Josephine Butler would later attest that a happy 'home is the nursery of all virtue, the fountain-head of all true affection, and the main source of strength of our nation' (Shanley, 1989, p. 191). But not all homes were happy. The romance hid what was often a more distressing and violent truth. It was for this reason that an increasing number of women, such as Barbara Leigh Smith Bodichon, were calling for the casting down of the 'sacred' juristic tablets and the raising in their stead of a 'bolder and more discriminating spirit, which is to judge calmly what is good and to amend what is bad' (Dolin, 2007, p. 127). The Preface to the second edition of *The Tenant of Wildfell Hall* is possessed of such a spirit.

'I suppose she doesn't mind it'

Twelve years before the publication of *The Tenant of Wildfell Hall*, in the summer of 1836, the journal readers of middle England were daily treated to accounts of the criminal conversation action taken by George Norton against the Prime Minister and royal favourite, Lord Melbourne. A suit for criminal conversation was actually pursued in the civil courts, seeking damages against a man who was alleged to have committed adultery with the claimant's wife.[3] Aside from the potential pecuniary loss, this case, as was common to many others, barely mattered to the defendant; indeed, it rather served to add a little lustre to the dimming reputation of an ageing Regency rake. It mattered an awful lot more, however, to Norton's wife. Spurred on by the realisation that she was unable to defend her own reputation in court, Caroline Norton proceeded to pen a series of barely fictional accounts of her marriage, together with a number of influential treatises on various associated issues of matrimonial law, including divorce, property holding and child custody. She became, in short, a putative feminist icon; even though she herself treated the 'ridiculous doctrine of equality' with scarcely veiled distaste.[4] In *English Laws for Women*, published in 1854, and a year later in *A Letter to the Queen on Lord Chancellor Cranworth's Marriage and Divorce Bill*, Norton argued that a wife was, in effect, a 'legal mistress', deemed by law to be 'non-existent', dragged along by the 'undercurrent of struggling lives' (Chedzoy, 1992, pp. 6, 193, 240–1). There is no evidence that Anne Brontë read Norton's writings, though it must remain a distinct possibility. Both the fiction and the polemic were widely read.[5] Conversely there is no evidence that Norton read *The Tenant of Wildfell Hall*, though if she did there was much she might have recognised.

Caroline Norton and Helen Huntingdon, rather, exist like twin sisters separated at birth but united by an eerily familiar coincidence of fate; except, of course, that there was nothing terribly unusual about Victorian men abusing their wives, and so the coincidence is not, perhaps, so remarkable.[6] Norton and Brontë wrote for audiences that were familiar with domestic tension, indeed for all those Carolines who feared the next beating and knew that there was little or nothing that could be done in law to save them. Evidently, the Norton marriage was not a happy one. Caroline, one of the famed 'three Graces', was intelligent, attractive, and comfortable in literary circles.[7] George was a dull minor aristocrat who, by all accounts, drank too much. Within months of marriage he started to beat his wife. Helen Huntingdon made an unhappy match too. She did not have to marry Arthur Huntingdon, and nor should she have done so.[8] Her aunt advised her against it, and Helen was fully versant with his reputation for being a 'bit wildish' (124, 128, 140–2). But that was half the fun, and her other suitors seemed to be so boring. And anyway, Helen was convinced he could be redeemed, recalled to the 'path of virtue' (141–2, 165–7). The fact that Arthur seemed to take particular pride in expressing contempt for all matters religious simply made the challenge all the more compelling (163, 166–7). Helen was, in short, 'infatuated', and she certainly did not want to run the risk, even at this young age, of becoming an 'old maid' (130, 154).[9] Glimpses of the kind of behaviour that was likely to beset her imagined domestic bliss did not deter; at least not until it was too late.

Helen's diary betrayed early doubts as to whether her affianced was quite as 'warm and generous' as she liked to think, whilst his enthusiasm for the 'orgies' and 'high festivals' of drink and gambling did nothing to settle her anxieties (175–6, 187–91). But the evangelist in Helen triumphs. She will redeem the sinner (Thormahlen, 1999, pp. 157–60). Helen marries Arthur Huntingdon and takes up residence at Grassdale. It is not long before the first cracks in the Huntingdon marriage occur. Eight weeks in, and Helen confesses that she was 'wilfully blind'. Arthur is 'selfish'. But still she is undaunted. The journey to redemption will just be all the more testing, for both of them; especially given that Arthur has apparently begun to weary of what he perceives to be Helen's excessive religiosity (191–5). A month later they have their first quarrel, over Arthur's earlier adulterous liaisons. He calls her a 'confounded slut' (202).

Arthur is not an easy man to live with. So much is obvious. Rather more subtle, perhaps, is the insinuation that Helen might be just as difficult; albeit in a different way. For, aside from her suffocating evangelism, Helen also displays a peculiar independence of spirit. Alighting at Wildfell Hall, craving privacy, rumours quickly circulate (58, 378–9). If the mysterious Mrs Graham was a 'proper person, she would not be living there by herself' (25, 89). If she had read her Sarah Stickney Ellis, it was clearly not often enough. On closer inspection, she appears to betray a 'lamentable ignorance' of the 'little niceties of cookery, and such things, that every lady ought to be familiar with' (13). She is, in sum, deemed to be an 'obstinate' woman 'ignorant of her principle duties' (54). The alternative view of domestic harmony articulated by Mrs Markham, of a wife who cooks well, and a husband who turns up for dinner in time and clears his plate, might seem to be somewhat simplistic (54). But it would not, in mid-nineteenth-century England, have been an uncommon view.

The Huntingdon marriage was not then destined to be a happy one. In one anonymous contemporary review of the novel, in the *Examiner*, it was suggested, with no apparent hint of irony, that what Helen Huntingdon really needed was a good lawyer (Allott, 1974, p. 260). It is not, however entirely clear what good a good lawyer could have done. Whether she remained within her marriage, or sought to fly from it, Helen was effectively cast outside the protection of the law. The fragmentation of the marriage is rapid. The mental and emotional abuse escalates. Her husband's 'predeliction for the pleasures of the table', as well as for the contents of his cellar, increases with each passing month (249, 254). Moral lassitude is pervasive at Grassdale, sexual impropriety forever smirking in the shadows. In time, Helen will be propositioned by Hargrave, one of Arthur's drinking companions who takes his host at his word when, in a fit of pique, he offers his wife to any who would care to 'have her'; a gesture that adds petty pimping to the litany of domestic abuses (340, 342–3). The mere offering of an unwilling wife to other men, needless to say, was not held in law to represent a form of mental cruelty.[10]

Sexual dishonesty rapidly emerges as a dominant motif in their increasingly bitter arguments, and the eventual uncovering of Arthur's relationship with Annabella Wilmot, Lord Lowborough's new wife, is a crushing blow (292). When confronted, Huntingdon is typically unapologetic, refusing to let Helen use the affair as a pretext for separation (294–5). Annabella is only concerned to extract from Helen an undertaking not to inform Lowborough; something which makes the appalled Helen a culpable accomplice after the fact to a 'connection' which, in echo of the familiar language deployed in civil adultery proceedings, she terms 'criminal' (299–300, 324). Even so, Helen does not, as yet, countenance separation. Of course, it would have been far from simple anyway; both in 1848 when the novel was published, and in the England of the 1820s when it was set.

As we have already noted, prior to 1857 divorce was generally consigned to the jurisdiction of ecclesiastical courts, which could grant decrees *a mensa et thoro* or *a vinculo*; the latter more effective in that it could ensure a complete break, but remaining dependent upon the successful prosecution of a civil action for 'criminal conversation'. Simple abuse was not grounds for separation as it did not amount in law to 'cruelty'. A husband, as Blackstone confirmed, was anyway entitled to use 'moderate correction' and reasonable 'chastisement' (Shanley, 1989, p. 42). If a wife had the misfortune to experience such correction, Judge Lushington advised Lady Dysart, her best recourse was to reconfirm her 'lawful obedience' to her husband (*Dysart*, 1847). Separation was rare, divorce prior to 1858 rarer still (Hammerton, 1990, pp. 270–1).

The 1857 Act was only passed after considerable, often furious, parliamentary debate, at the heart of which lay the culturally entrenched view that whilst a female adulterer sinned against God, a male one was merely a 'little profligate'.[11] It was for this reason, troubled by the thought that reform might encourage sexual impropriety on the part of women, that Parliament enacted a notorious legislative double standard, allowing husbands to petition for divorce on the grounds of adultery alone, but requiring wives to evidence 'aggravated adultery'; adultery compounded by at least one of incest, bigamy, desertion or prolonged physical 'cruelty'.[12] For this simple reason, despite its symbolic importance, the 1857 Act would not have helped Helen Huntingdon. Her husband was not a bigamist, merely an adulterer. There was no evidence of incest, and neither was she deserted. And, even if she was offered by her husband to his friends in a barely jocular invitation to rape, there is no evidence that she was subject to actual abuse.[13]

In this, in a sense, she was of course lucky; luckier certainly than Caroline Norton.[14] And luckier, too, than her friend Millicent Hattersley, who, it transpires, suffers periodic beatings at the hands of her husband, until, he confesses, 'she cries – and that satisfies me' (278). Hattersley's confession resonates:

> I positively think I ill-use her sometimes, when I've taken too much – but I can't help it, for she never complains, either at the time or after. I suppose she doesn't mind it.
>
> (277)

She 'does mind it', Helen retorts, whether or not she has the courage to complain. A wife-beater is a 'tyrant' (277–8). When Hattersley blusters another feeble if familiar justification, that a bit of a beating never really hurt anybody and that if anyone has been hurt it is he, it is Helen who again responds, painting the bigger picture. It is, she counters, 'a great matter', for:

> it is impossible to injure yourself – especially by such acts as we allude to – without injuring hundreds, if not thousands, besides, in a greater or less degree, either by the evil you do or the good you leave undone.
>
> (279)

Helen Huntingdon may not have been systematically beaten in the way poor Millicent was, but the reader is left to contemplate the likelihood of an abuse that is all the more terrifying for its spasmodic and unpredictable nature, and which moreover, leaves its victim in a state of perpetual anticipatory fear. In a later disquisition with a still blustering Hattersley, Helen confirms the 'terror and misery' of living a life of 'silent fretting and constant anxiety' on 'account' of an abusive husband (363). Later the narrator of the novel, Gilbert Markham, is struck by the extent to which Helen is fearful of strangers, prone to giving an 'electric start' whenever caught unawares (62–3).

Whilst she might have evaded physical beating, Helen Huntingdon was, of course, subject to systematic mental cruelty, not just in the instance of the invited putative rape, but in the embedded knowledge that spousal violence was endemic. Mental cruelty, however, was not recognised as grounds for abuse, the famous dictum of Sir William Scott resounding to the very end of the century:

> What merely wounds the mental feelings is in few cases to be admitted where they are not accompanied with bodily injury, either actual or menaced. Mere austerity of temper, petulance of manners, rudeness of language, a want of civil attention and accommodation, even occasional sallies of passion, if they do not threaten bodily harm, do not amount to legal cruelty: they are high moral offences in the marriage state undoubtedly, not innocent surely in any state of life, but still they are not that cruelty against which the law can relieve.
>
> (*Evans*, 1790, 467)

An abused wife, Scott concluded, must 'suffer in silence'. The dictum would only be challenged in the decades following the establishment of the new Divorce Court in 1857, and then only gradually as part of a wider promotion of an alternative ideal of 'companionate' marriage (Hammerton, 1992, pp. 4–5, 123–6). It was only with the 1878 Matrimonial Causes Act that a physically abused wife was granted the power to leave her husband and live, under the terms of an ecclesiastical separation, as *feme sole*.

A soul to educate

The arrival of little Arthur Huntingdon, after a year of marriage, marks a watershed in Helen's testament, providing her with a new priority in life just as it feeds her husband's sense of neglect.[15] It also gives the novel an added dimension; one that spoke to an emergent debate regarding the reform of child custody (Berry, 1999, pp. 105–10; Gruner, 1997, pp. 309–10). In her diary Helen writes:

> God has sent me a soul to educate for Heaven, and given me a new and calmer bliss, and stronger hopes to comfort me. But where hope rises fear must lurk behind, and when I clasp my little darling to my breast, or hang over his slumbers with unutterable delight, and a world of hope within my heart, one of two thoughts is ever at hand to check my swelling bliss; the one: He may be taken from me; the other: He may live to curse his own existence.
>
> (228)

Motherhood is a godly calling. But the world is saturated in sin. For every 'five hundred men who have yielded to temptation', Helen muses, 'shew me one that has had virtue to resist' (28). And the law will not help. Culture, as well as Scripture, confirmed the natural state of motherhood. There is certainly nothing natural about Arthur senior as a prospective father. 'I can't love it', he declares, 'what is there to love?' (231). But the law preferred fathers. Caroline Norton noted the incongruity between the 'specious' laws of England and the 'holier law ... of nature' (Craig, 2009, p.187). And so, it seems, did Anne Brontë.

Chapter three of the *Tenant* presents a long disquisition on the natural responsibilities of the mother in child-rearing.[16] Many of Anne's readers might have found something familiar in Mrs Markham's advice, that Helen will make a 'veriest milksop' of her son, 'a mere Miss Nancy of him' (28–9). If so, they would have found Helen's vehement response disconcerting. Speaking from experience, of 'those I do know', Helen retorts, only the close guidance of a good mother can prevent children, particularly sons, from falling into vice; for 'God knows he will have temptations enough to assail him' (29). In declaring alcohol to be one of the 'gifts of Providence', and in declaiming the 'criminal' responsibility of any mother who sought to deflect her child away from it, the Reverend Milward merely places himself amongst the array of unsatisfactory clerics who populate the pages of the Brontë canon (38). Helen is doing God's work. The semi-inebriate Reverend Milward clearly is not. And he is not alone in his misapprehension. Gilbert Markham's supposition that boys should indeed be encouraged to 'boldly' experience temptation earns Helen's equal disdain (30). Men are 'prone to err' in presuming that their sons should inherit an 'education properly finished by a little practical acquaintance with forbidden things' (31). The 'evil of transgression' does not need 'experimental proofs'. It can be readily seen in others. She would rather, she concludes, that little Arthur 'died tomorrow! – rather a thousand times!' than endure such an education (31).

It is when her husband indeed determines to expose little Arthur to 'forbidden things', to inculcate 'all the embryo vices' necessary to 'make a man of him', that Helen decides to take drastic action (335). When Arthur is thus cajoled into taking his first glass of wine, his mother responds with an abrupt exercise in aversion therapy, poisoning another glass in order to make little Arthur violently sick (354–5). The abuse is driven by a greater duty (Talley, 2001, pp. 139–42). Later Markham is particularly struck by young Arthur's peculiar 'terror and disgust' of the sight of alcohol (27). Only in time does it become apparent why. The same is true of the reasons why Helen seems to be so excessively protective of her son. The 'startling vehemence' that Helen betrays in defence of her son's security is one of the first things that Markham notes (18, 21, 25–6). Similarly pivotal is the earlier arrival at Grassdale of a governess, nominally to assume the education of young Arthur, but in reality to satisfy the lusts of his father; marrying in Helen the fear of ever greater moral laxity with the very real prospect of effective emotional detachment (366–7).[17] Feeling herself to be a 'slave, a prisoner', confined by a husband who increasingly fears the ignominy that will attend the concomitant loss of wife and child, Helen determines to flee Grassdale (352–3).

In doing so, of course, she was taking a huge chance. Whilst she might have been confident in her moral duty, Helen had no legal entitlement to her child. The common law position on custody was clear, developed through the eighteenth century in a series of cases such as *Eyre* and *De Manneville* (*Eyre*, 1722; *De Manneville*, 1804). In the latter case, commonly identified as providing a plotline for Mary Wollstonecraft's *Maria*, the court restated the 'life and limb' doctrine and approved the seizure of the infant by the father, 'not seeing any ground to impute any motive to him injurious to the health or liberty of the child'.[18] Fathers simply had to issue a writ of habeas corpus in order to secure judicial approval for such seizures. Only Chancery offered a notional respite to the rigours of the common law. During the final decades of the eighteenth century, Lord Mansfield, as Chief Justice of the King's Bench, had sought to modify the common law position with regard to abusive fathers. In *Delaval* in 1763, he accepted that a father who put his daughter into prostitution was abusive, and so ordered the child to be released from 'improper restraint' (*Delaval*, 1763). Four years later he gave a similar judgement in a case of wife-abuse in *Blisset* (1767). In both cases the powers of judicial discretion were clearly devised under the influence of Chancery, and the jurisprudence of the Court of Wards.[19]

But equitable remedies were always discretionary, and subsequent vice-chancellors were generally disinclined to follow Mansfield's lead, unless compelled by reason of securing settled interests in property (O'Halloran, 1999, pp. 14–16). We will investigate these latter kinds of interest shortly; for children, like settled estates, were commonly perceived to be a species of property first and humanity second. In the notorious case of *Ball*, in 1827, involving an adulterous father and a mother who had already gained an ecclesiastical separation, the vice-chancellor of the Court of Chancery confirmed that 'the court has nothing to do with the facts of the father's adultery, unless the father brings the child into contact with the woman'. Whilst the vice-chancellor was clearly keen to retain a residual jurisdictional discretion, he was not prepared to do much with it, concluding rather lamely that 'if any alternative could be found, I would most gladly accept it; for, in the moral point of view, I know of no act more harsh or cruel than depriving a mother of proper intercourse with her child' (*Ball*, 1827).[20]

Such was the law as it stood in the 1820s when Anne Brontë set her novel.[21] By 1848 the law had changed, and the debate regarding the legal custody of children had gained in intensity.[22] The 1839 Act, loudly declaimed by critics as the 'Robbery of Father's Bill', allowed mothers to petition in Chancery for custody of children under seven, and for periodic rights of access thereafter, with the singular exception that such provisions did not apply to women cited in a successful criminal conversation suit or an adultery action in an ecclesiastical court. Helen would, therefore, have been able to petition in Chancery for custody of her son. But she would have needed to show that his father was an inappropriate guardian, and she would have needed the money to mount the action in the first place.

And then a couple of years later she would have had to surrender custody anyway. Little wonder that contemporary as well as modern critics have concluded that the symbolic importance of the Act singularly outweighed the practical.[23]

Helen is clearly aware that her husband can demand the return of his son at any time. And, indeed, this is precisely what Arthur Huntingdon does. But by now he is near death, and so makes the demand from a position of physical, if not legal, weakness. Interestingly, Anne Brontë has Helen insist that her husband sign an agreement with which he passes custody of his son to her. At first he bluffs. But Helen is adamant. 'I cannot trust your oaths and promises', she declares, 'I must have a written agreement.' The dying Arthur is too weak to object. And so he signs, and is granted an audience with his son (410–11). The agreement has no legal force; though the illusion that it might was common, as Caroline Norton attested.[24] It is not clear whether Helen is aware of this. Perhaps more importantly, it could have represented a testamentary statement granting custody to Helen. As the law stood, the dying Arthur might have bequeathed his son away to anyone else, perhaps a relative, perhaps not.[25] He does not. And so, again, in this at least Helen Huntingdon could count herself luckier than some.

Caroline Norton, in contrast, was far less fortunate, only discovering on separation that she had no legal claim to custody of her children. And her attempts to abscond with them were nothing like so propitious either. Her husband, showing no comparable, and convenient, propensity to die, refused to accede to the request that he grant custody in return for a final estate settlement; perhaps knowing that he was under no obligation to do so. It was this circumstance, relating to child custody provision, which prompted Caroline's first polemical interventions. In a series of essays published in 1837 and 1838, she repeated the contradiction between the natural 'tie of love' between mother and child and the unnatural tie of custody preferred by the law.[26] The law, she supposed, relegated the role of a mother to little more than that of a surrogate, even a prostitute. 'To refuse the protection which would enable a blameless wife to continue her care for infants', she wrote in her *Separation of Mother and Child*,

> merely on the plea that the law will not interfere with the husband, what is it but to deny the position of the woman as

a rational and accountable creature? What is it but to adopt in a degree the Turkish creed, and consider her merely as the toy of the hour?

As it stood the law of child custody was 'despotic', a 'cruel tyranny'. It was a simple matter of 'humanity', or perhaps inhumanity; in 'making laws for the human race, the mothers of the human race were forgotten' (quoted in Shanley, 1989, p. 137; Acland, 1948, pp. 97, 107). Small wonder then that men were so worried that their wives might abduct their children and flee.

Apprised of the historic, if inconsistent, role of Chancery in moderating the rigour of common law jurisprudence, Norton argued strongly for statutory reform designed to confirm Chancery jurisdiction in all contested custody cases, and to operate with a presumption that mothers should have custody for the first seven years of a child's life. And this, of course, is precisely what happened in 1839. Here again, indeed, Norton's writings were extensively quoted by Serjeant Talfourd in his presentation of the Bill to the Commons (Chedzoy, 1992, pp. 159–60, 179–80). Not that the statute did Caroline much good; nor, it can be reasonably supposed, many other mothers. Threatened with a petition for custody in pursuance of the new Act, George merely sent his children to Scotland; periodically having them returned to London, so that he could torture his estranged wife with a series of inconsistently scheduled and necessarily uncomfortable home visits at the Norton residence.[27]

Further, if gradual, progress in child custody reform was realised in the collateral shape of the 1857 Act, which provided that the new Divorce Court had discretion to make final custody orders, though again only in instances where a husband was guilty of adultery, as well as one of incest, bigamy or excessive cruelty. In cases such as *Martin* and *Milford* during the 1860s the court gradually moved towards a 'fault' based principle in determining collateral custody disputes (*Martin*, 1860; *Milford*, 1869).[28] The 1873 Infant Custody Act, in turn, moderated the law so as to allow mothers to petition the court for custody of children under sixteen in exceptional circumstances. But perhaps the most significant statement, at least in procedural terms, could be found in the Judicature Act of the same year, section 25 of which provided that 'in questions relating to the custody and education of infants, the rules of equity shall prevail'.

Though even here the presumption in favour of paternal custody continued to operate; requiring petitioning mothers to show good reason why they should gain custody. The situation would only change more significantly in 1886, with the passage of a rather more significant Infant Custody Act, which, in the instance of a father's misconduct, allowed a mother to sue for full custody.

'Nursing a fine estate'

It was not, of course, just children who belonged in law to their fathers. Pretty much everything belonged to fathers. In an essay published in 1851, Harriet Taylor Mill noted that beaten wives more often stayed with husbands, not because they fondly hoped for their redemption, but because they would otherwise starve (Shanley, 1989, p. 160). Josephine Butler agreed, observing the 'material necessities of so many women's lives make them ready to accept almost any man who may offer himself' (Shanley, 1989, p. 61). For this reason, as we have already noted, the case for addressing the 'manifold evils' of matrimonial property law, which ran alongside that of infant custody, became a centrepiece of feminist agitation as the century drew on.[29]

As the property of a married woman belonged in common law to her husband, a putatively separated wife had to live by the terms of a separation which were more than likely dictated by the husband and which anyway were not enforceable in common law. To countenance reform, Parliament was regularly advised, was to countenance arrant 'discord and confusion'.[30] In the end, Caroline Norton could only secure such a settlement by bartering away some of her potential financial security for a sporadic access to her children. And even then, it was perhaps inevitable that George would renege on the agreement; which he could, and did.[31] When later approached to sign a petition organised in support of Lord Cranworth's Bill, Caroline signed but not before wondering how easy it would still be for a husband to 'coax, wheedle, beat or tyrannize his wife' out of her anticipated entitlement.[32]

Alongside the common law of property ran the equitable jurisprudence of settled estates. The female 'personification' of equity was part of the inherited iconography of English jurisprudence, and as with the interests of mothers, Chancery courts did seem willing to countenance the need for specific protection for the proprietary interests of married women (Watt, 2009, pp. 170, 181–3). Such protection was afforded most immediately perhaps to 'separate' trusts for 'use' devised to secure the long-term financial security of estates which passed as part of marriage portions or jointures. Noting their original purpose, which was to reassure anxious fathers against the hazard of wanton sons-in-law rather than to emancipate marriageable daughters, Bodichon dismissed the equitable fiction as another of those 'legal devices, patched upon a law which is radically unjust', which 'can only work clumsily', and which moreover could only be of value in protecting the heritable estates of wealthier women (Shanley, 1989, p. 32). Mill made precisely the same observation (Mill, 1988, pp. 32–3).

Even so, it was such an estate, inherited from her mother, that sustained Caroline Norton following her separation.[33] As a species of settlement trust, a 'separate' estate conveyed only a life interest, and commonly incorporated a 'restraint in anticipation' intended to prevent alienation of property. The 'strict' settlement was, of course, devised with precisely the same purpose; settling a life interest on a son, with an entail for successive generations, and only permitting alienation of estate by means of 'barring' the entail at the moment of successive re-settlement. Whilst they could be created by spousal contract, 'separate' estates were more commonly written into strict settlements, in general to reinforce prospective marriage jointures.

Whilst Chancery courts had supported 'separate' interests during the latter part of the eighteenth century, they had done so inconsistently, and only in the event of formal marital separation (Holcombe, 1983, pp. 37–47; Shanley, 1989, pp. 58–60; Okin, 1983, pp. 124–6, 134–5).[34] Law reformers commonly urged the need to resolve this unpredictability by means of statutory enactment. The Law Amendment Society made this recommendation, as did both the Civil Law Commission and Lord Lyndhurst's Select Committee in the run-up to the 1857 Act. Louder voices, however, advised that the incorporation of equitable principles into the common law of matrimonial property could only 'lead to perpetual discord' (Shanley, 1989, p. 46).[35] The failure of the 1857 Act to engage the anomaly caused considerable dismay amongst reformers.[36] A decade later, a Royal Commission established to further investigate the case for rationalising the relation of common law and equity revisited the same inconsistency and made the same recommendation. The enactment of the Married Women's Property Act in 1870 and the Judicature Act three years later finally resolved at least some of the residual inconsistencies between equitable and common law principles of matrimonial property.[37] Even then a morass of amendments, designed to distinguish personal earning and investments from heritable interests, rendered the statute in the words of one critic a legislative 'abortion'.[38]

Although she has saved a 'little hoard' of money, Helen Huntingdon's financial situation, as she arrives at Wildfell Hall, could only be described as precarious (347).[39] Devoid even of the dubious security of a separation agreement, she must try to earn her own living; something that could only add to the peculiarity of her position, at least in the eyes of her already suspicious new neighbours. Middle-class women were not supposed to paint for a living, any more than they were supposed to write. For this reason Helen Graham, like her creator, chose to retain her anonymity as an artist (42). It is significant that Arthur Huntingdon had taken a particular affront to his wife's painting, partly because he feared a source of financial independence, but also because he felt threatened by an aesthetic hinterland into which Helen might slip, and from which he was barred (349–5).[40]

Aside from Helen's personal earnings, which in terms of the common law belonged to her estranged husband, there is the matter of property. Whilst allusions recur throughout the novel, property real and settled takes on rather greater significance towards the end, speaking most obviously to the future prospects of Helen Markham. The Huntingdon estate is mostly settled; though there are a 'few mortgages on the rest' (162). Carrying only a life interest, unable to further alienate his estate in order to raise further capital and restricted in his ability to raise capital on his life interest, the seriously indebted Arthur is predictably frustrated. Much of the estate, Helen's uncle confirms, has been 'squandered away', in the main most probably encumbered by mortgage (168).[41] Rather later, Markham confirms that the estate remains 'entailed upon little Arthur'; something which prevents the further alienation of fee simple (452).[42] The recently widowed lady of Grassdale, it is also later reported, is 'nursing a fine estate' for her son; an undoubted allusion to the trust which would anyway have existed to manage the settlement, and which would have been further expected to deal with the eventualities of little Arthur's minority as well as, very possibly, administering Helen's jointure or portion in trust (456).[43] The metaphor, which was also used by her uncle, and which recurs in the novel, carries a particular consonance.[44] It is possible that the original motivation for Arthur marrying Helen was, at least in part, financial. Helen, her aunt had observed, was likely to attract suitors precisely because she had a 'considerable fortune and expectations' (124). At the same time, however, her marriage portion is reported to be 'small' (453).

The nature and extent of the fortune to which Helen's aunt alludes is rather uncertain. Of course, Helen may have been disingenuous in suggesting to her intended that she is 'not an heiress' (164). Certainly Helen's uncle hopes her father might be persuaded to leave her a 'decent fortune' (168). But such disingenuousness is not, at the time, in character; and Markham later confirms that her father 'had not given her much' aside from her modest marriage portion (453). Huntingdon's protestation, that he 'had never given' the matter of Helen's portion a 'thought', can be more easily disbelieved (164). There again, the Graham estate is also likely to be entailed, with Helen's brother enjoying a life interest, so Huntingdon was probably reconciled to the likelihood of his bride contributing a 'small' portion to the marriage settlement (453). Such portions had reduced dramatically relative to notional settlement value, as estates had become ever more encumbered during the eighteenth and early nineteenth centuries. Alternatively, the aunt may be referring to the prospect of Helen inheriting the Staningley estate from her uncle. It is later reported that the aunt 'advised her husband to it, they say: she'd brought most of the property, and it was her wish that this lady should have it' (456). The comment suggests an original jointure in trust, and it may well be that the estate is to be established, or confirmed, for 'separate use'. Whilst Markham finds it 'strange', Helen's aunt evinces a certain familiarity with marital economics and such a settlement would in fact have been eminently sensible.[45]

A further allusion to such a settlement is made in the ostler's discussion of the recent Hargrave marriage. Hargrave, it appears, had refused to marry a 'widow' with a 'rare long purse' who had declined to let him 'have it all'; a comment which implies a determination on the part of the prospective bride to establish a 'separate' estate by spousal contract, possibly incorporated into a settlement jointure. However another prospective bride, who 'isn't quite as rich – nor as handsome either', and perhaps most importantly was reported to be rather more desperate, has proved amenable to the demands of Hargrave, and his mother. 'They say', the ostler reports, that she already has reason to 'rue her bargain' (451).[46] It is reasonable to infer that Markham would have some sympathy with the Hargraves. It is certainly the kind of marriage settlement with which he would have been more familiar, and which he would more likely have preferred his prospective bride to accept.

We do not have any details as to the nature of the Markham–Huntingdon settlement. Markham is keen that Helen should not think that he wishes to propose merely to 'claim a share in her prosperity' which, it has become apparent, is now quite considerable (457). But we do know, from the very first page of the novel, that Gilbert Markham is acutely aware of his responsibility to 'transmit the paternal acres to my children' (9).[47] Markham takes 'comfort' in discovering that the Huntingdon entail remains, and so 'strictly speaking' the estate does not belong to Helen; something which confirms that Arthur did not die intestate, whilst also suggesting that there has been no attempt to bar the entail in anticipation of spousal re-settlement (452).[48] In more prosaic terms, this fact reassures Markham that, whilst there is a social distinction between 'Mrs. Huntingdon, the lady of Grassdale Manor' and 'Mrs. Graham the artist, tenant of Wildfell Hall', any financial disparity might not be so dramatic (433). He is equally relieved to discover that there is no formal 'restriction' in the entail which is designed to discourage Helen's re-marriage.[49]

Markham signs off his narrative with the observation that he and his wife have already produced a brood of 'promising young scions'; heirs to a now considerable estate (471). So a happy ending is implied. But we only have Markham's word for this; and Gilbert Markham, possessed of a wandering eye, prone to fits of jealous rage as well as the 'scruples of false delicacy and pride' has long caused critical unease (109–10, 116–20).[50] He seems to be genuinely fond of little Arthur, and is apparently deeply enamoured by Helen. But he is also determined to 'overcome' his beloved's 'uncompromising boldness' (47–8). Even if the Huntingdon entail is securely settled on little Arthur, and even if the Staningley estate has been passed separately,

Helen has taken a calculated gamble in marrying Markham, trading off a considerable measure of her personal and financial independence so that little Arthur might have a father-figure in his life once again.[51] Here at least it seems that Helen Huntingdon might indeed have benefited from the counsel of a good lawyer.[52]

'Foul and accursed'

Fictional perhaps, but the violence that consumed the Huntingdons was intended, as Anne confirmed in her Preface, to ring true. It was the kind of violence that William Dean Howells feared. 'No one will pretend there is not vicious love beneath the surface of our society', Howells advised, and 'if he did, the fetid explosions of the divorce court would refute him' (Leckie, 1999, p. 64). It was the kind that, Sarah Stickney Ellis agreed, was best kept out of sight, if not out of mind. 'There are', she advised her readers, 'private histories belonging to every family, which, though they operate powerfully upon individual happiness, ought never to be named beyond the home-circle' (Chase and Levenson, 2000, p.12). The *Tenant* was written in defiance of this vain hope. The cold brutality of tone, devoid of the Gothic gloss that covered sister Emily's account of life at Wuthering Heights, cut no compromises.

This brutality of tone troubled contemporary reviewers, even broadly sympathetic ones such as the reviewer in the *Athenaeum* who regretfully felt bound to concede that the *Tenant* was the 'most interesting novel which we have read for some time' (Allott, 1974, p. 251). It will certainly 'seize upon the public mind', the anonymous reviewer in the *Literary World* agreed (Allott, 1974, pp. 257–9). The same dilemma was felt by Charles Kingsley who, whilst troubled by the 'splenetic and bitter tone' admired the author's determination to expose the 'foul and accursed undercurrents' which lay beneath 'smug, respectable, whitewashed English society' (Allott, 1974, pp. 269–73). It is often remarked that the *Tenant* was set twenty years prior to its writing, in so doing aligning it with a distinct Victorian critique of perceived Regency excess (McMaster, 1982, pp. 352–62). But that did not, as Kingsley noted, insulate the novel. Whilst Arthur Huntingdon might have lived and died in a previous generation there are, Anne Brontë insinuated, plenty of other Arthurs still to be found walking the shires of Victorian England. And plenty of beaten wives too, many of whom might be tempted to reach the same conclusion as Helen Huntingdon, to seize their children and disappear into the night.

It is then unsurprising that the majority of contemporary responses to the publication of the *Tenant* were indeed negative; even though, in publishing terms, the novel was a striking, if unexpected, success. The *Spectator* was appalled by the 'morbid love for the coarse, not to say the brutal' (Allott, 1974, pp. 249–50). The reviewer in the *Rambler* thought it 'one of the coarsest books which we ever perused' (Allott, 1974, p. 267).[53] A similar distaste could be found abroad, in the *North American Review*, which bemoaned the fact that 'everywhere is seen the tendency of the author to degrade passion into appetite, and to give prominence to the selfish and malignant elements of human nature'. It was a 'disgusting' novel, written, the reviewer surmised, by someone who had spent too much time reading salacious reports of adultery proceedings in civil and ecclesiastical courts (Allott, 1974, p. 262). *Sharpe's London Magazine* was especially troubled by the thought that 'lady-readers' might actually stumble across the novel, adding the salutary rider that 'so revolting are many of the scenes, so coarse and disgusting the language put into the mouths of some of the characters, that the reviewer to whom we entrusted it returned it to us, saying it was unfit to be noticed in the pages of *Sharpe's*'. The same reviewer was just as troubled by the atheism and profanity that could be found in the novel, most readily apparent in Arthur Huntingdon's refusal to be consoled by Helen's assurance that redemption would guarantee 'joy and glory after' (Allott, 1974, pp. 263–5). Casual wife-beating is one thing, but to question the existence of God, as Arthur does, is quite another (429).[54] It was a pity, a rather later review, in 1857 in the *Christian Remembrancer*, concluded, that the author of *The Tenant of Wildfell Hall* had not come across more 'gentlemen' of a proper and godly disposition. Then she might not have written such a 'dreadful' book (Allott, 1974, pp. 369–70).

Anne felt the criticism 'keenly'. Hers was a 'thoughtful nature, reserved even', Charlotte confirmed in correspondence with the publishers; a conclusion that only served to underline one of the questions that most troubled critics, that of inspiration (Smith, 2007, p. 113). To a degree it resonates still. What made Anne Brontë write such a novel? Even her sister Charlotte felt the need to provide a posthumous apology, admitting that the 'choice of subject was an entire mistake', and seeking to reassure their audience that 'Nothing less congruous with the writer's nature could be conceived' (Allott, 1974, p. 274).[55] Where had Anne encountered these 'undercurrents'? Whilst many of the myths which attend to 'delicate' Anne gazing wistfully across the moors from the parlour windows of Haworth Parsonage, contemplating death and redemption and not much else, have been debunked, it remains true that she was, on the face of it, an unlikely author for such a brutal narrative. Three possibilities can be mooted.

First, whilst the more fantastical elements of the myth might have been debunked, the peculiarity of the Brontë family setting is relevant; not least in the obvious consonance between the essential themes that run through the three novels that the sisters were writing concurrently through 1846 and 1847. Each, albeit in rather different ways, was engaged in the broader 'woman question'. Each too, as we shall see in the following chapters, sought to portray dysfunctional marriages and families beset by myriad species of violence and abuse.[56] And, as critics have also long observed, there is a shared intellectual genesis, in particular a fascination with the likes of Cooper, Richardson and Scott. A second possibility relates to Anne's evangelical sympathies.[57] At the heart of early and mid-nineteenth-century evangelicalism was a belief in the 'cult of domesticity'. The *Tenant*, it has been argued, was written as a contribution to this particular genre of literary evangelicalism. It is for this reason, perhaps, that Anne appears to dwell longer on the possibility of spiritual rather than legal reform (Doggett, 1992, pp. 90–6; Thormahlen, 1999, pp. 13–23; Talley, 2001, pp. 129–38).

However, a third context is perhaps the most compelling. In her obituary for Charlotte in 1855, Harriet Martineau noted, in passing, that there had to be a reason why Anne and Emily in particular were determined to present such 'fearful representations' of men (Allott, 1974, p. 303). Anne's hurried departure from Thorp Green Hall near York, where she was employed as governess to the Robinson family, in 1845, has long engaged critical attention; forced to leave along with her brother Branwell, so the story goes, who had also been serving as a tutor in the family but who had been caught *in flagrante* with Mrs Robinson.[58] We shall revisit Branwell and Mrs Robinson in due course. 'Sick of mankind and their disgusting ways', Anne wrote in her diary. She had 'escaped' from Thorp Green Hall, having endured 'some very unpleasant and undreamt-of experience of human nature' (Wise and Symington, 1932, II, p. 52).[59] It is certainly possible to read a personal edge into the bold assertion in the Preface to the second edition that 'such characters' as Arthur Huntingdon 'do exist' (4).[60] It has been variously suggested that elements of Branwell can be seen in Arthur Huntingdon, as well as, in a slightly more optimistic vein, the ultimately redeemed Lord Lowborough (Barker, 2001, pp. 530; Gerin, 1959, pp. 246–7, 256; Diederich, 2003, p. 25). Whilst Anne may not have suffered the miseries that afflicted Helen Huntingdon, she had come to learn from bitter experience how easily men could fall, and how much easier still it was to fall prey to violent passions.

The ghost of Helen Huntingdon would continue to stalk the bedrooms and living rooms, and courtrooms, of England for the rest of the century, and beyond. As we have already noted, successive statutes would further reform married women's property rights. The 1882 Married Women's Property Act, which finally imported the principle of separate estates more fully into common law, would be hailed in some quarters as the 'Magna Carta' of women's liberties.[61] But its dynamic was procedural rather than moral; driven more by a determination to rationalise the relation between Chancery and the common law. A century would pass before the law would be changed so that all the assets of couples in divorce, separation and nullity cases would be regarded as jointly owned 'matrimonial property'.[62] Reform of child custody law followed too; though again only slowly. The 1886 Guardianship of Infants Act was similarly hailed as the harbinger of a new jurisprudential age, giving both parents an equal right to name testamentary guardians or to have the Court award custody after a legal separation, thus breaching the common law presumption in favour of a prior paternal right. It was, however, only later with the 1925 Guardianship of Infants Act that the law finally recognised that its primary concern ought to be the best interests of the child. As for the right to separation or divorce, here it was case law rather than statute which caused the greater excitement, most famously perhaps the *Jackson* case, heralded by Elizabeth Wolstenholme Elmy with the seemingly conclusive observation, 'Coverture is dead and buried' (Shanley, 1989, p. 182; *Jackson*, 1891).[63] Here again, however, time served to temper the enthusiasm. *Jackson* confirmed that an abused wife might petition a court for permission to leave her husband; nothing more.[64]

And, a century and a half after Anne Brontë abandoned her heroine to the uncertain charms of Gilbert Markham, the spirit of Helen Huntingdon is abroad still. As Mary Shanley observes, even if the law has been reformed, at least in part, the 'vision' projected by feminist campaigners during the nineteenth century is yet to be fully 'realized' (Shanley, 1989, pp. 20–1). This is certainly true of the three jurisprudential narratives that Anne Brontë wove into *The Tenant of Wildfell Hall*: reform of matrimonial property law, infant custody and, of course, domestic abuse. Each awaits a conclusion. Division of marital property on the occasion of divorce or separation remains a matter of considerable controversy, whilst child custody remains similarly fraught, even if the cause of the tension has been inverted, so that debate oscillates as much round paternal as maternal rights. And no one really thinks that spousal abuse is a thing of the past; quite the reverse. The 'tragedy of domestic violence', as Justice Bertha Wilson has recently confirmed, endures precisely because it is 'rarely spoken of, rarely reported, rarely prosecuted, and even more rarely punished' (*Lavallee*, 1990, 872). This was true in 1848, and it is just as true today.

2
Heathcliff's Case

In the Preface Charlotte Brontë provided for the second edition of *Wuthering Heights* in 1850 she admitted that the novel must 'appear a rude and strange production' (Brontë, 2009, p. 307). Her friend Ellen Nussey certainly thought so. It was, she declared, a 'dreadful book' (Miller, 2001, p. 201). 'Whether it is right or advisable to create a being like Heathcliff, I do not know', Charlotte responded in sympathetic agreement, concluding 'I scarcely think it is' (Barker, 2001, p. 534). In truth, there was much about *Wuthering Heights* that filled Charlotte with 'renewed admiration', or so she sought to reassure the publishers Smith Elder when she sent in her Preface (Smith, 2007, p. 177). But she was never reconciled to Heathcliff. A century and a half on, of course, and it can be fairly said that few novels are more firmly embedded in the canon of nineteenth-century English literature than Emily Brontë's *Wuthering Heights*. Few have more regularly topped lists of novels 'most read', few indeed have been more commonly re-written, few for sure more frequently translated onto stage and into film. The defining images Emily wrote into the pages of her novel have entranced generations of devotees: Lockwood encountering Catherine's tormented spirit, the brooding Heathcliff roaming the moors trying to reach it, their shared entombment in the decaying graveyard of Gimmerton Kirk, and so on. So much of the Brontë 'myth' owes its vigour to *Wuthering Heights*, and also to the peculiarly enigmatic reputation of its author.

Contemporaries tended to share Ellen Nussey's sentiments. A presentation of 'incidents', a reviewer in the *Spectator* concluded, 'too coarse and disagreeable to be attractive, the very best being improbable, with a moral taint about them, and the villainy not leading to results sufficient to justify the elaborate pains taken in depicting it' (Allott, 1974, p. 217). The pervasive violence caused especial concern. Wife-beating, child-abuse, drunkenness, Godlessness, licentiousness, myriad forms of delinquency; all removed from polite conversation in mid-nineteenth-century England, but all, rather too obviously, on show in the pages of *Wuthering Heights*.[1] A novel full of 'grim and terrible criminals', Elizabeth Gaskell observed, its author too obviously entranced by narratives of 'positive violence' (Gaskell, 1997, pp. 24, 104–5, 257). The reviewer in the *Britannia* warned his readers to be braced for 'scenes of brutality' that 'are unnecessarily long and unnecessarily frequent' (Allott, 1974, p. 225). So did the reviewer in *Jerrold's Weekly Newspaper*, confirming that 'In *Wuthering Heights* the reader is shocked, disgusted, almost sickened by details of cruelty, inhumanity, and the most diabolical hate and vengeance' (Allott, 1974, p. 228). 'How a human being', the reviewer in *Graham's Magazine* rejoined, 'could have attempted such a book as the present without committing suicide before he had finished a dozen chapters, is a mystery'. It is, he continued, 'a compound of vulgar depravity and unnatural horrors, such as we might suppose a person, inspired by a mixture of brandy and gunpowder, might write for the edification of fifth-rate blackguards' (Allott, 1974, pp. 242–3). *Wuthering Heights*, E.P. Whipple concluded, in the *North American Review*, presents a 'Pandemonium' of familial and human 'depravity' (Allott, 1974, p. 247).

Charlotte took the opportunity to provide some kind of excuse, if not apology, in the 1850 Preface. It was, she urged, a figment of metaphysical 'imagination' (Brontë, 2009, p. 308). There was certainly no claim to 'truth' of the kind that Anne had pointedly made in her Preface to *The Tenant of Wildfell Hall*. But the possibility that there might, all the same, be a deeper veracity did not escape more perceptive contemporary critics. G.H. Lewes agreed that there was a 'want of air and light in the picture', but also felt moved to add 'we cannot deny its truth; sombre, rude, brutal, yet true' (Allott, 1974, p. 292). G.W. Peck likewise suggested that it was precisely because Emily had 'lifted the veil' to reveal 'the dark side of our depraved nature' that her novel had secured such a 'rapid hold' in the public mind. It showed 'how much truth there is hidden under its coarse extravagance' (Allott, 1974, p. 240).

The identification of parallels between Emily's novel and Anne's, thematic as well as structural, has since become a commonplace of

Brontë criticism; the dysfunctional family, violent husband, abused children, framed narrative, oddly unsettling closure (Chitham, 2001, pp. 14–15; Berry, 1996; Jacobs, 1986). There are of course commonly noted differences, most obviously perhaps the rather more Gothic, even fantastical, tone that overlays *Wuthering Heights*. But the similarities are not to be denied; not least in the prescription of a narrative jurisprudence, however allusive. It might be that the law is rather more obviously present on the surface of the *Tenant*. But the fact that it is less obvious in *Wuthering Heights* does not make it any less significant; quite the reverse. The jurisprudential metaphors and allusions to legal instruments that make intermittent appearances in the text belie a more pervasive concern with the limits of law and justice. The narrative jurisprudence described in *Wuthering Heights* gauges the marginal presence and absence of law. For those who live at Wuthering Heights in an environment of seeming 'sour hatred' and 'aimless violence', the law remains evasive (Gilbert and Gubar, 2000, p. 260). It flits in and out of their lives, in the same way as it flits in and out of the novel. And in the same way, of course, as it would flit in and out of the lives of those who read it. There may or may not be a truth here. But there is a very real jurisprudential prescience.

'Neither of Lascar nor gypsy'

And this jurisprudence, like so much else in the novel, moves around the extraordinary character of Heathcliff, one of the grimmest and most terrible of criminals found, not just in the pages of a Brontë novel, but in the pages of any modern English novel.[2] Contemporary reviewers were particularly horrified by Heathcliff. The 'epitome of brutality' as one baffled reviewer observed (Allott, 1974, pp. 220–1). The reviewer in the *Examiner* concurred, the 'incarnation of evil qualities; implacable hate, ingratitude, cruelty, falsehood, selfishness, and revenge', his 'hardness, selfishness, and cruelty', he concluded in an oddly pedantic tone, being 'in our opinion inconsistent with the romantic love that he is stated to have felt for Catherine Earnshaw' (Allott, 1974, pp. 220–1). Whipple, in the *North American Review*, was driven to florid revulsion:

> He is a deformed monster, whom the Mephistopheles of Goethe would have nothing to say to, whom the Satan of Milton would

consider as an object of simple disgust, and to whom Dante would hesitate in awarding the honour of a place among those whom he has consigned to the burning pitch.

(Allott, 1974, p. 248)

Possible models for Heathcliff are various, and have long engaged critical reflection. Amongst the flesh and blood alternatives Byron and brother Branwell are most frequently commended.[3] Similarities with Charlotte's Rochester are also commonly noted, as well as Anne's Arthur Huntingdon (Armstrong, 1987, pp. 193–4).

Relatedly, much of the critical debate regarding the writing of Heathcliff has moved around the extent to which Emily might have engaged, consciously or otherwise, with an incipient debate regarding a 'failure' of masculinity; one which accompanied the emergence of the idealised companionate husband (Armstrong, 2001, pp. 101–8; Leavis and Leavis, 1969, pp. 113–14). The received image of the putatively despotic patriarch still had its adherents, of course. Charlotte Brontë could probably be counted as one, as we will see when we encounter her contemplation of alternative masculinities in *Shirley*. Problems arose, however, where the environment was dysfunctional and the despot wanting in benevolence. Heathcliff was such a despot; even if, or perhaps because, in the presentation of his emotional intensity, Emily appeared to endow him with traits that many of her readers might have perceived to be feminine (Aristodemou, 2000, p. 116; Gilbert and Gubar, 2000, pp. 293–40). Charlotte clearly preferred the idea that Heathcliff is flawed by an excess of emotion, 'a sentiment fierce and inhuman: a passion such as might boil and glow in the bad essence of some evil genius' (Brontë, 2009, p. 309).

It can certainly be concluded that, for whatever reason, Emily wrote Heathcliff to be exceptional. The doggedly prosaic reviewer in the *Examiner* concluded that it was 'with difficulty that we can prevail upon ourselves to believe in the appearance of such a phenomenon, so near our own dwellings at the summit of a Lancashire or Yorkshire moor' (Allott, 1974, p. 221). And in a sense it must have been. There is much about Heathcliff that seems to be peculiarly violent and demonic and terrifying. Yet the margins between the ordinary and the extraordinary are never quite so clear or so broad. Heathcliff is exceptional, in the same way that so many who found themselves in his circumstance in mid-nineteenth-century England might have felt themselves to be exceptional. For the whole novel moves, not just around Heathcliff, but around his origins; the brutal marginalisation of a category of persons, which was constructed by social prejudice and confirmed by legal prescription. The jurisprudence that lies perhaps nearest the surface of *Wuthering Heights* is that which addressed, or perhaps failed to address, the situation of bastards.

Illegitimacy mattered in nineteenth-century England, in the same way as adultery, for reasons of both property and propriety. Samuel Johnson was blunt on the importance of property. The chastity of a woman was 'of the utmost importance, as all property depends upon it' (Macfarlane, 1980, p. 75). So was Blackstone's *Commentaries*, which confirmed that an illegitimate child was *filias nullius*, and so could 'inherit nothing, being looked upon as the son of nobody', and was 'incapable even of a gift' from his or her 'parents' (Blackstone, 1828, p. 434).[4] Legal prohibition was justified by reason of moral propriety. Bastardy was proscribed in Scripture, most starkly in the story of Ishmael given in the book of *Genesis*. In the words of the angel to Hagar, Ishmael's mother: 'And he will be a wild man; his hand will be against every man, and every man's hand against him; and he shall dwell in the presence of all his brethren' (16:12).[5] Heathcliff is Emily's Ishmael.

For the same reasons of propriety and property, as well as parochial economics, legal provisions relating to bastardy had by the 1830s become a matter of considerable debate. Coating their prejudices with a gloss of moral perturbation, haunted by Malthusian images of rampant sexuality and demographic apocalypse, leading liberal and Whig politicians had agitated for a Royal Commission to investigate the efficacy of existing provisions enacted in the 1733 Poor Law which addressed the 'evils' of bastardy.[6] The 1733 Act had placed responsibility for maintaining illegitimate children upon fathers. Critics had long pontificated on the dangers of scheming women either seducing gullible young men in order to secure prospective maintenance payments or deliberately mis-attributing parental responsibility for the same end. Others just worried that there was too much sex, and urged that it be discouraged. The infamous bastardy clauses of the 1834 Poor Law, accordingly, shifted maintenance responsibilities to unmarried women, the 'pests of society' (Cody, 2000, p. 132). It was intended to serve as a crude, but hopefully effective deterrent to extra-marital sexuality. It failed. Illegitimacy rates did not decrease. Indeed, many contemporaries feared that divesting men of their financial responsibility had caused rates to rise. Popular protest grew, leading to the amended reforms of the so-called 'little' Poor Law of 1844, which transferred jurisdiction in bastardy proceedings from poor law commissioners to the civil courts, whilst also enabling women to apply to Petty Sessions for maintenance against named fathers.[7]

The extent to which Emily was familiar with these reforms and the debates that accompanied them is, as ever, uncertain. But it might be reasonably surmised that she knew something of them, and it is difficult to imagine that they were not in her mind as she contemplated Heathcliff. Some critics have surmised that Heathcliff could be Earnshaw's illegitimate son; something that might explain the latter's fondness for the waif, not to mention his otherwise inexplicable decision to bring him home (Chitham, 2001, p. 118; Solomon, 1959, pp. 82–3). Even so, the readiness with which Earnshaw appears to recognise the responsibilities prescribed at the time in law is striking, and given what befalls the family as a result, it might be surmised that Emily betrayed, consciously or otherwise, a certain scepticism of these provisions. More likely perhaps she just relished the possibility of depicting an Ishmael abroad in West Yorkshire.[8] Either way her depiction of the Earnshaw family after Heathcliff's arrival accords very obviously with the popular assumption that families tainted by illegitimacy were necessarily predisposed to violence (Frost, 2003, p. 298).

Seemingly a foundling, denied the Earnshaw patronym, Heathcliff occupies a curiously ambivalent place; neither inside nor securely outside the family (Kermode, 1975, pp. 123–4; Davies, 1994, pp. 210–12; Musselthwaite, 1987, p. 99).[9] Nelly's suspicion is, of course, symptomatic: 'We don't in general take to foreigners here' (39). Heathcliff is taken into the Earnshaw home, but never admitted to the intensely insular Earnshaw–Linton kinship circle. In time, following Hindley's assumption of patriarchal responsibilities in the household, he is further excluded, treated 'like the other servants', sent into the fields, like a slave indeed, to toil away (47). Most importantly, of course, Cathy chooses to marry Edgar Linton because marrying the obviously illegitimate Heathcliff would 'degrade' her (71). Heathcliff hates for a reason, and he will not, or cannot, be redeemed. He will remain 'Lonely, like the devil, and envious like him' (254). Other novels liked to romanticise the foundling who by reason of fortune or merit stakes a claim to respectability (Zunshine, 2005, pp. 7–14; Evans, 2005). But there is nothing romantic about Heathcliff's illegitimacy or its consequences. He remains 'other', in life and in death.

And he looks different too; something which adds an unavoidably racial edge to his depiction. He does not look like the other Earnshaws, or indeed any of their neighbours. On first encountering Heathcliff, Lockwood notes the 'singular contrast' which his host makes with the relative normalcy of his 'abode'. 'He is', Lockwood observes, 'a dark-skinned gypsy in aspect, in dress and manners a gentleman' (3). A 'dirty, ragged, black-haired child', as Nelly Dean confirms, speaking 'gibberish that nobody could understand', a 'gypsy brat' (31). Joseph makes the same presumption, a 'flaysome devil uf a gipsy' (77). The gypsy pejorative recurs.[10] It is Isabella's immediate assumption when Heathcliff is caught in the grounds of Thrushcross, and one reinforced by her father who, pondering the orphan's 'acquisition' in Liverpool, hazards that he might be 'a little Lascar perhaps, or an American or Spanish castaway' (44).[11] Critics have, accordingly, read a colonial referent; Heathcliff as the offspring of an escaped or freed slave perhaps (Meyer, 1996, pp. 98–101; Heywood, 1987). The slavery context would certainly have resonated with many in Emily's immediate audience (Heywood, 1987). Others have contemplated Irish origins, not least because of the Liverpool association (Eagleton, 1995, pp. 3, 11, 19; Chitham, 1986, pp. 123–3; Michie, 1992, pp. 125–6, 133–5).

Heathcliff's precise origins remain elusive, deliberately so. It is, anyway, the generic ascription that matters. Heathcliff, a boy without a name, or a history, or a family, living in a state of 'legal limbo', is an alien (Frost, 2003, p. 293; Witte, 2003, p. 328). He looks different, and speaks differently. And he feels different. At one point, Nelly tries to cheer him with the observation: 'You're fit for a prince in disguise. Who knows, but your father was Emperor of China, and your mother an Indian queen, each of them able to buy up, with a week's income, Wuthering Heights and Thrushcross Grange?' (50). The colonial resonances recur. In due course, Heathcliff will indeed 'buy up' Wuthering Heights, returning to sequester the estate, degrade the patrimony, and enslave the remaining progeny. In doing so he will realise the ultimate imperialist 'nightmare', the former slave turned slave-master (Meyer, 1996, pp. 117–19, 123–4). It is not, however, the only nightmare. There is something else about Heathcliff that is every bit as troubling.

Heathcliff is a rebel, possessed as Terry Eagleton puts it, of a 'furious insurrectionary energy', the kind of man for which middle England in the late 1840s was time and again advised to be vigilant, the kind of man who could easily prove to be a Chartist sympathiser or Irish confederate (1995, pp. 20–1). And it would certainly not have taken a much greater stretch of the imagination for Emily's readers to imagine Heathcliff as the kind of swarthy Jacobin terrorist conjured by the likes of Edmund Burke a generation earlier.[12] As the young Catherine Earnshaw confirms in her diary, 'we are going to rebel' (16). The alignment of the terrorist 'other' is ancient, and also very modern. The blood-spattered Jacobin has been replaced in the twenty-first-century imagination by the shadowy jihadist. But the capacity to entrance is the same. In this sense Heathcliff is the necessary 'other' upon which, as Edward Said has intimated, the western literary canon always falls back when it wants to terrify (2003). The fact that *Wuthering Heights* so obviously shares the same Miltonic root as so much modern terrorist literature is no coincidence (Gilbert and Gubar, 2000, pp. 189–95, 253–5). Emily was fascinated by the Miltonic 'fall', and the world of providential suffering presented in *Wuthering Heights* was one common to many late Gothic novels. At the very outset it is remarked that Heathcliff is 'dark almost as if' he 'came from the devil' (31). He is later reported to be praying to his 'own black father' (153). Heathcliff's is a 'diabolical violence', not least in that it is inflicted upon his own flesh and blood (239). Is 'he mad?' the newlywed Isabella Linton writes to Nelly in horror, 'And if not, is he a devil?' (120). As Charlotte concluded, her sister's creation was 'neither of Lascar nor gipsy, but a man's shape animated by demon life – a Ghoul – an Afreet' (Brontë, 2009, p. 309).

And yet Heathcliff's violence is intensely human too. Experience has nurtured his apparent 'aversion' to 'manifestations of mutual kindliness'. Heathcliff, Nelly rightly avers, has an 'utter lack of sympathy' for a reason (187). He is tutored in the strategic use of violence. And in this he is not at all exceptional. Certainly readers of Anne's *Tenant of Wildfell Hall* might have noted a resonance, and experienced a familiar thrill.[13] For Heathcliff is also that most terrifying of terrorisers, the calculating kind. Nelly realises as much, on witnessing his return to Wuthering Heights. 'His countenance', she observed, 'looked intelligent and retained no marks of former degradation.' Still, even if 'it was subdued; and his manner quite dignified', a 'half-civilized ferocity lurked yet in the depressed brows; and eyes full of black fire' (84–5). Heathcliff's vengeance will be cold, and ironic. The man diminished by law will wreak his apocalyptic revenge on his tormentors by the use and abuse of law; and it will be all the more terrifying for this.

The limits of law

The law in *Wuthering Heights* assumes an ambivalent, as well as an elusive, form. Allusions, literal and metaphorical, are frequent, but always compromised. Magistrates and lawyers hover; the former in the person of Edgar Linton impotent in the face of Heathcliff's demonic will, the latter in the shadowy form of attorney Green too easily corrupted by it. Its limitations are sharply drawn by Hindley, as he forces a knife between Nelly Dean's teeth, 'No law in England can hinder a man from keeping his house decent, and mine's abominable! Open your mouth' (65). The writ of law barely runs at Wuthering Heights, and so its very idea is treated with scarcely veiled contempt. The irony in Heathcliff's observation, contemplating Linton and his intended bride on the evening before their forced wedding is not of the light and airy kind, 'Had I been born where laws are less strict, and tasted less dainty, I should treat myself to a slow vivisection of these two, as an evening's amusement' (238). They would certainly not be the first members of the Earnshaw–Linton family circle that Heathcliff had emotionally dismembered for fun.

It is the failure of law in the face of 'purposeless power' that fascinates.[14] Writing a decade after its publication, Emile Montegut perceptively noted that the 'terror' that Emily Brontë had imagined was one bred of 'criminal passions' unrestrained by law (Allott, 1974, pp. 376–7). The sadistic intensity of violence constantly stretches the law (Aristodemou, 2000, pp. 108–9). Instances of physical assault are frequent (16–17, 40, 51, 63, 157). It is the Earnshaw way of life. Murder is repeatedly contemplated, metaphorically and literally. Hindley contemplates murdering Heathcliff (123–4, 155). Heathcliff, haunted by the thought that he has 'murdered' his beloved Catherine, is possessed by the thought that he might murder both Hindley and Edgar (53, 85, 148).[15] It would be easy to assume that this violence is 'aimless' (Gilbert and Gubar, 2000, p. 260).[16] But it is not. In a 'Lear-world of violence', as F.R. Leavis famously termed it, the law merely assumes a different guise, one that finds expression in Hindley's advice to Edgar Linton, to 'take the law into your own fists – it will give you an appetite!' (52; Leavis and Leavis, 1969, p. 89). Edgar does (102). The violence is 'habitual', as the horrified reviewer in the *Christian Remembrancer* observed (Allott, 1974, p. 368). Everyone is corrupted.

And pretty much everyone is a victim too. Children are regularly abused. So are servants. Nelly is imprisoned at the Heights for five days, in case her return to Thrushcross Grange might jeopardise the prospective nuptials of Linton and Catherine. There is a sorry inevitability about the serial abuse of wives. The law might have sought to limit rights of chastisement, but there is nothing, in practice, that can save Isabella from being assaulted by her husband (160). Having brought Isabella to Wuthering Heights, Heathcliff tells Nelly to inform Edgar that he will 'keep strictly within the limits of the law' in the governance of his new wife. Edgar can 'set his magisterial heart at ease', except of course that he too knows that the doctrine of coverture existed precisely to ensure that the law did not come between a husband and the governance of his wife (133).[17] Subsequently Heathcliff seeks to cheer Linton with the assurance that once he has married Catherine he will be 'able to pay her back her present tyrannies, with a vigorous hand' (241). The law will not protect Catherine Linton, any more than it did her aunt.

The irony in Heathcliff's observation, as he contemplates beating his new wife, is again of the grimmer kind:

> If you are called upon in a court of law, you'll remember her language, Nelly; and take a look at the countenance – she's near the point which would suit me. No, you are not fit to be your own guardian, Isabella, now; and I, being your legal protector must retain you in my custody, however distasteful the obligation may be.
>
> (134)

Husbands had every right to confine their wives, and Heathcliff will 'take care' his new wife 'does not disgrace me by rambling abroad' (132). Even when the law might be presumed to intervene, in an instance of forced marriage, it does not, or cannot, or will not. 'There's law in the land, thank God, there is! though we be in an out-of-the-way place', Nelly reminds Heathcliff when he seeks to force Catherine into marrying Linton (242). Perhaps; but it will not save Catherine Linton. The proscriptions of English canon law matter little in the further reaches of early nineteenth-century West Yorkshire. Catherine will belong to Linton, just as Linton is the 'property' of his father, and just as she was until her marriage the property of her father (182). Possession matters because it facilitates control and it sanctions violence. Wives are beaten for the same reason as doors are kicked in, windows smashed and crockery thrown.

The dispossessed Heathcliff craves property, personal and proprietary; a simpler vengeance spiced perhaps by a deeper belief in an entitlement to patrimony barred by the proscriptions of English inheritance law.[18] His 'sole consideration', Heathcliff informs Nelly Dean is 'the triumph of seeing my descendent [sic] fairly lord of their estates, my child hiring their children' (184). But there is more to it than that. Heathcliff craves property because control also facilitates destruction. Later, as death approaches, he confesses that his entire purpose has been to 'demolish' the Earnshaw–Linton estate (287). The fact that property matters so much is made plain to the rambling Lockwood, and the reader, on the very first page of the novel, 'Thrushcross Grange is my own sir' (1). The fact that it matters too much becomes just as obvious as the novel progresses, and as Catherine realises, 'you are too prone to covet your neighbour's goods' (94). And the law is too willing to condone the covetousness, she might have added. For whilst Heathcliff's strategy will incorporate all the darker arts of deception, intimidation and violence, it will also make much of the law's apparent preference for men like him. Emily Brontë, it is clear, was just as well versed in both the weakness of humanity, and the weakness of the laws that were devised to refine it.[19]

In the absence of any potentially inconvenient settlement, gaining control of the Earnshaw estate is relatively straightforward. As there is no settlement the fee simple appears to pass to Hindley unencumbered by any other charges. This means that Heathcliff, taking advantage of Hindley's spiral into alcoholism and personal debt, can become a mortgagee of the fee. Under the terms of mortgage at common law Heathcliff would be conveyed the fee and with it control of the estate (91–2). By the time of his death, Hindley has 'mortgaged every yard of land he owned' to Heathcliff (166). Heathcliff could pursue forfeiture, and seek to acquire the fee, most obviously perhaps after Hindley's death. But he does not need money. He has plenty of it 'and every year it increases' (29). What he craves again is control, and the conveyed fee gives him this, leaving Hareton little more than a 'beggar', his 'sole chance' being 'an opportunity of creating some interest in the creditor's heart, that he might be inclined to deal leniently towards him' (164). The equity of redemption would give Hareton the prospect of redeeming the mortgage at a later date.[20] But there is no sensible prospect of his being able to raise the capital to do this, at least not yet. Heathcliff might prove to be a 'cruel, hard' landlord mortgagor (174). But that is no concern of the law. The entire purpose of the legal 'fiction' of the mortgage, and of its equity, was intended to facilitate precisely this kind of arrangement; to allow estates to raise capital on security without having to alienate the fee in perpetuity (Cousins and Ross, 1989, pp. 8–12; Watt, 2009, p. 130).

The Linton estate is rather more complex, and so accordingly is Heathcliff's strategy. The Linton estate is settled, and appears to carry an entail general rather than an entail male; unusual perhaps, but not unknown. Heathcliff is careful to ascertain the nature of the settlement entail before marrying Isabella (94).[21] Nelly recalls that she 'mentally abused' old Linton for 'securing his estate on his own daughter, instead of his sons' (145). Catherine expresses similar sentiments, hoping that half a dozen nephews might 'erase' Isabella's 'title' (94). As an entail general, in default of male progeny, the life interest would descend to females in line. Edgar, without male progeny, is clearly aware of the nature of the Linton entail and is just as 'appalled' at the prospect of the life interest passing to Isabella and her son Linton in tail; meaning that it will, in the absence of any separate estate provision, in effect pass to the stewardship of Isabella's prospective husband. It is not just the 'degradation of an alliance with a nameless man' that horrifies Edgar. Rather it is 'the possible fact that his property, in default of heirs male, might pass into such a one's power' and, Nelly recounts, 'he had the sense to comprehend Heathcliff's disposition' (89).

Heathcliff is confident that there is 'no clause' in Linton's will to secure a separate settled estate against the passage of the entail. But there is still a potential hazard, in that the death of Linton Earnshaw before that of his father could re-route the entail, providing for the settlement of the equitable interest on young Catherine Linton, with a remainder to any progeny. It is for this reason, as a caution to 'prevent disputes', that Heathcliff is determined to force the marriage of Linton and Catherine, so that Thrushcross would in this event pass into his control (190). Ideally, as Heathcliff exclaims, Edgar will anyway 'go before' his nephew, not just to avoid a disputed entail, but also because Heathcliff is worried that he will not let them 'marry now' (237, 240). Interestingly, however, Nelly reports that Edgar is reconciled to his daughter's 'union' precisely because, in the likely event of his dying first, the marriage would furnish her with some prospect of returning to the 'house of her ancestors' (229). Catherine similarly suggests, albeit under a degree of duress, that her father is supportive of the marriage (242).

The settlement should anyway be secure, and the reader is reminded by the terms of Linton's will that whilst he could bequeath 'his, and what had been' his wife's 'moveable property' to his father, any settled 'lands, being a minor he could not meddle with' (261). The entail could not therefore be barred, or the property alienated. So the tail will pass to Catherine and any progeny. In the meantime, as Nelly reflects, legality and practicality are very different things. On Linton's death, Heathcliff assumes effective control, leaving Catherine for the present 'destitute of cash and friends' and in reality unable to 'disturb his possession' (261).[22] It is reported that Edgar had established a trust of personality, apart from the settled estate, 'a portion of his income for my young lady's fortune' (229). But it transpires that this has not in fact been as yet settled, and Heathcliff manages to bribe the lawyer into delaying his attendance at Edgar's deathbed in order to alter his will (250–1). Failing this, any 'moveable property' that attached to Catherine passes on her marriage to her husband, and then on his death to Heathcliff (261).

So Heathcliff's 'diabolical prudence' has succeeded, at least for now. Catherine Linton, like Hareton, has been 'cheated' (30). And she knows it, retorting when Heathcliff questions her replanting an uprooted hedgerow, 'You shouldn't grudge a few yards of earth for me to ornament, when you have taken all my land' (284). Except, of course, that it was never really her land, but rather a fictive jurisprudential interest which was passed, by the terms of the settlement, from her father to her husband, and on to the effective possession of her deceased husband's father. The impotence and the complicity of the law have been laid bare; and not just in the person of the corrupted lawyer Green. English property law was written to help men like Heathcliff consolidate estates. It is why the strict settlement was created, and the legal mortgage, and its equity of redemption. The problem, once more, lies in the fact that it is Heathcliff who does the consolidating. The shires of middle England were not supposed to be governed by nameless dark-skinned orphans. Illegitimacy was not a bar to magistracy. It was even possible in contemporary literature to discern a grudging admiration for the commercially-attuned orphan who overcame the disadvantages of unfortunate birth to make his fortune. But he was supposed to be virtuous not 'vile', the kind of man who could in time be integrated into decent society (Zunshine, 2005, pp. 17–20). Heathcliff is not such a man.

In the end Heathcliff is thwarted, and the reader is invited to contemplate a happier future, with Hareton having presumably inherited the fee and the equitable interest, and Catherine having inherited the life interest in the Linton estate. But any reassurance is tempered, as it was in the *Tenant*, and not simply because of residual distrust of the narrator. If there is a happier future it has been achieved by luck and circumstance, and the exhaustion which finally overcomes Heathcliff. It has not been secured by any institution devised by society, certainly not the Church and certainly not the law. It is perhaps significant that Heathcliff dies intestate; a final absence. He wanted to 'annihilate' the estate he now possesses, but overcome with the exhaustion of indecision leaves it too late (296). His estate will escheat to the Crown. The reader is left to infer that Hareton, now bolstered by income from the Linton settlement, is able to exercise his equitable right of redemption, discharge the mortgages held by the Crown and secure the re-conveyance of the fee.[23] Or maybe not.

'I am Heathcliff'

'Nelly, I am Heathcliff – he's always, always in my mind – not as a pleasure, any more than I am always a pleasure – but, as my own being', Catherine Earnshaw famously declares (73). He is 'more myself than I am' (71). It is a declaration of sublimation as well as affiliation, and much more too.[24] Determined to remain 'half savage and hardy, and free' Catherine Earnshaw consciously subsumes her identity with that of a violent Jacobin of uncertain racial origins and even less certain moral and sexual propriety. Of course, the declaration has no legal resonance. Following her marriage, Catherine's legal personality is subsumed into that of Edgar Linton. But her spiritual personality is not. Catherine assumes a metaphor, loaded with both religious and jurisprudential symbolism, and challenges the reader. She might have been Edgar's legal wife. But she was Heathcliff's spiritual lover. Whilst the merits of sibling affection were commonly championed in much eighteenth-century literature and polemic, the peculiar nature of the relationship between Catherine and Heathcliff, so violent and so thrilling, was calculated to discomfort. Catherine was 'too fond' (36). The thought that the violence and the thrill might have a sexual connotation was, of course, worse still.

And it was not just the violence, nor the broader insinuation of barely suppressed sexuality. There was something still more horrifying lurking just below the surface of *Wuthering Heights*, a species of sexuality that – quite literally in this instance – appears to be so perverse that it dare not speak its name. Foucault famously termed it society's 'dreadful secret', and Emily Brontë made her readers contemplate it (Foucault, 1990, p. 109).[25] Amidst the myriad horrors and violations that Emily wrote into her novel can be found, however evasively insinuated, the prospect of sibling incest, worse still perhaps cross-racial incest between half-siblings (Goetz, 1982, p. 363).[26] Anxious critics such as Sydney Dobell felt moved to reassure tender consciences, advising that even 'in the very arms of her lover we are not to doubt' Catherine's 'purity' (Allott, 1974, p. 278). Others, such as W.C. Roscoe and John Skelton, who depicted a 'half-savage child' bound in by a 'chain of fire' to the 'brawny young Titan', preferred to blame Heathcliff (Allott, 1974, pp. 337, 349).[27] If Catherine's virtue had been compromised it was his fault. The alternative, that she willingly embraced her role as Heathcliff's accomplice, that she craves violence and sublimation, and that in this sublimation she ultimately takes possession of him, was beyond the margins of decent contemplation.

Of course, because Heathcliff's origins are so uncertain, so is the nature of his sibling relationship. If he was indeed Earnshaw's illegitimate son then any relationship with Cathy would have been incestuous for reasons of consanguinity (Solomon, 1959, p. 82). If he was not – given the absence of any evidence of guardianship proceedings and the fact that legalised adoption would not follow for over a century – there would be no legal bar on their sexual engagement, provided of course it was sanctified by the institution of marriage. Nevertheless, the discomfort of the reader would have been barely assuaged. Whilst the intensity of inter-familial marriage between the Earnshaws and Lintons is indeed striking, it is again the absences which fascinate.[28] The evasion of the text has long entranced critics (Solomon, 1959, pp. 80–3; Paglia, 1990, pp. 444–51; Gilbert and Gubar, 2000, p. 258). The reader is left to surmise the implications of a relationship the nature of which remains elusive, but which, even if not uncommon in the romantic genre, here appears to be impervious to moral, scriptural or indeed legal injunction.

The law moreover was every bit as elusive. Incest might indeed be a primary cultural taboo. But the legal situation in nineteenth-century England, like the scriptural, was in fact far from certain. On the face of it, scriptural injunction seemed clear. Chapter 18 of *Leviticus* proscribed various degrees of incestuous relation. Sibling incest was specifically condemned in verse 9: 'The nakedness of thy sister, the daughter of thy father, or the daughter of thy mother, whether she be born at home, or born abroad, even their nakedness thou shalt not uncover.' The proscription of close sibling incest was relatively uncontroversial. Thereafter, however, it was apparent that within both clergy and laity there was a growing measure of uncertainty, even indifference.[29] Certainly whilst consanguineous incest was broadly disapproved, incest constructed through affinity was not. The demise of canon law jurisdiction further enhanced the sense of inconsistency.[30] Ecclesiastical courts generally preferred to deal with mooted cases of incest as matters of adultery or fornication, though they might also issue declarations which would render marriages within proscribed degrees 'voidable', which meant that they would have no further force in law.[31] When a case fell within the jurisdiction of the civil courts, most often in matters of property and probate, they would adjudge accordingly. However, the situation changed dramatically following the passage of Lord Lyndhurst's Act in 1835, a late amendment to which stated that all marriages that fell within the proscribed degrees would be void *ab initio*. Accordingly, if such a marriage was declared void, children would be retrospectively declared to be illegitimate and thus suffer all the equivalent disadvantages in probate. At the same time, the 1835 Act further removed the effective jurisdiction of the ecclesiastical courts in cases relating to alleged incest.[32]

As the eighteenth and nineteenth centuries progressed public concern regarding the disparity between the degrees of scriptural, legal and cultural prohibition grew, with many scholars minded to conclude that incest proscription was founded as much in custom as anything more jurisprudentially solid. Bolingbroke ascribed it to nothing more than legal 'prejudice' and 'habit', whilst Alleyne dismissed the Levitical injunctions as one of the prime 'absurdities of papal relicts' (Pollak, 2003, pp. 41, 44). One such absurdity caused particular concern and became the focus of reform debate, the situation of widowers who wished to marry the sisters of deceased wives.[33] Once again, this particular injunction found an original proscription in canon law, in *Leviticus* 8:7, which stated: 'The nakedness of thy father's wife shalt thou not uncover: it is thy father's nakedness.' The common law doctrine of coverture, which framed the juristic fiction of the sister-in-law, was derived from the second clause of 8:7 (Gullette, 1990, pp. 142–3; Anderson, 1982, pp. 74–5; Kuper, 2009, pp. 60, 73). However, *Deuteronomy* 25: 5, in suggesting that a surviving brother had a positive 'duty' to marry a bereaved sister-in-law lent scriptural support to those who anyway argued that such women were eminently suited to assume their sister's former responsibilities as housekeeper and mother (Pollak, 2003, pp. 28–30).

This, of course, was precisely what Aunt Branwell did; moving to Haworth following her sister's death and assuming all the effective duties of housekeeper to Patrick Brontë and mother to his children.[34] The Brontë children repeatedly bore witness to their appreciation of her sacrifice, clearly very aware of the peculiarity, at least in law, of their situation and hers. The theme of sisterly affections recurs throughout the novels, as does a concern for the welfare of orphan children (Corbett, 2008, pp. xi, 86, 92–6, 104–9; Lovell-Smith, 1994). And it is reasonable to assume that most readers of *Wuthering Heights* would have been just as familiar with the broader context set by the contemporary debate regarding the situation of deceased wives' sisters.[35] Most, it can be further assumed, would probably have shared the general view that such marriages posed little threat to the Victorian family, and might even serve its better interests. Although perhaps those readers of *Wuthering Heights* who harboured doubts might just have wondered if the acquiescence to too close a union between brothers and sisters, regardless of how it is constructed in law or Scripture, was indeed to tempt the wrath of God.[36]

Many of those who argued the case for legal reform ventured the question of consistency. It was frequently pointed out that whilst the law prohibited the marriage of widowers and sisters-in-law, it was untroubled by the marriage of cousins. Even though consanguineous, such marriages were not proscribed in *Leviticus*, and so not proscribed in canon or common law either. The radical John Bright was not alone in questioning 'Was there any man of common-sense who would not say that on every natural ground the marriage of first cousins was more objectionable than the marriage of a man with his deceased wife's sister?' (Kuper, 2009, p. 66). Whilst some, such as Paley, were troubled by the prospect, broader popular opinion was sympathetic to a prospective species of 'companionate marriage' which enjoyed the added virtue of serving to secure the family estate (Kuper, 2009, pp. 24–9, 107–10; Nixon, 2007, p. 137). Marriage between cousins was, accordingly, far from unusual, to some degree socialised indeed, and regardless of any jurisprudential inconsistency rarely seemed to disturb nineteenth-century sensibilities (Frost, 2008, pp. 63–4; Morris, 1991, pp. 235–6; Kuper, 2009, pp. 31–3). Readers of Austen were certainly inured to it, as were those of Thackeray, Gaskell, Barrett Browning, Trollope – even Beatrix Potter.

And readers of *Wuthering Heights*, if their attention was not blinded by the altogether more exciting passion of Heathcliff and Catherine, would have noted its recurring presence in the successive marriages of Catherine Linton in the closing chapters. It is difficult to read a clear line into these two marriages; at least with regard to the virtues or vices of cousin-marriage. Heathcliff justifies the first marriage, to Linton, in terms of securing their 'joint' succession and prosperity (189). Yet Heathcliff's motives are compromised, and the marriage proves to be fraught. Linton moreover is no recommendation for close familial inter-breeding, as any devotee of the latest essays in nineteenth-century eugenics might have noted.[37] Her second marriage, to Hareton, however, appears to be destined for a brighter future. The closing images describe a couple growing ever closer as they seek to restore harmony to the estates of Thrushcross and Wuthering Heights and to the lives of those who inhabit them. If anyone who reflected on these final images had any lingering doubts they could perhaps recall the similar resolution which Austen had prescribed in the marriage of Fanny and Edmund at the close of *Mansfield Park*; though whether or not they would as a result have felt any more reassured is a matter of conjecture (Corbett, 2008, pp. 25–7, 36–41).

A 'fierce book'

Charlotte famously did her best to detach her sister from the darker suspicions that troubled contemporary critics of *Wuthering Heights*.[38] In public, she sought to present a sister who was of a 'spirit more sombre than sunny', too easily fascinated by the 'tragic and terrible', who wrote out of naivety rather than a desire to terrify. The novel, as she affirmed in the 1850 Preface, 'was hewn in a wild workshop, with simple tools, out of homely materials', and having 'formed these beings, she did not know what she had done' (Brontë, 2009, pp. 308, 310). Charlotte's efforts were reinforced by Elizabeth Gaskell, who was keen to advise her readers of Emily's 'fierce, wild intractability' (Gaskell, 1997, pp. 257–8; Miller, 2001, pp. 202–5). It all enhanced the image of a literary 'genius', as Walter Swinburne termed her, composing paragraphs and stanzas as she walked the moors and cooked supper in the parsonage kitchen (Allott, 1974, p. 440). Emily is perhaps the most mythic element in the sometimes overwhelming mythology of the Brontë sisters.[39] 'Shakespeare's youngest sister', an awed Angus Mackay suggested in 1898 (Allott, 1974, p. 446). Later poetic paeans have all added further lustre to the mythic Emily, even where they have sought to do otherwise. Where Sylvia Plath mused on a seeming invitation to suicide, Ted Hughes wondered the power of such a 'fierce book'.[40] In so doing, each served to reinforce the sense that there is something mystic about both the novel and its author.

Georges Bataille famously observed:

> Emily Brontë of all women seems to have been the object of a privileged curse. Her short life was only moderately unhappy. Yet keeping her moral integrity intact, she had a profound experience of the abyss of evil. Though few people could have been more severe, more courageous or more proper, she fathomed the very depths of evil.
>
> (Bataille, 1990, p. 15)

The question of quite how Emily fathomed such depths has haunted contemporary and modern critics alike; just as the same critics have agonised over how Anne could fathom the particular 'truth' she chose to depict in the *Tenant*. Disregarding Charlotte's anxious apologetics, critics have found it hard to resist the thought that Emily wrote something of herself into the character of the 'half-savage' Catherine Earnshaw, just as she might have incorporated something of Branwell into the demonic Heathcliff.[41] Dante Gabriel Rossetti could only surmise that both author and creation were possessed of all the 'stronger' and unnatural 'female tendencies' (Allott, 1974, p. 300).[42] It is easy to see why some might wish to project a bit of Emily the 'wild pagan' onto Catherine the 'wild, wick slip', such a haunted, and haunting, soul (36; Jacobs, 1986, p. 204).

The pagan insinuation carries a particular charge of course; one closely aligned with the demonic pejoratives written into the character of Heathcliff. The anti-clerical tone of the novel has been long appreciated; the canting Calvinism of Joseph; the physical and metaphorical decay of Gimmerton chapel; the closing depiction of the sexton opening up Cathy's tomb so that she and Heathcliff may finally rest together, a symbolism which achieved the peculiar alignment of three of the most feared of contemporary Christian abominations, incest, necrophilia and sacrilege (297–300).[43] In a passage pregnant with Miltonic allusion, Catherine recounts a dream in which she was 'flung' from heaven 'and into the middle of the heath on the top of Wuthering Heights; where I woke sobbing for joy' (71). The dream obviously provides a metaphor for Cathy's removal from the 'heaven' of Thrushcross to the 'hell' of Wuthering Heights (Gilbert and Gubar, 2000, pp. 189, 252–5). If he can be trusted, Lockwood certainly reaches the conclusion that Cathy's love for Heathcliff is itself demonic. Following this lead, Albert Camus famously appraised *Wuthering Heights* as 'one of the greatest novels because it finishes in failure and revolt – I mean in death without hope'. The 'main character' in the novel, he added, 'is the devil', whilst the love that Emily vests in Cathy and Heathcliff 'can be continued only in hell' (Camus, 1979, p. 265).

It can be argued that Catherine Earnshaw appears to resemble exactly the kind of 'wild woman' whose image horrified so many contemporary critics of an incipient nineteenth-century feminist literature; the kind of cultural 'unbeliever', to adopt Mona Caird's ironic caricature, who is made to resemble the 'wicked sisters in a fairy tale, baleful creatures who go about the world doing bad deeds and oppressing innocence as it sits rocking the cradle by the fireside' (Hamilton, 1995, p. 291). Not only does Emily Brontë paint an apocalyptic picture of familial dysfunction, but in making Catherine such an enchanting heroine so too does she seek to lure young women into social as well as sexual transgression. And the damage is plain for all to see. Catherine Earnshaw is driven mad by passion, quite literally it seems, or so Isabella and Nelly Dean conclude (112, 120). Such a woman, as Caird noted half a century later, and with a due measure of irony, is properly termed a 'rebel', not necessarily because she was rebellious, but because she was perceived to be so (Hamilton, 1995, p. 291).

And the perception of an author possessed by a peculiarly feminist 'revolutionary ardour' has remained; a 'heretic', not just in her religion, but in her determination to challenge prevailing cultural and political norms (Aristodemou, 2000, pp. 126–8). Of course there is again the issue of narrative framing. What we know of life with the Earnshaws, we know by grace of Nelly Dean and Lockwood, two judges of distinctly disapproving disposition. Even so, and with that caveat in place, most modern critics have preferred to imagine a revolutionary, and putatively feminist, Emily Brontë. Stevie Davies hails an author driven by a 'spirit of perversity' to present before her readers a picture of 'fratricidal relations' and the 'dark violence' that lies at the 'heart of human affairs' (Davies, 1994, pp. xi, 28–30, 74).[44] In similar vein, Nancy Armstrong reads *Wuthering Heights* as a novel of sexual and political 'violation', written to disturb the cherished Victorian fantasy of happy homesteads, of angelic mothers and cherubic children (Armstrong, 2003, pp. 431–2). Of course, it can be argued that in deploying a male protagonist as the principle destroyer Emily Brontë disrupts any simple feminist critique. The strength of this argument rests squarely upon whether Catherine's famous declaration of love and affinity is a testament of submission as well as sublimation; and that is for the reader to decide.

The feminist implications of *Wuthering Heights* as a novel of more specifically jurisprudential 'resistance' have been drawn out by Maria Aristodemou. In describing the absence of law as much as its presence, a novel such as *Wuthering Heights* presents women, otherwise silenced, with their only entrance to the 'labyrinth' of law (Aristodemou, 2000, pp. 28, 270–2, 277). Invited to 'delve beyond the surface' of the text, Emily's readers encountered the irreducible relation of patriarchy and violence, as they did the prospective insinuation that when human passion engages the fragile pretence of law and reason, as it so often will, it is the latter that devours the former (Aristodemou, 2000, pp. 107–9). Aristodemou's ambition chimes with that of fellow post-modern jurists who prefer to imagine the law as a construct of 'human relationships' and human sentiments, of 'love and affection, pity and friendship', rather than the fictions of abstract jurisprudence (Douzinas, 2000, pp. 33, 341). Richard Rorty has suggested that such jurisprudence is written ironically, by 'strong poets' (Rorty, 1999, pp. 16–20, 60–1, 80; 2007, pp. 28–9, 108, 117). Emily Brontë, it might be argued, was such a poet.

In her Preface to the 1850 edition, Charlotte observed that on first encountering a draft of some of her sister's earlier poems, 'I looked it over, and something more than surprise seized me – a deep conviction that these were not common effusions, not at all like the poetry women generally write… To my ear, they had also a peculiar music – wild, melancholy, and elevating' (Brontë, 2009, 301). It is not difficult to discern, in lines from 'The Philosophy' for example, antecedents for the violent passion that will erupt in *Wuthering Heights*:

> No promised heaven, these wild desires,
> Could all, or half fulfil;
> No threatened hell, with quenchless fires,
> Subdue this quenchless will!
>
> (Brontë, 1992, p. 7)

Or in these from 'The Old Stoic':

> And if I pray, the only prayer
> That moves my lips for me
> Is, 'Leave the heart that now I bear,
> And give me liberty!'
> Yes, as my swift days near their goal.
> 'Tis all that I implore;
> In life and death, a chainless soul,
> With courage to endure.
>
> (Brontë, 1992, p. 31)

Strong poetry indeed.[45] Four years before commencing *Wuthering Heights*, in an essay entitled 'The Butterfly', Emily had reflected:

> All creation is equally insane. There are those flies playing above the stream, swallows and fish diminishing their number each minute: these will become in their turn, the prey of some tyrant of air or water; and man for his amusement or his needs will kill their murderers. Nature is an inexplicable puzzle, life exists on a principle of destruction; every creature must be the relentless instrument of death to the others, or himself cease to live.
>
> (Eagleton, 1975, pp. 98–9)

The affinity of nature and the 'principle of destruction' in a pre-social' world of irreducible 'dissonance' suggests more than a simple anti-clericalism. It confirms the 'underlying truth of violence' (Eagleton, 1975, pp. 98–100, 107–8). Deploying a metaphor of striking prescience, Hillis Miller suggests that these sentiments confirm Emily's view that in our 'patternless lives' violence is the 'sole law of life' (Miller, 1975, p. 164). A little over a century after Emily wrote these lines, in his notorious Preface to Frantz Fanon's *The Wretched of the Earth*, Jean-Paul Sartre commended its author for noting the role of violence in the drawing of 'humanity'. Fanon, he observed, 'shows clearly that this irrepressible violence is neither sound nor fury, nor the resurrection of savage instincts, nor even the effect of resentment: it is man recreating himself' (Fanon, 2001, pp. 18, 20). Such, according to Edward Said, is a 'literature of resistance' (Said, 1994, p. 331). Emily Brontë, the strongest of strong poets, wrote precisely such a literature. The triumph of passion over prejudice and patriarchy, necessarily liberating and necessarily violent, matters. And so does the intrinsic, and inevitable, failure of the law.

3
The Rochester Wives

Charlotte Brontë struggled to find a publisher for *Jane Eyre*. Its subject matter, which included not just insanity, but bigamy, adultery and various instances of domestic violence, obviously gave pause for thought; as, it seemed, did its sheer intensity. Charlotte's Jane confessed that the 'testament' might seem almost 'incredible' (347). Once published, contemporary critics were commonly appalled; again in much the same way as they were on first reading Anne's *Tenant* and Emily's *Wuthering Heights*.[1] Whilst the evident 'vitality' of the novel earned G.H. Lewes's cautious admiration, others, such as the reviewer for *Atlas*, worried rather more that such a 'sublime' passion as found amidst the pages of *Jane Eyre*, might 'make the pulses gallop and the heart beat' rather too fast (Allott, 1974, pp. 84–5).[2] Elizabeth Rigby was certainly concerned, concluding in the *Quarterly Review* that the novel was written with 'great coarseness' and in 'horrid taste', its protagonist 'unregenerate and undisciplined' (Allott, 1974, pp. 106–10). There was, the reviewer for the *Spectator* agreed, a rather 'low tone of behaviour' abroad in the novel (Allott, 1974, p. 75). Charlotte's publisher, George Smith, recorded hearing that Lady Herschel had forbidden her daughters from reading such an 'immoral' novel (Miller, 2001, p. 22).[3] At the same time, despite, or perhaps because of, this reception, *Jane Eyre* rapidly became a publishing sensation, selling 2500 copies in the first couple of months of early autumn 1847 (Glen, 2002, pp. 109–10, 134–6).

And it remains a publishing sensation, read by successive generations, firmly embedded at the very core of the canon of nineteenth-century English literature, and particularly cherished as a defining text in the emergence of a distinctive 'woman's' novel; a 'revolutionary' feminist testament according to Lucasta Miller, a defining 'story of a woman's struggle for independence' according to Heather Glen (Miller, 2001, p. 13; Glen, 2002, pp. 25–6, 52). Adrienne Rich famously termed it a 'feminist manifesto', confirming that the 'wind that blows through this novel' is a 'wind of sexual equality – spiritual and practical' (Rich, 1979, pp. 89, 97–8, 105). The same metaphor is enjoined by Cora Kaplan (Kaplan, 1986, p. 173). And it is easy, contemplating Jane's famous appeal for intellectual, if not political, liberation to see why the novel has attracted such approving epithets:

> Millions are condemned to a stiller doom than mine, and millions are in silent revolt against their lot... Women are supposed to be very calm generally; but women feel just as men feel; they need exercise for their faculties, and a field for their efforts as much as their brothers do; they suffer from too rigid a restraint, too absolute a stagnation, precisely as men would suffer; and it is narrow-minded in their more privileged fellow-creatures to say that they ought to confine themselves to making puddings and knitting stockings, to playing on the piano and embroidering bags. It is thoughtless to condemn them, or laugh at them, if they seek to do more or learn more than custom has pronounced necessary for their sex.
>
> (109)

Others, of course, are not so readily convinced by the feminist Jane. Anita Allen suggests that the Jane who emerges at the end of the novel is thoroughly conformist, a putative disciple of the Austinian school of legal positivism whose belief in the importance of rules, fairly and rigorously enforced, has been only enhanced by the series of injustices she has personally suffered over the years (Allen, 1992, pp. 176–8, 235–7).[4] Of course, the fact that Charlotte might have crafted an ultimately conformist protagonist does not preclude the possibility that she might also have crafted a putatively feminist novel. It was certainly Margaret Oliphant's supposition. *Jane Eyre*, she observed, was 'new' and 'startling', representative indeed of 'a kind of revolution' in women's 'fiction' (Wilkes, 2001, p. 42).

But there is a still closer context. The full title of the novel is *Jane Eyre: An Autobiography*, and even if it was not a 'regular autobiography', in Jane's testament Charlotte determined to write, not just about the condition of women like herself, but about their 'peace of mind', or lack of it (83, 347; Glen, 2002, p. 25; Ingham, 2006, pp. 172–3). It is again a matter of margins, of what lies beneath the surface. At the edge of human anxiety lies the horror of madness, and at the heart of *Jane Eyre* is the figure of Bertha Mason, the iconic 'madwoman in the attic'. In the presentation of Bertha Mason, modern critics such as Elaine Showalter have acclaimed a defining moment in the 'evolution from Romantic stereotypes of female insanity to a brilliant interrogation of the meaning of madness in women's daily lives' (Showalter, 1987, p. 66). Psychopathic metaphors pervade *Jane Eyre*. Everyone surveys, everyone diagnoses, everyone presumes to treat and to cure (Shuttleworth, 1996, pp. 15–17, 39–45, 173, 219–21).

Here again, however, contemporaries were nothing like so sure. The 1840s and 1850s were decades of 'enormous, even revolutionary, change' in both legal and cultural perceptions of madness (Showalter, 1987, p. 26). Public attention was rapt, the debate fierce. And novels mattered. Edward Seymour was not alone in bemoaning their apparent fascination with sensationalist accounts of supposed insanity:

> Still the feeling fostered by novel writers (who never, by the way, as far as I know, really depict a lunatic case), the feeling for absolute secrecy which pervades society, the idea that where there is secrecy there is the opportunity for injustices – all these operate on the public mind to decry similar institutions.
>
> (Suzuki, 2006, p. 176)

Joseph Mason Cox agreed, revisiting the thought that such literature actually rendered young impressionable women more susceptible to 'love-madness' (Small, 1996, pp. 44–8).[5] They may or may not have been justified in being so concerned. Certainly Jane is herself presented as an enthusiastic, even dangerously 'independent' reader of novels; the kind of woman who might indeed be susceptible to such persuasions (8, 21). But either way, *Jane Eyre* can and should be read as a strategic intervention in an often frenzied discursive struggle which engaged myriad questions regarding culture, ethics, science, and of course law.

Diabolical laws

The common law had presumed a role in controlling lunatics for centuries. Yet this presumption was oddly compromised. In more prosaic jurisdictional terms, up until the end of the eighteenth century its attention had been directed more towards the issue of criminal insanity (Bartlett, 2001, p. 107). In contrast, in matters of civil jurisdiction, including certificates of lunacy and commitment orders, the attention of the law seemed to be more evasive. Here, there were two matters of potential import: the question of the insanity of an alleged lunatic, and the collateral issue of their confinement. In both cases, recourse to the law was largely voluntary, itself the subject of considerable public unease, and confused by the increasingly confident pretensions of an emergent discourse of professional psychiatry.

With regard to proceedings for securing certificates of lunacy, families could petition the Lord Chancellor's Masters in Lunacy for an 'inquisition' or Commission in Lunacy in order to gauge whether an alleged lunatic was a 'a proper person to be taken charge of and detained under care and treatment'.[6] The reasons why they might choose to do so were various. Primary among them was the desire to secure entailed estates. The care of a committed lunatic passed to a 'guardian', whilst the management of his or her estates was vested in a 'committee'. Very often they were one and the same, more often still they were appointed from within the committed lunatic's family. Applicants could also seek to have marriages declared null. But such occasions were rare. Up until the 1857 Divorce Act, spouses who later discovered that they had married a lunatic had little recourse in law. As George Eliot observed, on reading *Jane Eyre*, the law which 'chains a man soul and body to a putrefying carcase' was indeed 'diabolical' (Grudin, 1977, p. 146). The greater public concern, however, was directed towards those who might be wrongfully certified and confined. In 1845, an Alleged Lunatics Friend Society was even established to press for legal reform in commission procedures (McCandless, 1983, pp. 86–8).

The possibilities for abuse and corruption were patent. Whilst the final decision in a commission case rested with the jury, it is clear that in many instances the power of medical evidence, alongside the direction of the Master of the Commission, had an awe-inducing effect.

An Act for the Regulation of Proceedings under Commissions of Lunacy, in 1853, was intended to address some of these abuses, but in seeking to rationalise proceedings, merely made committals easier. Up until 1853, moreover, lunacy certificates could be issued on the evidence of just two medical experts, commonly known as 'alienists', and notably without any need for a personal examination of the alleged lunatic.[7] This latter fact caused considerable disquiet, even within the medical profession. In his *Enquiry Concerning the Indications of Lunacy*, published in 1830, John Conolly had loudly adverted to the dangers inherent in a system that seemed so dependent on often semi-detached medical opinions and so ready to confirm the incarceration of family members who might, in reality, be more inconvenient than mad (Suzuki, 2006, pp. 73–7). Conolly's view was further supported by other prominent psychiatrists such as Henry Monro, and increasingly, and perhaps most importantly, by successive editors of the *Lancet* (Suzuki, 2006, p. 171; McCandless, 1983, pp. 90–1).

At the same time, however, counter-polemics, such as James Prichard's *Treatise on Insanity*, published five years after Conolly's *Enquiry*, just as vigorously defended the notion that families were best placed to adjudge the nature and extent of any 'moral' lunacy found in their midst, just as it also recognised their complementary capacity to ascertain the precise threat that such a lunatic might pose to their property and estates (Scull, 1981, pp. 7–10).[8] Such justification, however, did little to allay popular suspicions regarding the relation of mutual dependency that existed between families who wanted relatives committed and 'alienists' who wanted to be hired to provide such certificates.[9]

The attitude of the courts, particularly in prominent cases of appeal from Lunacy Commissions, was far from consistent; oscillating between periods during which it articulated a greater concern for individual liberty and periods when it was clearly inclined to defer to medical opinion. For much of the eighteenth century, courts had tended to be more active in protecting individual liberty. Lord Hardwicke's judgement in *Lord Donegal's Case* is often presented as the most famous example (*Lord Donegal's Case*, 1751). By the early nineteenth century, however, courts seemed altogether more sensitive to the concerns of anxious families keen to secure their estates. Lord Eldon's notorious judgement in *Ridgway* in 1802, that in assessing mental capacity, a court or a commission should first and foremost look to an ability to properly manage an estate, was confirmed four years later by Lord Erskine in *Cranmer*, who agreed that an inability to properly conduct business as well as personal 'affairs' was itself evidence of an 'unsound mind' (*Ridgway*, 1802; *Cranmer*, 1806).

Half a century on, certain judges were prepared to articulate a rather greater scepticism, particularly in the matter of the supposed sanctity of medical evidence. In *Nottidge* in 1849, Baron Pollock commented that courts should reject the 'notion' that 'any person may be confined in a lunatic asylum or a madhouse who has any absurd or even mad opinion upon any religious subject', whilst the Lunacy Commissioners should 'liberate every person who is not dangerous to himself or others' (*Nottidge*, 1849). In the main, however, judges remained willing to countenance medical evidence which was often couched in nothing more solid than vague notions of 'love-madness' or an 'unsound mind' (Suzuki, 2006, pp. 156–8; Williams, 2005, pp. 132–7).[10] Moreover, in his pointed response to Pollock's comments, published in the respected *Journal of Psychological Medicine*, the famous Forbes Winslow flatly countered that any 'insane person is both dangerous to himself and others, whatever may be the degree of his mental disturbance' (McCandless, 1983, pp. 93–4). For men such as Winslow, the court and the family remained the twin guardians of public safety, possessed of a shared responsibility to keep the insane off the streets of England; a point affirmed by the Lunacy Commissioners themselves in their own response to Baron Pollock (McCandless, 1983, p. 94).

It is clear that in the matter of securing certificates of lunacy, whilst courts and Commission retained a nominal jurisdiction, the dominant discourse was fashioned by the alienists and the families who hired them. And it was not, of course, limited solely to securing certificates. The second, necessarily collateral, issue was that of confinement. And it was here, in the matter of supposedly 'wrongful confinement', that public concerns were greatest. Having secured a certificate, a guardian might then seek to have their ward placed in a public or private asylum; neither of which, up until 1845, were subject to any coherent system of public inspection.[11] There again they might not; and there was no legal requirement that they should. Strategies of 'domestic psychiatry', of what Suzuki terms 'discreet and invisible control', had obvious attractions (Suzuki, 2006, pp. 114, 138, 151, 174–5). Perhaps most importantly, they evaded public embarrassment; and few ailments caused middle-class Victorians greater concern than familial insanity. In 1860, a Parliamentary Select Committee on the Care and Treatment of Lunatics sympathised that 'Insanity under any shape is so fearful a malady, that the desire to withdraw it from the observation of the world is both natural and commendable' (McCandless, 1983, p. 96).

More positively, there was a strong evangelical literature that supported strategies of 'unbossoming' ('unbosoming'); a confessional as well as redemptive process which was presumed to work most effectively within the supposedly more receptive and nurturing environment of the family (Suzuki, 2006, pp. 113–17). Thackeray chose to pursue this approach in the case of his intermittently psychotic wife. At the same time, myriad accounts of ill-managed, brutal asylums, public and private, contributed a further dimension of concern; encouraging, as Conolly regretted, families to incarcerate their relatives 'in garrets, or in the secluded wings of country mansions' (McCandless, 1983, p. 97). In such circumstances, families would very often seek to employ the services of professional 'keepers', generally men or women who presented themselves as having had experience of dealing with lunatics in public or private asylums. All in all, as Sir Robert Peel concluded, for reasons of both principle and practice, it was always 'preferable to leave' lunatics 'in the custody of their relations, than to lock them up in madhouses' (Suzuki, 2006, p. 174). It was a solution that chimed, moreover, with received perceptions of the sanctuary and indeed sanctity of the mid-Victorian family. As Lord Brougham confirmed, it was 'better to trust to the relatives, wives, husbands, or children of persons unhappily afflicted' than to the Lunacy Commissioners (Suzuki, 2006, p. 1174).

But not always, of course; for whilst some may have recommended strategies of 'domestic psychiatry' for their redemptive potential, for their capacity to facilitate 'unbossoming' perhaps, or maybe just to avoid placing loved ones in brutalising institutions, for many others, the abiding virtue of 'domestic psychiatry' was its extra-legal quality. The fact that courts consistently refused to intervene in cases where husbands were alleged to have committed acts of violence against supposedly lunatic wives confined in their private homes speaks volumes; both of the reticence of the courts and of the particularly perilous conditions in which unwanted Victorian wives might find themselves.[12] The common law was evasive, the civil jurisdiction particularly so; and that evasion was reciprocal. Many Victorians preferred not to engage the law and it, by and large, preferred not to engage their lunatic relatives.

Moral madness and morbid perversions

In this, the presence of so many alternative, often conflicting, discourses clearly played a determinate role. This was, as Andrew Scull has suggested, an age of scientific 'professional imperialism', an age in which the public discourses of the medical profession enchanted contemporaries, just as it has entranced later historians and historiographers (Scull, 1981, p. 17). What doctors said tended to matter most; even if what they said was so often contradictory. At the end of the day the simple truth is that there was no ready agreement as to what constituted insanity, no agreement as to how it might be treated, no agreement as to the most suitable strategies of confinement, no agreement, as we have already noted, even as to whether alleged lunatics should be examined by those with the power to issue committal certificates.

The implications were obvious. In his essay *On Liberty*, John Stuart Mill articulated the common fear that anyone who fails to do 'what everybody does' ran the constant risk 'of a commission *de lunatico*, and of having their property taken away from them and given to their relations' (Mill, 1955, pp. 99–100). The extent to which necessarily 'elastic' measures of what constituted lunatic behaviour were dependent on the perceived transgression of presumed cultural norms is patent; especially so in the context of debates that oscillated around the original idea of 'moral' insanity and its later pseudo-medical mutations, such as hysteria and neurasthenia (Suzuki, 2006, pp. 138–9). In this context, moreover, it is all too easy to see why such apparently transgressive behaviour on the part of young women in particular, especially that which appeared to carry a sexual connotation, could be reinterpreted by horrified family members, and titillated jurors, as evidence of madness.

Mid-Victorians were fascinated by madness, and obsessively so by female madness. Charles Dickens relished the chance to spend an afternoon gazing at supposedly deranged young women in his local mental hospital (Showalter, 1987, pp. 51, 90). Newspaper editors, like Dickens indeed, also knew that few things sold as well as lurid accounts of Lunacy Commission proceedings, or stories of wrongly confined young women, particularly if they could boast a sexual perversion or two; such as the 'Portsmouth case', with its stories of sexual debauchery amongst the more deranged quarters of the English aristocracy, or that of the famous heiress Rosa Bagster whose family alleged that an unhealthy sexual proclivity had led their daughter to elope and to make an unsuitable marriage (Suzuki, 2006, pp. 12–18, 122–7). There was, as one recent historian has noted, a vital 'sense of tragicomedy' in such accounts (Suzuki, 2006, p. 32). John Bucknill might well bemoan a journalistic genre that fed popular hysteria. Accounts of supposedly 'sane people confined in lunatic asylums', he declared in the *Journal of Mental Science* 1858, were merely the 'ghosts of newspaper readings' (McCandless, 1981, p. 356). But no one was listening really; at least no newspaper editors were.

Both the Portsmouth and Bagster cases engaged a particular species of madness that was very obviously as much the construct of social prejudice as of scientific veracity: 'moral madness' (Scull, 1981, pp. 7–10: McCandless, 1981, pp. 354–6; Suzuki, 2006, pp. 80–7). In his rather florid, but highly influential, definition of this kind of insanity, James Prichard depicted 'moral madness' as a 'morbid perversion of the natural feelings, affections, inclinations, temper, habit, moral dispositions, and natural impulses, without any remarkable disorder or defect of the intellect' (Showalter, 1987, p. 29). It was, Prichard insinuated, the kind of madness to which young women like Rosa Bagster might be peculiarly susceptible. A propensity to fall in love too much and with the wrong type of men was, in much of the accompanying cultural literature, perceived as being just as aberrant in principle as any of the more thrilling examples of rampant sexuality presented to the courts and Lunacy Commissions. A telling expression could be found in Alexander Morison's *Outlines of Lectures on Mental Diseases* in 1825, which advised that in its ability to produce 'febrile symptoms, and increased sensibility, love' when 'hopeless' could be categorised as 'a form of madness' (Small, 1996, pp. 33, 36–8).

Such determinations of madness might today seem rather whimsical. We might smile at Mr Brocklehurst's sage advice to the young Jane Eyre and her classmates at Lowood, that the greatest threat to their earthly peace of mind, not to mention their later salvation, lay in 'lusts of the flesh' (64). But few would have laughed in mid-nineteenth-century England, when such prejudices, endorsed by commissions and courts, assumed an altogether darker resonance. The emergence, as the century progressed, of further clearly gendered determinants of insanity, most obviously hysteria, affirmed a seeming scientific authority to moral prejudice. John Cheyne and Henry Maudsley both advised that instances of perceived female mental disorder might be commonly traced back to improper sexual behaviour, most readily forms of sexual self-abuse, but also including complications arising from irregular menstruation. Women who were found to swear incessantly, or who displayed a propensity for 'nymphomania', were generally assumed to suffer, in particular, from the latter alleged affliction. In this way the discourse of 'moral madness', as Elaine Showalter suggests, was all too readily translated into a specifically gendered 'female malady' (Showalter, 1987, pp. 3–4, 18–19, 29–31). In such a way, it can also be situated within the broader array of discourses that engaged the wider political and social 'question of women'. Frances Power Cobbe's ironic conflation in her essay *Criminals, Idiots, Women and Minors* is justly renowned; a conflation, she pointedly advised, that was enshrined in the 'common law of England' (Hamilton, 1995, pp. 108–221).

Cobbe's essay is important for more than its prescient irony; for at its heart was a collateral desire to promote a counter-strategy, of raising female voices. The same aspiration lay at heart of Josephine Butler's appeal for a 'literature of our own', and Mona Caird's advice that only female testament could overcome the historical 'fetishes' of patriarchy (Hamilton, 1995, pp. 9, 287–304). Such testaments might, for example, include poetic confession, a strategy particularly recommended by advocates of evangelical 'unbossoming', as well as diaries; in both instances documents which were, paradoxically perhaps, often seized upon as *prima facie* evidence of 'love-madness'. The value of such testaments today, however warily they may have been treated by contemporaries, is that they can raise voices, breaking through what Luce Irigaray has termed the 'mutism and mimicry' imposed by the discourses of medico-jurisprudence (Irigaray, 1977, pp. 136–7).

In this context, the emergence of a distinctive genre of 'madness' and 'wrongful confinement' in mid-Victorian fiction is striking, and has, of course, been well chronicled: Edward Bulwer Lytton's *Lucretia*, Mary Elizabeth Braddon's *Lady Audley's Secret* and Wilkie Collins's *The Women in White* as well as Charles Reade's *Hard Cash* and Sheridan

LeFanu's *The Rose and the Key*. And it is instantly apparent too that female protagonists dominate the genre, either as madwomen, or as women wrongly confined on the pretence of madness. Early precursors of the genre could be found in Mary Wollstonecraft's semi-autobiographical novellas *Maria* and *Mary* and Mary Hays's *Victim of Prejudice*. But by the middle of the nineteenth century, as Gilbert and Gubar confirm, the gendered image of madness and confinement had become culturally 'all-pervasive'. The 'madwoman in the attic', the 'mad double', was everywhere:

> Images of enclosure and escape, fantasies in which maddened doubles functioned as asocial surrogates for docile selves, metaphors of physical discomfort manifested in frozen landscapes and fiery interiors – such patterns recurred throughout this tradition, along with obsessive depictions of diseases like anorexia, agoraphobia, and claustrophobia.
> (Gilbert and Gubar, 2000, p. xi)

And one semi-autobiographical testament quickly assumed an iconic status in this emergent genre of 'female malady' or 'wrongful confinement' literature, both in terms of contemporary audience and critical reputation: *Jane Eyre*.

Its author, as critics have long noted, was clearly fascinated by these myriad narratives and debates, reading widely in the area, even visiting institutions such as the Bethlem Hospital in London (Showalter, 1987, pp. 69–70). Not that Charlotte needed to travel far. Rumours, as well as reported cases, of insanity in the Haworth area, most of which were dealt with behind closed doors, were far from uncommon. The story of the curate of Oakworth incarcerating his mad wife in his parsonage was notorious, as were similar rumours with regard to the Sidgwick family of Norton Conyers (Barker, 2001, pp. 511–12). On a more personal level, Charlotte also knew of the committal of her friend Ellen Nussey's brother to a private asylum near York. Ellen kept Charlotte informed of his condition, providing regular updates in her letters. It is also possible that Charlotte might have been aware, however dimly, of the travails of William Makepeace Thackeray, whose own wife was subject to increasingly common fits of *postpartum* insanity.[13] Even closer to home, of course, was the sorry demise of brother Branwell, whose final months were characterised by alcohol induced moments of often violent delirium, and then the collapse in health of sister Emily, whose intermittent bouts of depression and anorexia nervosa were chronicled by an anxious Charlotte (Ingham, 2006, pp. 13–14; Gilbert and Gubar, 2000, pp. 284–5). A reading of private correspondence from 1846 and 1847, confirms the suspicion that Charlotte herself may have suffered from similar nervous disorders.[14] The depictions of madness that were written into *Jane Eyre* were not written from chance or ignorance, of that we can be sure.

A 'clothed hyena'

Whilst allusions to madness pervade *Jane Eyre*, contemporary critics tended to focus their attention elsewhere, primarily on the implications of Rochester's scandalous proposals and Jane's struggle to resist them. Of course, to some the ferocity with which the young Jane resists patriarchal authority would itself have seemed dangerously close to mental instability. She is, Bessie observes, a 'mad cat' (12). And she is confined as one too, at Gateshead, at Lowood, even at Thornfield (14, 50–2). Rochester too reveals a worrying propensity to moments of irrational violence (302). But in terms of engaging contemporary debates around associated questions of insanity and confinement, the defining figure in *Jane Eyre* is, of course, Bertha Mason.

The nature of Bertha's malady is never explicitly stated. The reader is left to infer it. In this Bertha remains almost ephemeral, a physical force that is, as Adrienne Rich suggests more 'sensed than seen' (Rich, 1979, p. 99). Various suppositions are intimated. Rochester, clearly sympathetic to the broader notions of 'moral insanity', ascribes his wife's condition to genetic disease. Bertha's mother was 'both a madwoman and a drunkard', whilst her daughter descended into a state that was 'intemperate and unchaste', possessed of apparently monstrous sexual 'propensities', and given, the insinuation also runs, to the ultimate sin of masturbation (291–2, 305–6). To this extent, Rochester's depiction chimes with contemporary presumptions, seemingly shared by Charlotte, with regard to sexual excess leading inexorably to mental instability (Shuttleworth, 1996, pp. 11–12). Her 'vices', Rochester affirms to Jane, 'sprung up fast and rank', the 'germs of insanity' already evident in her rampant sexual energy on their catastrophic wedding night (306–7). There is, of course, a patent racism in Rochester's chronicle, as there must be too, by imputation, in Charlotte's (David, 1995, pp. 108–10). We will revisit this issue shortly.

In private correspondence with her publishers, Smith Elder, Charlotte defended herself against the complaints of some critics with regard to the presentation of Bertha Mason:

> The character is shocking, but I know that it is but too natural. There is a phase of insanity which may be called moral madness, in which all that is good or even human seems to disappear from the mind and a fiend-like nature replaces it. The sole aim and desire of the being thus possessed is to exasperate, to molest, to destroy, and preternatural ingenuity and energy are often exercised to that dreadful end. The aspect in such cases, assimilates with the disposition; all seem demonised. It is true that profound pity ought to be the only sentiment elicited by the view of such degradation, and equally true is it that I have not sufficiently dwelt on that feeling; I have erred in making horror too predominant. Mrs Rochester indeed lived a sinful life before she was insane, but sin is itself a species of insanity: the truly good behold and compassionate it as such.
>
> (Smith, 2007, p. 96)

The concession, that the depiction might be too brutal, and too horrific, is striking. Bertha's is, for sure, a peculiarly intense form of 'moral madness', certainly far removed from the kind of semi-comic depictions of 'love-madness' found in *Northanger Abbey* or *Sense and Sensibility* (Shuttleworth, 1996, pp. 14–15, 52–5). There is nothing romantic about Bertha Mason.

The description that Charlotte provides of Jane's first glimpse of Bertha is designed to perplex and to horrify:

> In the deep shade, at the furthest end of the room, a figure ran backwards and forwards. What it was, whether beast or human being, one could not, at first sight, tell: it grovelled, seemingly, on all fours; it snatched and growled like some strange wild animal: but it was covered with clothing; and a quantity of dark, grizzled hair, wild as a mane, hid its head and face.
>
> (293)

There is something physical and brutal, obviously animalistic, about the 'horror' of Bertha Mason. She is a 'strange wild animal', a 'wolfish thing', a 'clothed hyena' (293–4).[15] Nancy Armstrong argues that such a rampantly aggressive sexuality, so obviously capable of destroying the domestic harmony of the family home, represented a critique, albeit perhaps unconscious on the part of its author, of the fragility of the early Victorian domestic idyll (Armstrong, 1987, pp. 164, 174). The physicality of Bertha Mason is intense.[16] Corporeal and sanguinary images are prevalent, particularly in the passages following her attack on her brother Mason, allowing Charlotte to conjure up familiar Gothic images of vampyric demons, whilst also attaching contemporary associations between female insanity and disturbed menstrual cycles. 'She sucked the blood', Mason wails, 'she said she'd drain my heart' (213). Later Jane will make the same allusion, to the 'foul German spectre – the Vampyre' (284).

Curiously perhaps, Jane's perception of Bertha, which might be expected to confirm her creator's preconceptions, is in fact rather evasive; the product on the one hand of Jane's own status as an outsider and, on the other, of an ambiguity which reaches across Charlotte's corpus, between the alternative lures of sense and sensibility, reason and romance. Initial encounters with Bertha are written to tempt, to entice her heroine into a more Gothic sensibility, one which might lure the 'romantic reader', but which Jane must resist; the 'demoniac laugh' from one of the rooms off the long passage 'with its two rows of small black doors all shut, like a corridor in some Bluebeard's castle'; Mason's allusion to being attacked by a vampire; Jane's own recollection of Bertha's 'fearful and ghastly' face as she leant over her bed two nights before her intended marriage to Rochester, a recollection which, she confesses, momentarily disrupted her own reason, rendering her 'insensible from terror' (147–8, 213, 282–3). All quite 'creepy' as Queen Victoria famously observed (Allott, 1974, pp. 147–8).[17]

It has been suggested that this Gothic sensibility might have been impelled by Charlotte's desire, conscious or subconscious, to reproduce a 'fairytale' romance, replete, not just with a putative princess rising from her place at the hearth, but with a monster incarcerated at the top of the castle. The fact that Rochester might also, in this paradigm, be depicted as the 'beast' to Jane's 'beauty', merely reinforces the thought that there is a deeper psychological and sexual contest in play; the pilgrim Jane destroying the monster that has cast a spell over her 'beast' and his enchanted home (113).[18] There is, of course, a different fairytale tradition which critics have subsequently projected into the fate of Bertha Mason; that of the sexually alluring concubine and the voracious oriental despot. Here again, Jane's allusion to Bluebeard's castle would have had an unmistakable resonance.[19]

But the plainer 'truth' must out; the fairytale must give way to the personal testament (Rowe, 1983, p. 89; Eagleton, 1975, pp. 17–20, 75–8). There is no 'ghostliness', no 'curious cachination', even if the 'clamorous peal' of laughter, as 'tragic, as preternatural a laugh as any I ever heard', seemed to 'echo in every lonely chamber' (107). Silenced she might be, but Bertha's voice ultimately reinforces her animality. At the moment of her death, as the innkeeper recalls, she 'yelled, and gave a spring, and the next minute she lay smashed on the pavement', as 'dead as the stones on which her brains and blood were scattered' (427–8).[20] Bertha Mason may indeed appear to be a 'shocking', even fantastical lunatic. But she is also, as Charlotte readily admitted in her letter to her publisher, an ordinary and familiar one, a 'natural' lunatic.

A second question, made all the more pressing by the 'natural' state of Bertha Mason's condition, is the efficacy of Rochester's strategy of trying to confine his wife's insanity within the boundaries of the home. Certainly the theme of 'constraint', physical, emotional, intensely gendered, dominates *Jane Eyre* (Shuttleworth, 1996, p. 148; Grudin, 1977, p. 145). For much of the time, Jane consciously resists Rochester's supposition that she has merely become Thornfield's latest 'inmate' (124). Equally, the confinement of Bertha Mason was clearly intended to make a contribution to a current debate of likely interest to readers. Bertha is confined like a 'prisoner in his dungeon' (164).[21] H.F. Chorley, reviewing the novel for the *Athenaeum*, observed that the 'mystery' of Thornfield was no 'exaggeration', for 'We, ourselves, know of a large mansion-house in a distant county where, for many years, a miscreant was kept in close confinement'; an observation that revisits the supposition that Charlotte and her audience would probably have been quite familiar with such apparently dubious incarcerations (Allott, 1974, p. 72).

Aware that the common law would not countenance his divorce from Bertha, Rochester confesses that this solution appeared to be his only credible strategy; a supposition which, as we have again noted, would have accorded with the thoughts of many readers (306–7). Rochester even contemplates his strategy in terms of a moral injunction, convincing himself, 'Let her identity, her connection with yourself, be buried in oblivion: you are bound to impart them to no living being' (309). Incarceration at Thornfield has the virtue, above all, of being discreet; allowing Rochester not merely to hide his wife from public view, but himself too. Rochester, as Mrs Fairfax confirms, withdrew from his own family and his own 'society' on discovering the predicament in which he was placed by the terms of his father's estate settlement (127–8). Thornfield is a house full of different inmates, all enduring different forms of confinement and alienation (141–2, 146).

Indeed, there is much in Rochester's strategy of confinement that would have conformed to contemporary attitudes, not least the recruitment of an experienced 'keeper', Grace Poole, to whom he is more than willing to convey responsibility for the care of his first wife.[22] The same might be said of the apparent reluctance, wherever possible, to use physical restraints, a comparative gentleness that was commended by Conolly in his *Treatment of the Insane without Mechanical Restraint*; though again, in the context of Bertha's final acts of destruction, the wisdom of this strategy is rendered rather less certain (Showalter, 1987).[23] Interestingly, Conolly actually cited the 'case' of Bertha Mason in his treatise, precisely to warn against such domestic confinement. Whilst the relationship between the Rochesters, he observed, became ever more 'fierce and unnatural', Thornfield itself was rendered:

> Awful by the presence of a deranged creature under the same roof: her voice, her sudden and violent efforts to destroy things or persons; her vehement rushings to fire and window; her very tread and stamp in her dark and disordered and remote-chamber, have seemed to penetrate the whole house; and, assailed by her wild energy, the very walls and roof have appeared unsafe, and capable of partial demolition.
>
> (Small, 1996, pp. 54–5)[24]

Thornfield is rotten, literally and metaphorically.[25] It must be destroyed. Bertha's fate suited the plot, not least in opening up the possibility of an eventual, and legal, marriage between Jane and Rochester. It was the ending that, as Charlotte knew, her audience would expect. But it was also an ending that made a statement as to the efficacy of Bertha's confinement; as indeed Conolly's commentary testifies, and as Charlotte must, again, have appreciated. Familial confinement at Thornfield does not work. Grace Poole turns out to be a drunk, whilst Bertha Mason roams the upper stories of Thornfield seemingly at will, assaulting and maiming her husband, terrifying Jane, destroying the house and eventually killing herself (427).[26]

The casting of Rochester as Bluebeard reinforces the thought that Charlotte had her doubts about her hero. Later, in a slightly different perspective, Rochester confesses to Jane that 'Concealing the madwoman's neighbourhood from you, however, was something like covering a child with a cloak, and laying down near a upas-tree: the demon's vicinage is poisoned, and always was' (300). There again it might be argued that Rochester's strategy appears to have been effective, at least for a while; so much so that the local clergyman subsequently confesses himself astounded by the thought that there might have been a wife lurking in the attic for years (291). Moreover, the audience is clearly supposed to sympathise with the incarcerator's predicament. The insanity with which he had to deal was clearly no ordinary form of 'love-madness'. Bertha's degenerative insanity, within which the audience is clearly supposed to discern a violent sexuality, is apocalyptic. Small wonder, perhaps, that Rochester's first inclination was to hide a wife who, not just in her apparent illness, but also in her original physiognomic condition, might have appeared to his contemporaries to be semi-savage.

The manner of Bertha Mason's confinement, moreover, speaks to a larger evasion; one that resonates with Irigaray's famous alignment of madness and the denial of voice. It also resonates with Virginia Woolf's identification of a 'twisted' rage in the novel; a temptation to self-immolation which must be resisted (Woolf, 1998, pp. 90–5).[27] The Bunyanesque theme of temptation and its resistance has been commonly traced, from the young Jane herself, incarcerated in the Red Room at Gateshead Hall and driven to hysterical rage, to the parallel incarceration of Bertha Mason's howling fury in another conspicuously red room in Thornfield (17–18, 23). It enjoins the familiar reading of the novel which sees Bertha as Jane's 'secret-self', her 'darker double agent' (Gilbert and Gubar, 2000, pp. 341–2, 348, 359–62;

Rich, 1979, pp. 90–1; Grudin, 1977, pp. 152–3). The veil that is 'rent' by Bertha is the veil that threatens to shroud Jane Rochester (283–4).

Here the twin suppression, of voice and of vice, resonates with the simpler proposition that Bertha's silence articulates Jane's deeper subconscious anxieties and anger, that in Bertha's fate Jane might have detected a premonition of her own if she were to succumb to Rochester's suggestion that they might live an adulterous liaison. Jane resists with the aside that 'I will hold to the principles received by me when I was sane, and not mad – as I am now' (317). In a prosaic sense, she will, as critics have noted, uphold the principles of the common law and social order (Allen, 1992, pp. 235–8; Gilbert and Gubar, 2000, p. 364). But more importantly, perhaps, she will also uphold the principles of the moral law, or at least the moral law as it was imagined by mid-nineteenth-century middle England, and in so doing resist the deeper temptations of bigamy, adultery and 'moral insanity'. And the resistance proves to be agonising, leading indeed to a famous fainting fit in which Jane hallucinates Rochester's voice from afar.[28]

In this dominant interpretative paradigm, the two questions, of the nature of Bertha's madness and of the manner of her confinement, come together, even as they articulate a vivid and empowering testimony of silence and disempowerment. Critics have, of course, disputed the authority of this paradigm. According to Helen Small, the greater symmetry in the novel is between the overt sexuality of Bertha Mason and the barely suppressed sexuality of her frustrated partner, whilst Jane actually represents her 'alterity'; the silence and unconstrained sexuality of Bertha contrasting sharply with the articulacy, self-control and strength of will of Jane (Small, 1996, pp. 166–70, 174–5, 178). Yet, alterity does not preclude complementarity; indeed it might be said to sustain it.

Either way, and such interpretative subtleties aside, it can be surmised that there was in the presentation of Bertha Mason pretty much everything that the incipiently neurotic mid-Victorian audience might have expected to find when invited to consider the phenomenon of the 'madwoman in the attic'. All the prejudices are written in: that madness in a woman is peculiarly bestial, and threatening and downright odd; that it is rooted in a moral or sexual deficiency; that the desire to domesticate its constraint was powerful, and preferred by many contemporaries; that the necessary form of constraint would be mental rather than physical, the gaze directed towards internal as much as external strategies of surveillance; that such a strategy might well lead to catastrophic results; and that lunacy can creep up, or indeed arrive abruptly, and destroy any family, no matter how watchful it might be.

'Same thing as slavery'

The after-life of *Jane Eyre* is relatively easy to trace. As we have already noted it was an immediate publishing success, and within a couple of years critics were confirming its nascent canonical status (Ingham, 2006, pp. 206–11). Margaret Oliphant, writing as soon after its publication as 1855, noted that 'the most alarming revolution of modern times has followed the invasion of *Jane Eyre*', continuing perceptively that:

> Nobody perceived that it was the new generation nailing its colours to the mast. No one would understand that this furious love-making was but a wild declaration of the 'Rights of Women' in a new aspect... Here is your true revolution. France is but one of the western powers; woman is the half the world... And this new Bellona steps forth in armour, throws down her glove and defies you – to conquer her if you can.
> (Allott, 1974, p. 312–13)

Charlotte herself, we can suppose, would have been appalled by the thought that she might have written a feminist 'manifesto', worse still that she might be appraised as a revolutionary writer. But she had, and she was.[29]

There is a particular paradox here; one that moves around the literary redemption of Bertha Mason.[30] Elizabeth Gaskell sought to marginalise Bertha; and for a century or more she seemed to have largely succeeded.[31] During the second part of the twentieth century, however, it was Bertha Mason who emerged at the centre of critical consideration, just as Jane was despatched to the shadows (Baer, 1983, pp. 131–3, 147–8; Emery, 1990, pp. 65–7). The publication of Jean Rhys's novel *Wide Sargasso Sea* in 1966 was a critical moment in this redemptive process; as was the subsequent intervention two decades later of Giyatri Spivak, determined to redress the apparent neglect of the novel's colonial context by both contemporary and modern critics. According to Spivak, Charlotte's Bertha is a 'figure produced by the axiomatics of imperialism', first and foremost the product of her colonial background, a Creole of mixed blood, and someone whom it was all too easy for Rochester to depict as a sexual enchantress. From the very outset, Spivak argues, Rochester is above all obsessed with his wife's race. She was, he recalled to Jane, 'tall, dark and majestic', and chosen because 'her family wished to secure me because I was of good race' (Spivak, 1985, pp. 247–8).

Duly chastised, Brontë critics have since uncovered various colonial referents across the canon, from the uncertain origins of Heathcliff in *Wuthering Heights* to passing comments on 'sordid savages' in *Shirley* (Meyer, 1990, p. 247). More immediately, in *Jane Eyre* they have contemplated the prevalence of racially inflected images of slavery and submission: in the younger Jane's allusion to herself as a 'rebel slave'; in her later musings on the situation of 'servitude' that defines women in her society; in her haughty rejection of Rochester's suggestion that he might prefer 'one little English girl' to a 'whole seraglio'; in the alignment of the 'mystery' of violence breaking out in the 'deadest hours of the night' at Thornfield with contemporary accounts of night-time slave riots; and, of course, in the missionary imperialism of St John Rivers (12, 85–6, 107, 133–4, 269–70; Meyer, 1990, pp. 254–5, 258–63; Zonana, 1993).

Overall, however, matters of race in the novel, like indeed those of sexuality and insanity, remain oddly allusive. The depiction of Bertha Mason, it has been suggested, represents an evasive anti-colonialism; one that is founded not on any laudable sense of injustice, but on an altogether less edifying fear of racial contamination (Meyer, 1990, p. 261). Bertha Mason is dangerously mad, the insinuation runs, not just because she is a woman, but because she is a black woman, and one, moreover, who has married into the English gentry; forever threatening to seduce her paranoid husband and breed mentally degenerate, mixed-race children. The importance of Rhys's prequel, as Spivak urged, lies in the original alignment of female insanity with questions of race and imperialism. It frames a triple exclusion, of Bertha as woman, as madwoman and as colonial.[32]

Musing on her motivation for writing *Wide Sargasso Sea*, Rhys later aligned the peculiar injustice of this triple exclusion:

> The madwoman in *Jane Eyre* has always interested me. I was convinced that Charlotte Brontë must have had something against

the West Indies and I was angry about it. Otherwise, why did she take a West Indian for that horrible lunatic, for that really dreadful creature? I hadn't really formulated the idea of vindicating the mad woman in the novel but when I was rediscovered I was encouraged to do so.

(Baer, 1983, p. 132)

The defining strategy of vindication in *Wide Sargasso Sea* is reversal. The torching of Thornfield becomes not an act of madness, but one of liberation; as does Bertha's leap from the roof. In Jamaica it is Rochester who feels confined, who feels 'bought', who flirts with despair and depression, who betrays symptoms of neurosis and paranoia in his attempt to comprehend his own sexual inhibitions (Rhys, 2000, pp. 42, 47, 67, 109–11). The love-potion, which momentarily impassions Rochester on his wedding night, might induce a transitory state of 'moral madness', but it is his madness, and his morality. It is he who succumbs to the alternative charms of Amelie, just as it is he who, betraying his growing paranoiac insecurity, chooses to believe malicious imputations directed against the virtue and chastity of his new wife (Rhys, 2000, pp. 59–60, 83, 89–90, 106–7).

The most important reversal, of course, albeit a necessarily parallel one, is that which retrieves the voice of Bertha and which casts Jane into the shadows. And with the retrieval of her voice, comes the reassertion of something more. Antoinette Cosway retrieves her name and her identity; an exact reversal of the 'violent' erasure of both enacted by Rochester in *Jane Eyre* (Rhys, 2000, p. 71; Spivak, 1985, pp. 249–50). In this humanising process, Rhys immediately dilutes the caricatures of insanity, animalistic or moral. Antoinette is a real flesh and blood human being; one moreover who is fully comprehending of the injustice to which she, like other women and other Creoles, is subject. 'Justice', she muses, 'it looked like a damned cold lie to me' (Rhys, 2000, p. 94). The Bertha Mason incarcerated in the attic of Thornfield may be denied expression, but Antoinette Cosway is not. She is human and she has a voice. It is she who, in the final passages of *Wide Sargasso Sea*, chronicles her own desperate collapse into despair and hallucination (Rhys, 2000, pp. 117–23).

Rhys recovers something else too from Antoinette's testament, something which again in *Jane Eyre* remains elusive. For unlike

Charlotte Brontë, who only imputes the 'force' of law, to borrow Derrida's appellation, Rhys foregrounds it. Antoinette is confined by this force. It is because of the law, because her dowry will resuscitate the ailing Rochester estate, that she has been married. Not that Rochester is particularly relieved at the prospect. He may have saved his inheritance, but he is haunted by the thought that he has also 'sold his soul' ((Rhys, 2000, pp. 42, 97–8, 101). It is the law that conveys Antoinette's property, and her person, to Rochester; even if the latter inclines to view the transaction more in terms of contamination than resuscitation (Rhys, 2000, p. 101). Antoinette is a chattel; passed by one man, her brother, to another, her husband. 'She's mad', Rochester later agonises, 'but mine, mine' (Rhys, 2000, p. 106). Charlotte's Jane has a similar presentiment of the fate which awaits any prospective bride (259).[33] There are repeated allusions to the failure of Antoinette's brother to arrange a protective legal settlement (Rhys, 2000, pp. 69, 72; Le Gallez, 1990, pp. 142–6). 'I am not rich now', the newly married Antoinette informs an uncomprehending Christophine, 'I have no money of my own at all, everything I had belongs to him.' 'That' she confirms 'is English Law' (Rhys, 2000, p. 69).

A further parallel is obvious. The sequestration of an estate through marriage in nineteenth-century Jamaica, or indeed nineteenth-century England, is no different in substance than the purchasing of a slave. 'The Letter of the Law', as Christophine observes, 'Same thing as slavery. They got magistrate. They got fine, they got jail house and chain gang. They got tread machine to mash up people's feet' (Rhys, 2000, p. 69; Thomas, 1999, pp. 10–11). When Antoinette later appeals to her brother to redeem himself and to save her, Christophine's deeper suspicions are again vindicated. 'I cannot interfere legally between your husband and yourself', Richard Mason replies. Bertha, an uncomprehending Jane records, then 'flew at him' (Rhys, 2000, pp. 119–20). As Spivak notes, it was not perhaps only the simple matter of confinement that triggered Antoinette's violence. It was the 'dissimulation' that she 'discerns in the word "legally"' (Spivak, 1985, pp. 249–51).

Rhys's Rochester becomes the physical embodiment of the laws of patriarchy, cultural and jurisprudential, all their various dissimulations, all the 'masquerading'. It is the 'letter of the Law' that permits Rochester to return to England with his hated wife, and her estate; disregarding Christophine's desperate plea that he might at least leave his wife behind, with some remnants of her estate, and her freedom (Rhys, 2000, pp. 101–2). Christophine has anticipated Rochester's likely strategy: 'It is in your mind to pretend she is mad. I know it. The doctors say what you tell them to say' (Rhys, 2000, pp. 103). And it is the law, as Christophine also appreciates, that precisely allows him, even encourages him, to confine Antoinette to the third floor of Thornfield. The very day following his final altercation with Christophine, Rochester is writing home, instructing his lawyers to engage a 'discreet' staff and to expect his return (Rhys, 2000, p. 105). Rochester needs the law, not just to secure his estate, or to allow him to hide his mad wife, but to justify the violence he inflicts on her, when he makes love to her, and when he later incarcerates her. It furnishes another set of collateral excuses for the original sin into which he fell, providing an emotional prophylactic for the paranoid self-loathing into which he is, thereafter, prone to falling.[34] The laws of patriarchy make men like Rochester feel a bit better about themselves; though not always, as Rhys implies, that much better.

Of course the very fact that Rhys's novel has attained such a critical prominence confirms the extent to which its progenitor succeeded in disrupting precisely the kind of public–private demarcation that Rochester, and those who thought like him in mid-nineteenth-century England, were so keen to maintain. It brings into the open not just the cruelty inflicted upon Bertha Mason, the writing of a 'widow-sacrifice', but the responsibility of lawyers and doctors, and husbands too, like Rochester, perhaps even the ultimate evasion of an author and a literary genre (Spivak, 1985, p. 259; Sharpe, 1993, 14–15, 47–9).[35] The allusive, degenerate, almost inhuman Bertha Mason in *Jane Eyre* has become the irreducibly vivid, intensely human Antoinette Cosway. This again was Rhys's aspiration; to bring to the fore the personal narrative that Charlotte Brontë, in the final analysis, preferred to keep in the shadows of the attic. Charlotte's Bertha, Rhys later reflected, 'seemed such a poor ghost, I thought I'd like to write her life'.[36] In this re-writing, the madness of Antoinette is raised by a paranoid husband, and then validated by a legal order that exists to mask deeper anxieties regarding female sexuality and power. In like terms, the manner of her confinement, the stripping away of her voice and humanity, leads as it only can to an apocalyptic moment of self-immolation, one that liberates as well as maims and destroys, and that provides a symbolic rejection of a strategy of confinement that prioritises familial security and public reticence over the care and compassion of its individual members.

Wide Sargasso Sea was published in 1966; a critical period in the evolution of attitudes towards women and insanity, as Laingian theories of female schizophrenia, which situated mental ill-health in deeper forms of cultural oppression, emerged to challenge the supposed triumph of Freudianism (Showalter, 1987, pp. 195–6, 222–32, 243–7). In more recent decades, the reassertion of Freudian prejudice in psychiatric medicine has witnessed the determination of newer supposedly female species of mental instability, most obviously, and in the context of the Brontës, most presciently perhaps, anorexia nervosa (Williams, 2002, p. 76). The debate moves back as it tries to move on. Certainly there is much in modern debate regarding insanity and treatment which resonates with the 'case' of Bertha Mason. And the degree of confusion is familiar too; as evidenced in the often tortured debates that surrounded the progress of the recent Mental Health Bill in the United Kingdom, or more broadly the merits or demerits of 'care in the community' initiatives. As one modern commentator has concluded, 'We, like the Victorians, are still baffled by the nature of insanity and the best way to deal with it. Moreover, we, like them, are still sceptical of the ability of medicine to diagnose and treat it effectively. As long as these conditions exist, the fear of wrongful confinement is likely to continue' (McCandless, 1983, p. 104).

There is a still deeper resonance too; for the mad were, and are, only one category of those silenced by the public discourses of law. Women are another, the racial 'other' another still (Crenshaw, 1988). There is, for example, a striking resonance between the sentiments embedded in Patricia Williams's autobiographical account of life in the legal academy, *The Alchemy of Race and Rights*, and the narrative which Rhys chose to re-imagine in *Wide Sargasso Sea*; not least in recalling the nascent sense of being 'born in the fearsome, loathsome packaging of an "other" body' which opens Williams's personal testament (Williams, 1991, pp. 4, 10–11, 60–73). Raising these voices, whether they are the bitter rejoinders of fictive victims or the reflective memorials of female jurists, speaks to a larger aspiration. As Maria Aristodemou concludes, deploying a metaphor of peculiar pertinence in the context of this chapter:

> While man was running away, or hiding in his own self-created prisons, in labyrinths variously called law, reason, knowledge, God, woman has travelled the world. From the prison he imposed on her called home she has been on a journey that does not return back to oneself, or lead to death, but reaches out towards the other.
>
> (Aristodemou, 2000, pp. 270–1)

4
The State and Shirley Keeldar

In a review which has assumed notoriety in the canon of Brontë criticism, G.H. Lewes condemned Charlotte Brontë's *Shirley* for its 'random' construction, its overarching 'coarseness', its peculiarly masculine tone, and its lingering preference for describing the 'habits and manners of Yorkshire' rather than the proper 'principles of human nature' and 'good taste' (Allott, 1974, pp. 160–70).[1] Its notoriety is perhaps based as much on Charlotte's horrified response, 'God deliver me from my friends!' (Gaskell, 1997, pp. 339).[2] Charlotte, it should be noted, rated *Shirley* as equivalent in quality to *Jane Eyre* or anything else she had previously written.[3] But Lewes was not alone in his temper; a 'feeble effort', according to the *Westminster Review* (Allott, 1974, pp. 158–9).[4] Charles Kingsley famously expressed himself so 'disgusted' with the opening passages on the bickering curates that he refused to read on (Allott, 1974, p. 343).[5] The reviewer in the *Daily News* expressed a like concern regarding 'vulgar' depictions of the clergy (Allott, 1974, p. 117).[6] Charlotte's defence, typically, was grounded in a claim to experience. Such a species of curate existed. She had encountered some at Haworth, finding their manner so disagreeable 'that my temper lost its balance, and I pronounced a few sentences sharply' (Smith, 2007, p. 61). We will revisit the bickering curates in due course.

In truth, however, most contemporary reviews of *Shirley* were rather more equivocal; the 'adventures', according to one reviewer, were 'simple, brief and few'; a 'slender' story, according to another, nicely 'written', but lacking 'power'; the presentation of a 'strange little world', according to a French reviewer; a novel of 'infrequent brilliancy' marred by an 'unsightly ... surrounding gloom' according to the reviewer in *The Times* (Allott, 1974, pp. 117, 121, 137, 151, 373). A novel that would hardly 'enhance' the reputation of Currer Bell, but hardly 'detract from it' either, was perhaps the epitome of such critical indifference (Allott, 1974, p. 151). In time Charlotte conceded that its 'dryer matter' might not appeal to 'novel-readers', at least not those who had been 'charmed with *Jane Eyre*' (Zlotnick, 1991, p. 282). And, with one or two notable exceptions, modern criticism has been similarly equivocal; again tending to condemn *Shirley* to the margins of the Brontë canon. Much of the criticism that the novel has attracted centres on its lack of focus, together with its essentially static form and limited character development (Eagleton, 1975, pp. 80–1, 95; Shapiro, 1968, pp. 74–5; Qualls, 1982, pp. 70–1).

Just a few, however, thought that they had detected something rather more interesting in *Shirley*. The reviewer in the *Atlas* was perhaps alone in discerning the 'stamp of genius' (Allott, 1974, p. 120). But there was perception in Albert Fonblanque's suggestion that there was something of import in the author's evident 'strong sympathy' for the principles of 'Toryism and High Church' (Allott, 1974, p. 129). Equally perceptive was William Howitt in the *Standard of Freedom*. The novel, Howitt confirmed, is about what it means to be 'English' (Allott, 1974, p. 133). There is a resonance here, of course, with later critical reflections on the 'condition of England' novel, a genre of mid-nineteenth-century literature that we have already encountered. Whilst we know that neither 'England' nor its 'condition' lends itself to easy determination, we also know that many in mid-Victorian England were increasingly unsettled by the thought that their green and pleasant land was neither as green nor as pleasant as they had been led to suppose. And Charlotte Brontë it seems was no exception.

Shirley has assumed a modest presence in the 'condition of England' genre and there can be little doubt that its author wished to address rather different themes to those which had been engaged in *Jane Eyre*, or indeed in *Wuthering Heights* or *The Tenant of Wildfell Hall*.[7] It would be a mistake, however, to assume that Charlotte was no longer interested in matters of private politics and morality. Whilst the more fantastical images of madwomen in attics, of incestuous siblings and glowering Byronic heroes might be absent, there is much in *Shirley* that is familiar. There is much about marriage and love, more broadly still the proper place of women in mid-Victorian England. But the aspect is different. Where *Jane Eyre*, and *Wuthering Heights* and the *Tenant of Wildfell Hall* too, explored the fissures underlying the veneer of Victorian private life, *Shirley* looked outward, to fissures that appeared to be opening up in the frame of public governance. And if the image presented was not, in terms of textual composition, quite so confident or so coherent, it was very probably because its author was rather less reassured by what she felt obliged to depict.

Glory and emulation

Anxiety about the 'condition' of England is a periodic affliction.[8] Of course, Englishness has always enjoyed a maddeningly elusive quality. But on certain occasions, commonly when contemplating significant constitutional reform, the anxiety becomes acute. Early twenty-first-century England evinces precisely these symptoms. The closing years of the twentieth century witnessed a raft of statutes intended to reform the 'British' constitution. One set in particular engaged head-on with questions of national identity; the series of devolution statutes which established and empowered new representative assemblies in Edinburgh, Cardiff and Belfast. It is not that England was forgotten. But it was neglected. Denied a shiny new statute, the English were left to experience a kind of virtual devolution, leaving constitutionalists to ruminate over the 'West Lothian question', whilst others contemplated bigger questions about an intrinsic English identity, if such a thing existed (Ward, 2004, pp. 158–9). And as they did they were drawn beyond questions of constitutional consistency into a more poetic realm of what Robert Colls terms 'history and myth' (Colls, 2002, pp. 7, 19–20).

Peter Ackroyd ruminated over the idea of England as 'an island of visions', of competing and irreducible mythologies, an 'enchanted circle' indeed, that is 'endless because it has no beginning and no end' (Ackroyd, 2002, pp. xix, 20–1). The governance of Ackroyd's Albion is a form of 'art' and a matter of 'sensibility'; one that draws its strength precisely from its mythic lineage (Ackroyd, 2002, pp. 126–9). Short of a framing text such as the American Constitution, and a set of suitably revered constitutional 'framers', English constitutional history has been shaped by poets and polemicists, the likes of Bede and Blake, Spenser and Shakespeare, and lesser poets too, such as

Stanley Baldwin who liked to evoke the 'sounds of England, the tinkle of the hammer on the anvil in the country smithy, the corncrake on a dewy morning', and John Major who, though blissfully unaware of the inherent irony, preferred Orwell's depiction of 'old maids bicycling to Holy Communion through the morning mist' (Ackroyd, 2002, pp. 49–53, 255; Clarke, 1996, pp. 134–5; Orwell, 1984, pp. 116–17). This England, regardless of nominal political affinity, is an intensely conservative England. As it peers anxiously, reluctantly, into the future, it looks longingly backward. And when it seeks constitutional assurance, it looks as often as not to its poets first, and to its jurists second.

As it contemplated its own particular 'age of reform', mid-nineteenth-century England did exactly this, vesting in Shakespeare another renaissance, in Milton another reformation. Tennyson reached back into the metaphoric mists of time to retrieve Mallory's Arthur. Soldier heroes, the more poetic the better, were much vaunted. One such hero, hardly poetic in temperament, but verging on the mythic even as he lived, assumed a dominant presence: Wellington, the Iron Duke. The England of Charlotte Brontë idolised the Iron Duke. Charlotte certainly did, establishing him in heroic pose in the juvenile *Tales of Angria*, and then in private correspondence confirming her admiration for a man who, in pointed comparison with Napoleon, was of 'conscience', who 'shrinks from eulogy', who 'rejects panegyric', whose 'character equals grandeur and surpasses in truth that of all other heroes, ancient or modern' (Gaskell, 1997, pp. 70, 80–1, 387–8; Rogers, 2003, 157–8, 173).[9] And the admiration was not dimmed by time.[10] Indeed, a revival of Wellingtonian masculinity is presented as the surest means of England's redemption in *Shirley*. The eponymous heroine dreams of marrying Wellington, or someone very much like him, 'the soul of England', as the Reverend Helstone confirms, the 'right champion of a good cause, the fit representative of a powerful, a resolute, a sensible, and an honest nation' (34).

Rather less heroic perhaps, but conversely altogether more poetic, was another much admired castigator of the French, Edmund Burke. It was the 'Genius of Burke', as Wordsworth put it, to have reminded the English, when momentarily tempted by the 'dances of liberty' glimpsed across the Channel, of the altogether greater wisdom written into their constitutional tradition. Wellington and Burke were brothers in arms, both in their respective ways responsible for the destruction of the French revolution, one by force of sword and musket, the other by force of pen and polemic (Furniss, 1993, pp. 2, 21; Sacks, 1993, pp. 90–9, 249–53, 257–8; Kramnick, 1977, pp. 4, 41). Others, most obviously Carlyle, deployed the French Revolution to warn their compatriots of the singular horrors that might attend ideological zeal. But it was the rather more subtle, intensely nostalgic refraction of English constitutionalism found in Burke's *Reflections on the Revolution in France* which came to define what Geoffrey Best has termed the 'Protestant Tory Constitution'; the constitution of a distinctive English commonwealth sanctified by the revolutions of the seventeenth century, nurtured during the long eighteenth century, and now perceived to be the rock against which the raging torrents of radicalism and Jacobinism, popery and dissent, swirled during the early decades of the nineteenth century (Best, 1958). The spectres raised in *Reflections* continued to haunt the febrile imagination of mid-Victorian England. Pre-Tractarian Church Tories constantly invoked Burke as the great interlocutor of the Hookerian tradition of 'sacral monarchy' (Nockles, 1994, pp. 47–9, 60–3, 69). Others, such as Henry Buckle, simply lauded 'the greatest thinker who ever devoted himself to English politics' (Kramnick, 1977, p. 42). Another of his Victorian hagiographers, George Croly, agreed, advising his countrymen and women that in Burke:

> The politician was elevated into the philosopher, and in that loftier atmosphere from which he looked down on the cloudy and turbulent contests of the time, he soared upward calmly in the light of truth and became more splendid at every wave of his wing.
> (Kramnick, 1977, p. 41)

Whilst Charlotte Brontë's veneration of Wellington was repeatedly confirmed, there is no testamentary evidence of a comparable reverence of Burke. But there can be little doubt that her natural political sympathies were essentially Burkean, innately conservative, evidently Church Tory even if somewhat evangelical in temper.[11] Charlotte may have resisted the appellation 'high Tory' in correspondence with Hartley Coleridge, but neither particularly vigorously, nor particularly convincingly (Smith, 2007, p. 27). To the extent that Charlotte was prepared to adhere to a cause that might be termed political, it was anyway defined by the interest of the established Church. Half a century after Charlotte's death Mary Ward suggested, with the same perception as Fonblanque and Howitt, that the 'main stuff' of all Charlotte's writings was 'English, Protestant, law-respecting, conventional even' (Allott, 1974, p. 453). And whilst an anxiety with regard to progress and in particular to industrialisation was certainly not the preserve of the conservative or the Church Tory, there were relatively few conservatives or Church Tories who were not so troubled. As Terry Eagleton has confirmed, novels such as Charlotte's *Shirley* betray an anxiety that in many ways defined a 'tradition of radical conservatism'; one that can be readily traced back to Burke (Eagleton, 1975, p. 76). In this, Charlotte was very much a Burkean, someone who, when she sought to navigate a safer passage for her beloved England did so by charting backwards. It is for this reason that history was so critical to her strategy in *Shirley*.

Famously, in *Reflections* Burke deployed the English constitution as a metaphorical construct, the 'representative' enactment of a quintessentially English 'state of mind'; the product not of abstract 'adulterated metaphysics' or juristic principle but of historical memory and established institutions. There was nothing unusual in preferring metaphorical constitutions. The revered 'ancient' constitution was an entirely fictive piece of narrative jurisprudence, whilst Blackstone famously likened the English constitution to a 'Gothic castle' (Chaplin, 2007, p. 40; Colls, 2002, pp. 19–20). And there was nothing unusual in preferring metaphysical ones either. Samuel Johnson suggested that all constitutions, and here England provided a supreme example, are 'states of being'; an observation that echoed Sir Matthew Hale's observation, in his *History of the Common Law of England*, that the 'common law' was a 'disposition of the English nation', an expression of its 'Temperament' and 'Manner' (Blakemore, 1988, pp. 6–7; Colls, 2002, p. 26).[12] *Reflections* ratified a constitution and a constitutional culture that was both metaphorical and metaphysical (Ward, 2010).[13]

The constitution Burke eulogised, in both Parliament and polemic, was 'entailed' and prescriptive, 'Inherited' from generation to generation, secured by a common law of indelible precedent and an array of institutional 'prejudices' (Burke, 1986, pp. 116–17, 119–20, 187; Hill, 1974, pp. 5–7). Two such 'prejudices', related yet distinct, were of particular importance: Church and family. The constitutional authority of the former, finding original expression in Hooker's *Laws of Ecclesiastical Polity*, was testimony to the 'profound and extensive wisdom' of the English people, to the 'sublime' beauty which a commonwealth founded on faith could express (Burke, 1986, pp. 188–9). The presence of the second, though rather more metaphorical perhaps, enjoyed an equally revered place in English, particularly Protestant, constitutional thought; the image of an English 'commonwealth of commonwealths', constituted of myriad God-fearing families, governed by their respective patriarchs, each guided by the example of God's anointed, the 'affectionate father' of the nation (Burke, 1986, p. 117). Whilst constitutional royalists contemplated the elevated virtues of 'sacral monarchy', in her *Women of England, Wives of England* Sarah Stickney Ellis ventured to advise her female compatriots of their 'divine' duty to realise on earth 'the union of the great family of heaven' (Chase and Levenson, 2000, p. 82).

This intensely familial, and familiar, iconography framed what Burke termed the 'impression' of the English 'mind', its 'conscious dignity, a noble pride' and its 'generous sense of glory and emulation' (Burke, 1986, pp. 137, 198). In a particularly resonant passage in *Reflections*, Burke opined:

> The institutions of policy, the goods of fortune, the gifts of Providence, are handed down, to us and from us, in the same course and order ... By adhering in this manner and on those principles to our forefathers, we are guided not by the superstition of antiquarians, but the spirit of philosophic analogy. In this choice of inheritance we have given to our frame of polity the image of a relation in blood; binding up the constitution of our country with our dearest domestic ties; adopting our fundamental laws into the bosom of our family affections; keeping inseparable, and cherishing with the warmth of all their combined and mutually reflected charities, our state, our hearths, our sepulchres, and our altars.
>
> (Burke, 1986, p. 120)

The value of such collective imagery, Burke knew, lay in its capacity to 'engage' the 'affections' of the 'commonwealth'. Preserving the idylls of Albion, accordingly, becomes a matter of restoring the sanctity of the hearth, of retrieving and reinvesting images of happy families and cherubic children. Three years before the publication of *Shirley*, *The English Matron* confirmed that 'the government of a household, for the sake of all the inmates, should be a monarchy, for 'of all forms a democracy is the most uncomfortable in domestic life' (Ingham, 2006, p. 120). Margaret Oliphant went further still, opining that the 'constitution of the household is more entirely representative than even that glorious constitution which keeps our ship of state afloat' (Doggett, 1992, p. 97). Albeit with rather greater irony, Walter Bagehot did precisely the same, observing in his *English Constitution* that a 'family on the throne is an interesting idea' precisely because it 'brings down the pride of sovereignty to the level of petty life' (Bagehot, 2001, p. 85). The monarchy, at once glorious and petty, was the supremely 'dignified' aspect of Bagehot's constitution.

The Burkean idyll, then, shaped mid-nineteenth-century conservative sentiment. The England Tennyson recalled was innately Burkean in its recourse to jurisprudential metaphor:

> A land of settled government.
> A land of just and old renown,
> Where Freedom slowly broadens down
> From precedent to precedent.[14]

Of course, Burke had his critics. Those of a dissenting disposition would have shared Tom Paine's caustic rejection of the constitution Burke prescribed in his *Reflections*; nothing more than a fantastic 'burlesque' (Paine, 1985, pp. 118–22, 172–4). But they remained a minority. And Charlotte Brontë, for one, would certainly not have counted herself amongst their number. The Burkean idyll, if not Burke himself, pervades *Shirley*; for a nation, as Charlotte reminded her readers in its final passages is best governed when 'the humblest of its inhabitants tastes a festal feeling' (534). Such sentiment might today seem whimsical. Constitutional law textbooks are rarely written in verse. But then the English state of mind has not been shaped by constitutional jurists. It has been imagined by its poets.

A new and strange world

Shirley, like any novel, was written at a certain point in time, and in a certain place. For reasons we shall encounter shortly, its composition was fragmented, running through 1848 and into early 1849. It was published a year later. The temporal context of the novel is further refracted by the fact that it is set in 1811–12; a historically appropriate prism through which, Charlotte clearly surmised, to contemplate the 'condition' of England in the late 1840s, or more particularly the 'condition' of West Yorkshire, for *Shirley* is also, as Lewes noted, a regional novel.[15] Of course, the regional context in particular tends to fuel more romantic images of Charlotte and her sisters, tucked away in Haworth, inspired, in the famous words of Virginia Woolf, by little more than 'solitary visions over distant fields' (Woolf, 1998, p. 91). And it is perhaps true that the gritty realism of other 'condition of England' novels, such as *Mary Barton* or *Hard Times*, is missing. Certainly *Shirley* lacks a convincing working-class voice. In correspondence a couple of years after the publication of *Shirley*, Charlotte recounted reading Mayhew's *The London Poor*. It was, she commented, a 'new and strange world – very dark – very dreary', one that 'I scarcely dare imagine' (Smith, 2007, p. 185).

But the Brontë 'myth', as we have already noted, is distracting. Charlotte read widely, attended local bodies such as the Keighley Mechanics Institute and engaged her father and sisters in informed political and social conversation.[16] It was in the latter, undoubtedly, that the Church Tory instincts written into *Shirley* were nurtured and refined.[17] We will revisit these instincts in due course. Patrick Brontë, moreover, had lived through the Luddite riots which Charlotte chose to depict in her novel and about which she had read in archived copies of the *Leeds Mercury*.[18] These accounts revealed that rioting had begun in the area in early 1811, and spread rapidly. Church Tories had united with Whig captains of industry to raise local militia and reinforce the defence of their mills and factories (Thompson, 1991, p. 613). The attack on William Cartwright's Rawfolds mill was particularly notorious, and provided the model that Charlotte recast in her assault on the Moore mill in *Shirley*.[19] Victorian families lived their history, especially their local history, with a peculiar intensity, and in the parlours and parsonages of West Yorkshire in the late 1840s the semi-mythic history of the assault on Rawfolds mill retained its power.[20]

For a generation who believed that the next bloody insurrection was just around the corner, it was living history in every sense.[21] After all, as Elizabeth Gaskell confirmed in her *Life of Charlotte Brontë*, the West Riding was still renowned in the 1840s as a haven of incipient republicanism, and the Brontës would not have been alone in pondering the notorious slogan of the *Northern Star*, 'Peaceably if we can, forcibly if we must' (Gaskell, 1997, pp. 19, 83–4; Newsome, 1998, p. 44). Whilst *Shirley* was set in 1811–12, it was, of course, composed in the context of later renewed Chartist unrest; something which becomes, as Terry Eagleton suggests, the 'unspoken subject' of the novel (Eagleton, 1975, p. 45). For much of 1848 rumours of Chartists drilling on the moors carried an eerie resonance of events forty years earlier. And Charlotte was fully cognisant of these rumours, in personal correspondence expressing her fear that 'convulsive revolutions put back the world in all that is good, check civilization, bring the dregs of society to the surface' (Eagleton, 1975, p. 46; Rogers, 2003, pp. 159–61).

The historical refraction is then critical. The past reaches into the present, allowing Charlotte to direct her audience's gaze to a particular historical event that can gesture, if only allusively, to the present and to the future. Such a literary strategy became increasingly familiar in early and mid-nineteenth-century literature, situating Charlotte and her sisters at the cutting edge of a nascent schism between the providential and historical 'aesthetic'; trying to balance a necessary affection for the former with a growing awareness of the irresistibility of the latter. In this context, many critics have argued that *Shirley* can be read as an ongoing struggle between the faculties of reason and the imagination; between the desire to depict human experience, and its necessarily impressionistic reception (Ermarth, 1997, pp. 3–8, 25–7, 68–72, 77). No one better appreciated the peculiar agonies which attended this tension, of course, than Burke, whose *Philosophical Inquiry* had famously supposed that 'authentic histories' should always be written to move the political imagination in the same way as 'romances or poems' (Burke, 1990, pp. 42–6; Furniss, 1993, pp. 92–3). *Reflections* was written as a testament to precisely this philosophy of history.

At its outset *Shirley* famously eschews the romantic for the real:

> If you think, from this prelude, that anything like a romance is preparing for you, reader, you never were more mistaken. Do you anticipate sentiment, and poetry, and reverie? Do you expect passion, and stimulus, and melodrama? Calm your expectations; reduce them to a lowly standard. Something real, cool, and solid,

lies before you; something unromantic as Monday morning, when all who have work wake with the consciousness that they must rise and betake themselves thereto.

(5)

From her very first fictional writings, Charlotte had expressed a desire to deploy 'plain and homely' realism in order to better excavate human experience (Christ, 1979, p. 289). The fear that *Shirley* depicts is real fear; febrile rumours of 'regiment after regiment' training on Nunnely common and marching off towards Brierley, rumours that lead the bickering curates to arm themselves before setting off home through the dark, and which persuade Robert Moore to reinforce his mill so that it resembles a 'castle' (15–16, 22). And the violence is real violence too; as the eponymous heroine informs her friend Caroline Helstone, when the latter countenances going to aid her beloved Robert in defence of his mill. It 'is not a tilt at a tournament we are going to behold, but a struggle about money, and food, and life' (288). On perusing the 'ruinous' mill the following morning, the narrator notes that amidst the residual carnage 'more than one deep crimson stain was visible on the gravel: a human body lay quiet on its face near the gates; and five or six wounded men writhed and moaned in the bloody dust' (292).

The England that Charlotte duly describes in *Shirley* is distressed, weary of war, and of the restrictions that the continuing Orders in Council, designed to counter Napoleon's 'continental' trading regime, betokened. Its people 'cried out for peace on any terms'. 'National honour', as such, 'was become an empty name, of no value in the eyes of many, because their sight was dim with famine; and for a morsel of meat they would have sold their birthright' (26–7). It is no coincidence that Charlotte places the most desperate invocation of the situation in the voice of her most moderate working-class character in the novel, William Farren. Addressing the mill owner Moore, and speaking of the impact of the new machine frames in particular, Farren explains:

> It's out o'no ill-will that I'm here, for my part; it's just to mak' a effort to get things straightened, for they're sorely a crooked. Ye see we're ill off, – varry ill off: wer families is poor and pined. We're thrown out o'work wi'these frames: we can get nought to

do: we can earn nought. What is to be done? Mn we say, wsiht! and lig us down and dee? Nay: I've no grand words at my tongue's end, Mr Moore, but I feel that it would be a low principle for a reasonable man to starve to death like a dumb cratur' I will n't do't ... Invention may be all right, but I know it isn't right for poor folks to starve. Them that governs mun find a way to help us: they mun make fresh orderations. Ye'll say that's hard to do: – so mich louder mun we should out then.

(117–18)

Assailed by the hated frames, beset by failed harvests, haunted by unemployment and starvation, men such as Farren had reached the end of their tether, and the 'throes of a sort of moral earthquake were felt heaving under the hills of the northern counties' (27).

'But', the authorial voice confirms, 'as is usual in such cases, nobody took much notice.' The starved were left to 'their destiny'; so they just 'ate the bread and drank the waters of affliction', and died in the streets (27). Some notice. Hiram Yorke, 'a Yorkshireman par excellence', does (39). But too many do not.[22] What is missing, not just in the Hollow, but across the county and the country, is not closer government, but a 'want of general benevolence' (41). Alongside her study of the archived holdings of the *Leeds Mercury*, Charlotte would very likely have come across Richard Oastler's notorious essay *Yorkshire Slavery*, published in 1830. According to Oastler, the condition of Yorkshire factory workers was 'more horrid than are the victims of that hellish system' (Gallagher, 1985, pp. 3–4). The alignment of factory worker and slave was far from uncommon in the literature and journals of the 1830s and 1840s, and was particularly favoured by evangelicals campaigning for reform of the legislation relating to both. Charlotte Brontë may not have been an overt campaigner for either. But her sympathies were evident. The needs of such workers, she confirms in later correspondence, 'should not indeed be neglected, nor the existence of their sufferings ignored'. If 'the government would act' to alleviate their condition, she advised, 'how much good might be done by the removal of ill-feeling and the substitution of mutual kindliness in its place' (Eagleton, 1975, p. 46).

It is again an intensely Burkean insight; public politics reduced to private sentiment. It is for this reason that Terry Eagleton has rightly depicted Shirley Keeldar as a true Burkean 'Romantic conservative'

(Eagleton, 1975, pp. 10, 51). The fact that Charlotte's perception of the state of England was shaped by editorials in the *Leeds Mercury* or by conversations engaged in the streets of Haworth does not detract from its acuity. Politics is always local. Magistracy is a human endeavour, its failure a human failing. Much of *Shirley*, as we shall see, is about the failure of magistracy, and more particularly the failure of paternal and parochial magistracy. Yet there is in *Shirley*, as in each of Charlotte's other novels, a still deeper testamentary context. The composition of the novel was protracted and painful, interrupted first by the death of Emily in December 1848, and then by the death of Anne six months later. A 'great part of it', Charlotte later attested, 'was written under the shadow of impending calamity and the last volume, I cannot deny, was composed in the eager, restless endeavour to combat mental sufferings that were scarcely tolerable' (Moglen, 1984, p. 157). When Charlotte returned to this last volume, in the summer of 1849, the desire to personalise its politics had become compelling. The political context still mattered, the desire to reflect upon the condition of England, and more particularly still the condition of West Yorkshire. But the personal mattered even more, reinforcing in Charlotte the fundamental belief that politics is not just a local experience, but above all a familial and sentimental one.

The elision of the public and the private is most readily apparent in the testamentary characterisation of the two female protagonists, Shirley Keeldar and Caroline Helstone. Impelled by Elizabeth Gaskell's assertion, traditional Brontë scholarship has liked to see in Shirley a testament to Emily Brontë. So much was acknowledged by Charlotte (Gaskell, 1997, pp. 299, 412).[23] The young Henry Moore thinks Shirley might be 'a kind of white witch'; an observation which resonates with the pagan licentiousness with which readers viewed the author of *Wuthering Heights* (392). Unsurprisingly, contemporary reviewers tended to prefer the altogether 'sweeter' and 'gentler' Caroline Helstone.[24] The *Daily News* found in Caroline the epitome of 'variety, beauty, and truth' (Allott, 1974, p. 118). Some even preferred to think of *Shirley* as a novel about Caroline.[25] Later critics have commonly read in the 'sweeter' Caroline a complementary testament to Anne Brontë. There is certainly a resonant spirituality, along with a common affection for the 'voice divine' of Cowper, and long walks in the country (178–9, 189–91, 295). As the novel unfolds, it becomes ever clearer that Charlotte presents her readers with two very different visions of femininity, both intensely personal and both intensely political. And whilst we might prefer to eschew the more mythic in this envisaging, it can be suggested that both were shaped, first and foremost, in the now rather more sombre and solitary parlour at Haworth parsonage.

'The healing voice of Christian charity'

In the received conservative tradition, there were two natural and supposedly complementary magistracies, both intensely and irreducibly masculine. One was composed of the local landed elite, who were increasingly accruing industrial wealth. The other was the established Church; a central pillar of the English constitution since the great Elizabethan statutes of Uniformity. The role of the Church, binding the English commonwealth together in common faith was, as we have already noted, central to the Burkean state of 'mind', the magisterial consonance of hearth and altar (Himmelfarb, 2006, pp. 4–7). The idea might seem rather quaint today, though by reason of the 1700 Act of Settlement the established Church remains an intrinsic part of the English constitutional settlement.[26] A century and a half ago, however, the idea of an English constitution was indistinguishable from the idea of an established Anglican Church (Chadwick, 1977, pp. 1–3, 103–4, 476–7). Every holder of public office, from monarch to municipal corporation member, swore a solemn oath of fidelity to the Church. Constitutional settlement, however, did not necessarily guarantee parochial content. Indeed, it was increasingly supposed by many that the converse might be true.

Certainly, many would have shared the opinion of Charlotte Brontë's Hiram Yorke, that the Church of 1811, and by implication of 1848 too, was in a 'bonnie pickle' (308). The 1851 census confirmed that 5 million of the registered 18 million Englishmen and women regularly attended an Anglican Church. But it also confirmed that 5 million preferred to go to dissenting chapels or attend the Catholic Mass, whilst 8 million did not regularly pray anywhere (Moorman, 1973, p. 357; Best, 1970, p. 46). Reasons were various, some metaphysical, others rather more earthy. Whilst the great cathedrals might repose contentedly on their settled endowments, far too many parishioners spent their Sunday mornings staring at broken windows and dodging the rain coming through the chancel roof, or indeed trying to work out who was preaching the sermon. Patrick Brontë's parishioners were here rather luckier than some. Their heads stayed dry and their vicar was resident. But such fortune was as much the exception as the norm. Parochial mismanagement, material decay, absent clergy; it all 'smelt of the middle ages' as Owen Chadwick put it, of a Church that had returned to its pre-Reformation state and which, the logic presumed, needed to be reformed once again (Chadwick, 1977, pp. 35, 38–42).

Moreover, the mid-Victorian had begun to doubt (Chadwick, 1977, p. 1; Wilson, 1999, pp. 8–10). Not all mid-Victorians of course, perhaps not many; but enough. Darwin's *On the Origin of Species* was only half a generation away. The Benthamites had already set up their secular academy at University College London. Intellectual debate within the Church was alternately considered and frenzied, if more often frenzied; finding elevated expression in debates between Oxford dons and Tory bishops, and more prosaic variations in myriad literary and journalistic media. Most importantly perhaps, for a period during the middle of the century, peaking in the 1850s, the Anglican Church was assailed by the spirit of evangelicalism. The sense of need to reinvest the principles of national reformation was not evenly shared of course. Indeed some within the Church did not feel the urge at all. But the inhabitants of Haworth parsonage, albeit to varying degrees, did, and it seems reasonable to suppose that the same was true of many of their fellow parishioners.[27]

In response to the growing tide of anxiety, variously metaphysical, moral and material, the government of Sir Robert Peel established an Ecclesiastical Commission in 1835 (Chadwick, 1977, pp. 126–41; Moorman, 1973, p. 329). Of all the great institutions of the realm, it seemed, none was in greater need of reform than the Church. The condition of the English parish was very obviously and very intimately related to the condition of England itself. The Reform Act of 1832 may not have touched the Church directly. But it reflected and enhanced a tone. Little wonder that Tory bishops should have expressed such hostility during the tortuous passage of the bill. And little wonder that the country in turn should express such hostility towards its bishops. An incipient mood of populist anti-clericalism took hold. The 1832 Act, moreover, was not an isolated expression. Amongst the raft of legislative reforms that passed through Parliament during what Whig historians like to term the 'age of reform' a number were intended to address the myriad perceived failings of the established Church. The Test and Corporation Acts had already been repealed in 1828. A year later, a sobbing George IV assented to an Act confirming an equivalent 'emancipation' for Roman Catholics; something which, it has been suggested, relegated the established Church to little more than a 'department of state' (Wilson, 1999, p. 42).

And so it went on. A new Poor Law, its seeming necessity an implication that the Church could no longer be entrusted with the sole responsibility for alleviating the starving condition of its least fortunate members, was enacted in 1834. A year later Russell's bill to reform municipal corporations confirmed the possibility that non-Anglicans sitting on corporations might administer charitable Church trusts. Three further statutes were enacted on immediate recommendation of Peel's Commission, the 1836 Established Church Act, the Pluralities Act of 1838 and the Dean and Chapter Act of 1840.[28] A similar genesis could be traced for the 1836 Tithe Commutation Act, which provided statutory regulation of tithe collection, and a new Registration Act of the same year which permitted dissenting chapels to be licensed for marriage. The 1840 Church Discipline Act, moreover, could only be read as a blatant attempt by the state to reinforce the constitutional as well as ecclesiastical authority of the Book of Common Prayer and the Thirty-Nine Articles against the perceived challenges of the Tractarians and their Ritualist acolytes.[29] Taken together these statutory reforms represented, in the words of one recent commentator, nothing short of a 'constitutional revolution' in the governance of the Church and its relation with the state (Nockles, 1994, p. 79). The only substantive recommendation that did not make it onto the statute book was Church rate reform. But even here the common law intruded, the House of Lords in *Gosling* confirming that whilst each parish might indeed be responsible for financing the repair of its church buildings, there was no effective penalty should any decline to do so (*Gosling*, 1850; Chadwick, 1977, pp. 155–8).

Another piece of civil jurisprudence, the judgement of the Judicial Committee of the Privy Council in the *Gorham* case, caused still greater consternation. High Churchmen and Tractarians united in their horror at the willingness of the committee to reverse a Court of Arches decision which had confirmed that the Bishop of

Exeter was not obliged to provide a confirmatory testimonial for a curate presented to a living in the gift of the Lord Chancellor. The bishop had consistently declined to provide such a testimonial for a renowned evangelical on the grounds of 'unsound doctrine' (*Gorham*, 1849; Jordan, 1998; Nockles, 1994, pp. 93–8).[30] Little wonder perhaps that talk of disestablishment should spread beyond the margins of radical polemic and dissenting congregations into the very heart of the Tory Church establishment.[31] For those who defined their Loyalism in terms of the original Elizabethan settlement, articulated by Hooker and reaffirmed by Burke, it did indeed seem as though the balance between Church and state had been lost. The purpose of a second reformation was not merely to finance the rebuilding of decaying chancels. It was to reassert the spiritual integrity of God's 'chosen people' against the political subversion of their own Church.

In time, the Church would emerge revitalised, in large part benefiting from the reforms recommended by successive generations of commissioners, as well as the missionary zeal of evangelicalism.[32] By the time Charlotte Brontë died in 1855, the signs of rejuvenation were already apparent. A decade earlier, however, the more sober prospective articulated by Thomas Arnold would have seemed darkly compelling, the 'church as it now stands no human power can save' (Chadwick, 1977, p. 47). Charlotte, like so many of her compatriots, would have reflected on these reforms and very probably in similarly sober tones.[33] *Shirley* is conspicuously concerned with the fate of the Church.[34] And the reason is not difficult to discern. For someone whose life was so indelibly wedded to its rhythms, the health of the English commonwealth was dependent, in very substantial part, on the health of the Church. If the Church was in crisis it was hardly surprising that the 'condition' of England was a troubled one. 'No sound ought to be heard in the Church', Burke advised in his *Reflections*, 'but the healing voice of Christian charity' (Burke, 1986, p. 94). Charlotte concurred, emphasising in private correspondence that the greatest need in her bit of England was for a 'healing voice', one that would drown out the Babel of dissent and schism.[35] In a very obvious sense, *Shirley* is written as a Bunyanesque quest for this healing voice, part of what William McKelvey has termed a distinctive Victorian 'cult' of evangelical literature (McKelvey, 2007, pp. 251–77).[36]

Charlotte's personal religious sympathies are well documented; her dislike of Puseyite pomposity, a particular loathing of Catholic ritual, an evident sympathy for the kind of moderate Church evangelicalism toward which her father, and younger sister Anne, leaned.[37] The cause of Christian charity defined such evangelicalism, the 'spirit of the Gospel' as Charlotte put it in private correspondence (Gaskell, 1997, p. 221). Politics, faith and love; the ideal of a living community with God was set by these coordinates. In *Shirley*, it finds expression in Reverend Hall, the one cleric who seems to know his flock, understand their plight and contemplate a resolution of their distress (119–21).[38] It finds further allusion in the repeated recommendation of Cowper, a particular favourite of Anne Brontë. And another still in the depiction of the Briar-chapel which, although a 'new, raw, Wesleyan place of worship', is one in which 'singers passed jauntily from hymn to hymn and from tune to tune, with an ease and buoyancy all their own' (123). The Briar-chapel, we can surmise, is precisely the kind of place where Charlotte and her sister might have felt at home.[39]

At the same time, of course, the author of *Shirley* wrote as a confirmed, if critical, supporter of the established Church.[40] 'I love the Church of England', Charlotte confirmed in private correspondence, 'with all her faults' (Thormählen, 1999, p. 203). It is the same voice that can be discerned in chapter sixteen, where the narrator observes:

> Let England's priests have their due: they are a faulty set in some respects, being only of common flesh and blood, like us all; but the land would be badly off without them; Britain would miss her church, if that church fell. God save it! God also reform it!
>
> (254)

The observation presages the famous battle of rival clerical processions at the Whitsun feast; an event which marries the comedic with an altogether darker sub-text. The dissenters are vanquished, the Church militant triumphant. But it is also very silly, a patent failure of magistracy and hardly consonant with the received idylls of a 'chosen people' of common godly sentiment (254–7; Thormählen, 1999, pp. 173–4).

The opening of the novel famously confirms that a 'shower' of beneficent curates would in time descend on West Yorkshire (5). The Church will indeed be reformed once again. But those who meanwhile populate *Shirley* spend far too much time on 'frivolities which seemed as empty as bubbles to all but themselves', and far too little in administering to a flagging flock. Theirs is a 'mucky pride', as the perceptive, if destitute, William Farren comments (274). It is an unsavoury picture, as the reader is warned, of 'unleavened bread with bitter herbs'; a view which echoes closely Charlotte's own contempt for the various curates who had passed through Haworth Parsonage over the years, 'a self-seeking, vain, empty race', as she confided in correspondence with Ellen Nussey (5; Smith, 2007, p. 147; Barker, 2001, p. 586).[41] It is not hard to discern an authorial tone in the anxieties voiced by Shirley in chapter twenty-one:

> When I hear Messrs Malone and Donne chatter about the authority of the Church, the dignity and claims of the priesthood, the deference due to them as clergymen; when I hear the outbreaks of their small spite against Dissenters; when I witness their silly narrow jealousies and assumptions; when their palaver about forms, and traditions, and superstitions, is sounding in my ear; when I behold their insolent carriage to the poor, their often base servility to the rich, I think the Establishment is indeed in a poor way, and both she and her sons appear in the utmost need of reformation.
>
> (310)

In similar tones Helstone despairs of the young curates, of their 'confusion of tongues which has gabbled me deaf' (11–12). Helstone may not be the kind of cleric with whom Charlotte would have shared an immediate affinity.[42] But he is honest and perceptive; not least in his awareness that whilst Anglican curates wander their disenchanted flock cadging free suppers, dissenters and Methodists are in the 'thick of a revival' (12). Helstone too realises the need for another reformation.

His observations with regard to the wider responsibilities of civil magistracy are equally acute. In conversation with Robert Moore on the subject of starving machine-breakers, he casts a biblical analogy, to the 'poor Hebrew wanderers' of the Old Testament, armed only with 'shepherd's crooks, or the masons' building-tools'. The Lord saved them, or more immediately the 'right hand of the Lord' did (34–5). Moore, he insinuates, should aspire to be that hand; standing shoulder to shoulder with the local clergy, aligned in a common appreciation of their magisterial duty to heal and settle. Moore however is an avowed man of 'manufacture', comfortable only with 'my trade, my mill, and my machinery'. These are his 'gods' (22). And they, in the opinion of the narrator, have proved to be a singular disappointment:

> All men, taken singly, are more or less selfish; and taken in bodies they are intensely so. The British merchant is no exception in this rule: the mercantile classes illustrate it strikingly. These classes certainly think too exclusively of making money: they are too oblivious of every national consideration but that of extending England's (ie. their own) commerce. Chivalrous feeling, distinterestedness, pride in honour, is too dead in their hearts.
>
> (142–3)

The echo of Carlyle's complaint, in *Sign of the Times*, is sharp. 'Mechanical' men are 'guided only by their self-interest', by 'rule and calculated contrivance' (Himmelfarb, 2007, pp. 34, 39). Robert Moore is such a man, even if he is a dimly self-aware one:

> When a man has been brought up only to make money, and lives to make it, and for nothing else, and scarcely breathes any other air than that of mills and markets, it seems odd to utter his name in a prayer, or to mix his idea with anything divine.
>
> (106)

The relation between money and faith is not a readily comfortable one. Robert is a zealot for the law, but not for justice. He reveals scant interest either in those who were riding his wagons and who were beaten on Stilbro' moor or in William Farren's reasoned appeal for benevolence; a 'missed chance he was lord of', as the narrator puts it, wondering how he 'could turn from such a man without a conciliatory or a sympathizing expression' (118–19).

Robert Moore can, however, be saved. Critically Charlotte vests in him a heroic Wellingtonian masculinity. He is decisive, a natural leader of men, possessed of energy and zeal, one who 'ever wanted to push on' (26). When his mill is attacked he acts with resolve. A 'cooler commander' Helstone admits, 'I would not wish to see'. The same is true when he is faced with Moses Barraclough's deputation (116–18). The redemption, moreover, will be fashioned by Caroline Helstone. It is the evangelical Caroline who appreciates that good magistracy must 'cherish hope', wed the 'heart' and the 'head' and admit the presence of love as the supreme 'divine virtue' (62, 73, 80). A critical moment comes in Caroline's determination that Robert must read *Coriolanus*.[43] It is this voice, the voice of humanity, that Robert must come to appreciate:

> You must have his spirit before you; you must hear his voice with your mind's ear; you must take some of his soul into yours ... It is to stir you; to give you new sensations. It is to make you feel your life strongly, not only your virtues, but your vicious, perverse points ... Now, read, and discover by the feelings the reading will give you at once how low and how high you are.
>
> (77)

Moore's confession – that he now realises that a good magistrate must learn to accommodate his 'two natures; one for the world and business, and one for the home and leisure' – seems to reassure (215). There is, he finally concurs, something 'to look to, beyond a man's personal interest':

> To respect himself, a man must believe he renders justice to his fellow-men. Unless I am more considerate to ignorance, more forbearing to suffering, than I have hitherto been, I shall scorn myself as grossly unjust.
>
> (454)

The rhetoric is appropriate. But doubts, as we shall see, remain.

Quite a woman and something more

Robert Moore might be destined to govern, eventually. But the common law of property and probate demands an alternative magistracy, that of 'Captain' Shirley Keeldar:

> Business! Really the word makes me conscious I am no longer a girl, but quite a woman and something more. I am an esquire: Shirley Keeldar, Esquire, ought to be my style and title. They gave me a man's name; I hold a man's position: it is enough to inspire

me with a touch of manhood ... You must choose me for your churchwarden, Mr Helstone, the next time you elect new ones: they ought to make me a magistrate and a captain of yeomanry.
(172)

Magistracy is thrust on Shirley. She has inherited the responsibility and seems to comprehend its essentials; the ideal consonance of 'private conscience' with her 'landed-proprietor and lord-of-the-manner conscience'; the harsh reality of 'suffering and desperation'; and the duty of the magistrate to 'allay the suffering' (222–6, 244).[44] But her rhetoric carries a self-conscious ironic inflection. 'Captain' Keeldar is fatally compromised, and when real violence threatens, when the 'romance of female paternalism' passes, she readily concedes her commission to 'Captain' Moore (209; Harsh, 1994, p. 115; Bodenheimer, 1998, pp. 22–3, 48–9).[45] Much though we are supposed to admire Shirley Keeldar, so too are we supposed to be disturbed; by the thought that England might be governed by what Joe Scott in the novel declaims as the 'petticoat' pretensions of a 'generation' of women who appear to be rather too 'kittle' and 'froward' (275–9). Charlotte, notably, would most likely have encountered many editorials which sought to damn Chartism precisely because women appeared to assume such a prominent role in its organisation.

Centuries of cultural and constitutional history, as well as myriad statutory enactments and judicial pronouncements, militated against the idea of female churchwardens and captains of yeomanry. Home 'duties', Elizabeth Gaskell confirmed, should always be 'paramount'; and Charlotte, Gaskell assured the readers of the *Life of Charlotte Bronte*, felt the same.[46] Perhaps, but even if the author of *Shirley* would have found little to dispute in the idea of 'separate spheres' the novel she wrote asked questions.[47] *Shirley*, as Eugene Forcade observed in his review, was first and foremost about the 'condition of women in the English middle-class' (Allott, 1974, pp. 143–5). It was, another reviewer accorded, a conspicuously 'womanly book' (Allott, 1974, pp. 120–1)[48] Margaret Oliphant, as we have already noted, appraised it in precisely these terms (Allott, 1974, pp. 390–1; Miller, 2001, p. 91). Charlotte Brontë may not have set out to write a subversive novel. But she did, all the same.

Heather Glen suggests that the deeper significance of *Shirley* rests in the juxtaposition of 'inarticulate private suffering and public official history' (Glen, 2002, p. 144). Time and again, she argues, the novel subverts the presumption that there might be a distinct private sphere where women live in comfortable seclusion, insulated from the horrors of public life (Glen, 2002, pp. 156–7). The strategy is feminist, even if the author was not. Notorious in this context is Shirley's disquisition on the subject of Milton and Eve in chapter eighteen.[49] The first woman, Shirley here opines, bred Titans. She 'yielded the daring which could contend with Omnipresence'. She spoke to God, with the same alacrity as Adam. It was this woman that Milton failed to see and it is this woman who, Shirley continues, 'I love', for 'Heaven may have faded from her brow when she fell in paradise; but all that is glorious on earth shines there still.' Her friend Caroline is quick to dismiss such a 'hash of Scripture'. But the echo lingers: 'Hush, Caroline! You will see her and feel as I do, if we are both silent' (269–71). It is this sentiment that has inspired feminist critics to read *Shirley* as a testament of 'revolutionary fervour'.[50]

It is certainly tempting to discern, yet again, an authorial voice in Caroline Helstone's tangential plea:

> Men of England! Look at your poor girls, many of them fading around you… You would wish to be proud of your daughters and not to blush for them – then seek for them an interest and an occupation which shall raise them above the flirt, the manoeuvrer, the mischief-making tale-bearer. Keep your girls' minds narrow and fettered – they will still be a plague and a care, sometimes a disgrace to you: cultivate them – give them scope and work – they will be your gayest companions in health; your tenderest nurses in sickness; your most faithful prop in age.
>
> (330)

Caroline's might be a different feminism, but it retains, as Shirley appreciates, a 'force and a depth somewhere within, not easily reached or appreciated' (222).[51] It is Caroline who articulates the relation, familiar most obviously perhaps from Jefferson's essay on the subject, of the 'heart' and the 'head' in matters of governance. It is she too who appreciates that 'hate' is born of 'misery' and desperation, and that it would 'be better' for her intended to be 'loved' by his 'workpeople than to be hated by them, and I am sure that kindness is more likely to win their regard than pride' (27, 80).[52]

Most importantly, Caroline has an innately Burkean sense of her responsibilities as prospective wife and mother; a prospective which was being presently shaped in the nascent cult of Victoriana (Homans, 1998, pp. 26–7). The institution of marriage dominates the closing chapters of the novel. It is the natural state, the 'great wish – the sole aim' of every girl, Caroline declaims (329). Not everyone agreed, as we have already noted. But most did, approving Lord Kames's pronouncement, that 'it is the chief duty of a woman to make a good wife', to 'please her husband, to be a good economist, and to educate their children' (Dolin, 2007, p. 121). There are alternatives. Shirley and Caroline might remain spinsters; as Charlotte did until very nearly the end of her life. But the thought is not to be countenanced. 'What was I created for, I wonder? Where is my place in the world?' Caroline muses, anticipating such a terrible fate. The role of 'old maids', flitting around in the background, devoting their lives to the care of those more fortunate, might seem noble in its 'abnegation of self', but is 'there not a terrible hollowness, mockery, want, craving in that existence?' (149). She might, in such circumstances, even have to become a governess. Whilst there was a growing literature, particularly evangelical, which sought to applaud the idea of working women, in *Shirley*, the thought of becoming a governess, far and away the most likely form of employment for a middle-class spinster, is viewed with nothing less than horror. Shirley compares it to the life of a 'slave' (203).[53]

So marriage it must be. Whilst there is a whiff of something darker in Helstone's observation that 'Millions of marriages are unhappy', concluding 'perhaps all more or less so', as there is in Mrs Pryor's lecture on the 'illusions' of marriage, those prescribed in *Shirley* seem to be rather happier events (363–5). The more brutal masculine view of marriage is rebuffed; the Reverend Malone's crude recommendation of an 'advantageous connexion' echoed in the opinion of Shirley's uncle that marriage is a 'question of common sense and common prudence' rather than 'sympathy and sentiment' (21, 463). Shirley intends to be choosy.[54] Samuel Fawthrop Wynne, deemed by her uncle to be 'decidedly suitable' and in possession of a 'fine unencumbered estate' is rejected with alacrity. Whilst she would never marry someone who was poor, Shirley advises her uncle, she is determined to marry for love and, she adds, neither he nor the 'common law' can stop her (394). The advances of Sir Philip Nunnely are despatched in the same tone, as is Robert Moore's percipient and ill-judged proposal, couched in terms of pity and patronage. Such a proposal, Shirley declaims, is 'obnoxious to a woman's feelings' and 'warped' (500). Shirley's uncle assumes that his niece has read too many 'French novels' (460). Contemporary reviewers suspected as much of the novel's author. Eugene Forcade could only wonder at such a 'revolutionary' approach to matters of marital politics (Allott, 1974, p. 146).

In the end, Shirley marries Robert's rather bookish brother, Louis; the latter's attempts to resist the 'secret ecstasy' of romance duly overcome (422). There is an obviously reciprocity here, one that seems to realise the ideals of companionate marriage; the headstrong Robert complemented by the reflective Caroline, the wilful Shirley complemented by the poetic Louis. And it provides a closure to a novel which, as critics have often argued, lacks any other. All will, in the end, be well. Or will it? Despite the apparent neatness with which Shirley and Caroline are married off, there is something discomforting about the manner of Shirley's subjugation to marital norms, and the willingness of her conformity too.[55] Shirley craves not just a husband, but a 'master', someone who can 'hold me in check', who is 'able to control me' (461). Louis, it seems, is just the man. He wants to 'break in' his wife, to replicate in his home the relationship which defines his calling as a tutor, the relation of master and pupil (519). Shirley is duly reassured, 'glad I know my keeper' (522). Charlotte leaves her readers with the closing image of a Shirley duly tamed, desperate for her submission to be sealed by the institution of marriage:

> Thus vanquished and restricted, she pined, like any other chained denizen of deserts. Her captor alone could cheer her; his society only could make amends for the lost privilege of liberty: in his absence, she sat or wandered alone; spoke little, and ate less.
> (534)

The metaphor Shirley deploys is pointed; crediting her husband in showing how to properly apply the 'powers of the premier' at home (535). 'Am I always to be curbed and kept down?' Caroline reflects. It is Shirley's turn to counsel. 'For his sake, yes', she replies (292). The sense of closure is thus compromised. Marriage comes at a price, rendering the female partner as a 'species of ghost, who haunts her husband, and only becomes half solidified when he is no more' (Glen, 2002, p. 28). Patricia Ingham is not alone among modern critics in wondering why, in apparent contradiction of its earlier realist pretences, *Shirley* closes with its female protagonists confined to a patriarchal 'dreamworld' (Ingham, 2006, p. 137).[56]

And they are not the only dreamers. The novel concludes with Robert Moore indulging his 'Extravagant day-dreams', musing on what he hopes might happen so long as 'I succeed as I intend to do'. He will 'lay wiser and more liberal plans'. Provided he can make some money, bolstered by the estate that Shirley will bring to the family by marrying Louis, the two brothers will be able to carve up the parish between them, rebuild the mill, dig up the copse in the Hollow, and replace it with 'lines of cottages, and rows of cottage-gardens'. If all goes well Robert will also secure a parliamentary statute with which he can enclose the common. It will help him home the 'houseless' and feed the starving (539–40). He might become another Robert Owen. Then again, he might not. The 'good time seemed to come', the narrator observes; and the 'seemed' is important (534).

It is all a bit elusive; critically compromised perhaps by what Helene Moglen terms the 'haunting cry of personal alienation' (Moglen, 1984, p. 154). Certainly there is a sense that Charlotte, in the end, preferred to return to concerns of the human rather than the political condition. The hasty run through events since 1811–12, including the repeal of the hated Orders in Council fails to convince, and anyway somehow barely seems to matter now. The Hollow has been dug up and a 'mighty mill' has arrived, 'and a chimney, ambitious as the tower of Babel'. It is no longer a 'bonnie spot' (541–2). Critics have suggested that the final passages evidence the triumph of the new over the old, the public over the private, the male over the female (Argyle, 1995, pp. 752–3; Zlotnik, 1991, pp. 294–5). Perhaps; but as Asa Briggs implied half a century ago, it may be that the real genius of *Shirley*'s author lay in her refusal to pretend that there could be easy resolutions (Briggs, 1958, pp. 214–16). An apparent inability to decide whether the future should be imagined in darker or lighter shades compromised the final passages of both Charlotte's final novels; for as we shall now see, when Charlotte contemplated once again the inner recesses of the female condition, and their outer appearance, in *Villette*, a surer resolution proved to be just as elusive.

Conclusion: The Trials of Lucy Snowe

The first edition of Elizabeth Gaskell's *The Life of Charlotte Brontë* was published by Smith Elder in March 1857. It was a considerable success, the initial print run of just over 2200 copies sold out in a month. Another 2200 were produced by early May. On the 26th May, however, all unsold copies were recalled. The reason for this sudden turn of events was one particular passage in chapter thirteen. It addressed the peculiar circumstance of Branwell's hurried departure from his employment as tutor to the Robinson children at Thorp Green Hall. The reason, Gaskell opined, was his taking 'the fancy of a married woman, nearly twenty years older than him', one 'so bold and hardened, that she did it in the very presence of her children, fast approaching to maturity'. Poor Branwell was dismissed when the husband of this 'mature and wicked woman' found them in a compromising position. A 'black gloom' descended on the 'brightest hope' of the family, never to be raised (Gaskell, 1997, pp. 205–6). Still haunted by his 'yearning love', his peace of mind further disturbed by her later pleas that they should elope together, but equally devoured by his sense of guilt at committing such a 'deadly crime', Branwell descended into drugs, debt and an early death (Gaskell, 1997, pp. 211, 213–14).

And the fault, as anyone with the slightest knowledge of the Brontës, or York society, would have known, lay with Mrs Lydia Robinson, 'still flaunting about to this day in respectable society; a showy woman for her age; kept afloat by her reputed wealth' (Gaskell, 1997, p. 212). Not that she was named of course. But within days Newton and Robinson, the solicitors representing the now remarried Lady Lydia Scott had written to Smith Elder threatening legal action unless all unsold copies were recalled, the offending passage excised from further editions, and a suitable apology published in the press. The problem had been anticipated. 'Do you mind the law of libel?' Gaskell had inquired of George Smith, her publisher. Lady Scott, 'that bad woman who corrupted Branwell Brontë', would not be 'named by name', she added, but she was to be 'gibbetted' along with the publisher Newby and Lady Eastlake (Uglow, 1999, pp. 403–4; Barker, 2001, pp. 800–1).[1] They did mind, George Smith confirmed in reply. But the commentary remained, at least until communication was received from Messrs Newton and Robinson. William Gaskell, in his wife's absence, signalled his accord to the meeting of all terms, provided that alongside the retraction the solicitors published a letter confirming Elizabeth's good faith (Uglow, 1999, pp. 425–6).[2] Of course, by then the damage was done, as Gaskell consoled herself (Miller, 2001, p. 77).[3]

We are left to speculate upon what might have happened if Smith Elder had not recalled their unsold copies of Gaskell's *Life* and printed their retraction. There were two routes open to the Scotts. But one was closing, whilst the second was not enticing. The law of libel, like so much else it seems in mid-nineteenth-century jurisprudence, was not particularly coherent. The first option was an action for defamation in the ecclesiastical courts. Such actions could only be pursued if the defamation related to an activity otherwise proscribed in canon law, most obviously sexual misconduct (Waddams, 2000, pp. 8–9, 27–9). This was the case here of course. But the available penalties were archaic.[4] And anyway the appropriateness of ecclesiastical jurisdiction in such cases had attracted increased criticism as the century progressed (Waddams, 2000, p. 11–13).[5] It was to be curtailed by statute in 1855.

The second option was a civil action for defamation; an action which under the doctrine of coverture would have been taken by Sir Edward Scott, and which could lead to the award of damages (Waddams, 2000, pp. 18–24).[6] But such actions were as embarrassing as they were expensive; not least because so much depended on showing that a particular person was readily identifiable to his or her peers. Again, this could probably have been achieved in the case of Lydia Scott. But whether Sir Edward wanted to spend days in court whilst his lawyers tried to prove that his wife was the married woman with whom Branwell was wrongfully alleged to have committed adultery is doubtful. The ritual of libel law, defamation, threat of action, mutually agreed retraction, was intended to replace the need to be thus embarrassed, financially or otherwise, and in this instance Newton and Robinson and Smith Elder played their roles in precisely the fashion intended.

Critics commonly trace the origins of the Brontë 'myth' to Gaskell's *Life of Charlotte Brontë* (Jay, 1997, p. ix; Miller, 2001, pp. 1–2, 25). Certainly Gaskell felt an acute sense of responsibility. She was a chosen biographer, selected by Patrick Brontë as the person best placed to address the various factual errors and 'malignant falsehoods' that were swirling round the family reputation in the months that immediately followed Charlotte's death (Jay, 1997, p. xiv; Uglow, 1999, pp. 391–2).[7] And if aspersions had to be cast in order to restore Charlotte's reputation, and that of her siblings, Gaskell was evidently quite prepared to do so. The extensive use of private correspondence reinforces the sense that as Charlotte's biographer, Gaskell became a kind of refracted autobiographer.[8] But it was still her Charlotte that emerges from the pages of the *Life of Charlotte Brontë*; and her Emily and Anne too, and her Lydia Scott.[9]

A perilous course

Gaskell was concerned then with fashioning and preserving reputations. She was not alone. So were Sir Edward and Lady Scott. And so too was Charlotte Brontë. Charlotte was obsessed with her reputation, by what others – particularly other writers and reviewers – thought of her and her novels and those of her sisters (Miller, 2001, pp. 2–3). The opinions of friends mattered as well, particularly informed ones, such as George Smith, her publisher. Craving his opinion of the final draft of *Villette*, Charlotte begged, 'I can hardly tell you how much I hunger to have some opinion besides my own, and how I have sometimes desponded and almost despaired because there was no one to whom to read a line – or of whom to ask counsel' (Smith, 2007, p. 207). But it was the opinion of critical reviewers that mattered most. Their reviews were eagerly anticipated and devoured, and where necessary just as urgently rebutted, as Charlotte's correspondence repeatedly confirms (Smith, 2007, pp. 123, 140–1, 154, 156).

By the middle of the nineteenth century the review article had assumed a dominant place at the heart of Victorian culture; one that has perhaps never since been equalled (Himmelfarb, 2007, pp. 22–4). Its gaze was steady and uncompromising, and its gentler subjects, particularly its female ones, lived in fear of its withering aspect. There was, after all, as Margaret Oliphant warned, a 'shame' in women writing, particularly if they were adjudged to have written the wrong sort of novel (Thompson, 1996, p. 14).[10] Charlotte was, as Gaskell confirmed, forever 'anxious about the impression' her writings produced 'on the public mind' (Gaskell, 1997, p. 305). In reply to an inquiry from a teenage Charlotte as to the suitability of women writing, Robert Southey had warned that 'so perilous a course' is 'likely to induce a distempered state of mind', so much so that it might render a woman 'unfitted' for her proper role in life, to run a household (Gaskell, 1997, p. 117). The misogyny is obviously discomforting today, as it must have been to Charlotte at the time, even if she did later attest that Southey's advice 'did me good' (Gaskell, 1997, p. 118).

Given the pejorative that worked against the idea of women writing at all, it is unsurprising that women writers might have been peculiarly sensitive to their identities being revealed. It was for this reason, along with a sense of conventional propriety, that Acton, Currer and Ellis Bell published *The Tenant of Wildfell Hall*, *Jane Eyre* and *Wuthering Heights*. Necessarily, of course, the fact that any author might seek to mask their identity only sharpened the thrill of chasing down true authorship. Gaskell later attested to the veritable 'ferment' that accompanied attempts to find out who the author of *Jane Eyre* might be, just as she likewise recorded Charlotte's determination, as far as possible to 'preserve her incognito' as the author of *Shirley* (Gaskell, 1997, pp. 251, 306).

Along with reputation, Charlotte's other great concern was with 'truth'. Truth mattered, both in its presence and its denial. A 'faithful allegiance to Truth and Nature' against the 'jargon of conventionality' is the 'first duty of an Author' (Smith, 2007, p. 115, 118). It was for precisely this reason that Charlotte was so determined to compose a Preface to the second edition of Emily's *Wuthering Heights*. It was written to aid the 'reader' in achieving 'pleasure' and avoiding 'distress', and to disabuse any who might have inclined to think that there was some kind of more prosaic truth to be discerned within

(Thompson, 1996, pp. 43–5). Prefaces were commonly accepted as places wherein an author might seek to define the relative veracity of a novel; something which imported a particular intensity in the context of novels which claimed to be testamentary. They were sites of 'mediation' between audience and author, places where the latter might strive to limit the interpretative latitude of the former (Chaplin, 2007, p. 38). And, it might be added, a site of invention too. Charlotte certainly invented a new Emily, as she did again in *Shirley*, where she also invented a new Anne. Likewise, Anne used the Preface to *The Tenant of Wildfell Hall*, as we have already noted, to do much the same, to mediate, to instruct and to prospectively re-invent.

Anecdote and correspondence confirm the intensity of Charlotte's concern regarding truth. Suggestions that parts of *Jane Eyre* might be rather melodramatic invariably met with a fierce riposte. Gaskell recalled that when someone had 'objected, in my presence' to the passage wherein Jane 'hears Rochester's voice', Charlotte had 'replied, in a low voice, drawing in her breath, "But it is a true thing; it really happened"' (Gaskell, 1997, p. 319). When Lewes dared to venture the same, he was curtly reminded that 'Nature and Truth' were the author's 'sole guides' (Smith, 2007, p. 90). Charlotte's publishers had met a similar response when they dared to suggest that she might wish to rewrite some of the earlier passages in the novel. It may prove to 'suit the public taste better than you anticipate', Charlotte replied, 'for it is true and Truth has a severe charm of its own' (Smith, 2007, p. 86). A similar plea from the same publishers in the context of the notorious opening to *Shirley* fared no better, and when Lewes again ventured a disapproving comment, Charlotte's response betrayed a sensitivity to the fact that her adherence to truth might exact a price, 'All mouths will open against that first chapter; and that first chapter is true as the Bible, nor is it exceptionable' (Gaskell, 1997, p. 305). The fact that Charlotte wrote from experience strengthened her resolve. *Jane Eyre*, she reminded Lewes, was 'an autobiography, not perhaps in the naked facts and circumstances, but in the actual suffering and experience' (Miller, 2001, p. 13).

Charlotte's defence of truth and authorial integrity was uncompromising. But it was also prickly and defensive; for she knew that the claim, necessarily compromised in the context of romantic fiction, was equally subject to the vicissitudes of subjective judgement. Any text invites the judgement of its readers. But if the claim of the text is to truth, the invitation is pointed. The author can reach through to the reader, hoping somehow to sharpen the frame of interpretation and judgement. But the reader can reach back just as readily. Author and reader engage in a process of reciprocal judgement and surveillance. And again, nowhere is the desire to regulate the reception of the text seemingly more urgent than in the presentation of testament (Flint, 1993, pp. 187–91; 2001, p. 35). Here again Charlotte was acutely sensitive to the peculiar authorial responsibilities that attached to the writing of testamentary novels (Jay, 1997, p. x; Miller, 2001, p. 13). *Jane Eyre*, as we have already noted, was subtitled *An Autobiography*. 'Speak I must', Jane declares at the outset. *The Professor*, unpublished until after Charlotte Brontë's death, was to some degree autobiographical. And so, of course, was Charlotte's final novel, much of which sought to rework the autobiographical sketches written into *The Professor*. It has been suggested that Charlotte Brontë's defining achievement as a novelist was to resurrect the literary, as opposed to scriptural, expression of 'confessional art' (Gilbert and Gubar, 2000, pp. 439–40).

As a number of critics, contemporary and modern, have noted, *Villette* is in many ways the most personal of Charlotte's literary testaments.[11] Certainly Charlotte was keen to confirm that the reader of *Villette* would not be distracted by any 'matter of public interest' (Smith, 2007, p. 208).[12] At a superficial level this might be true. Law and politics are even harder to discern on the surface of *Villette* than is the case with her earlier novels. But it is precisely this invisibility that matters. It is the silence of Lucy Snowe, the intense introspection, the anxiety of self-reflection that makes *Villette*, at a necessarily deeper and perhaps necessarily more elusive level, a testament of real political import.[13] In fact, it has been argued that in the presentation of the thoroughly 'defeated' and 'dispossessed' Lucy Snowe, Charlotte penned not just her own most 'despairingly feminist novel', but also one of the most terrifying of her generation. Lucy is the ultimate 'woman without', engaged in a constant struggle not just with the machinations of those around her, but with her own sense of crushing isolation and mental frailty (Gilbert and Gubar, 2000, pp. 399–400).[14] If there is indeed rather more to *Villette* than meets the eye, it is intriguing to reflect on how far Charlotte was cognisant of the fact, and how much she perhaps embraced it (Ciolkowski, 1994, pp. 219–20).

Moreover, if the claim to truth is nowhere more urgent than in the writing of a testamentary novel, so too is the reciprocal need for the reader to distrust. There is much about Lucy Snowe, as there is indeed about Jane Eyre, and Gilbert Markham, and Lockwood and Nelly Dean, that recommends caution. Indeed Lucy Snowe does not even trust herself, something that is made all too starkly apparent in her ongoing struggle to resist the lures of Catholic confession and its attendant rites of sublimation. The denunciation of Catholic 'priestcraft' is a constant rhetorical refrain in *Villette*: all the 'tales that were nightmares of oppression, privation, and agony' and which constitute Roman theology (117). Yet, driven by an enervating sense of alienation, craving the ritual and reassurance of any 'spectacle of sincere worship', Lucy enters a confessional (160–2). The reader is assured that Lucy finds the experience repellent, particularly the priest's invitation that they should meet again in private. Lucy recoils from 'walking into a Babylonish furnace', troubled in considerable part by the possibility that she might indeed have been tempted by 'popish superstition', and perhaps by the sense that she was in the process being somehow seduced (163; Gilbert and Gubar, 2000, pp. 214–15).[15] However Lucy's spiritual thirst is not assuaged, as the reader comes to realise, and in time Lucy finds herself in the priest's company once again, at the home of the 'evil fairy', Madame Walravens (388, 394). And the seduction continues too, not so much in the priest's eerie stalking, but in M Paul's collusive attempts to effect her conversion (417–21). In the closing passages, Lucy seeks to reassure her reader that M Paul has given up this futile endeavour. But Lucy is not a reassuring narrator, and the reader is only too aware that she remains both enamoured of and entranced by her 'master' right up until news of his death in the final passages of the novel (494–6).[16]

It is interesting that a number of contemporary critics were troubled by the intense tone of the confessional passage in *Villette*. Charlotte took particular exception to Harriet Martineau's suggestion that the author had abandoned 'calm disapproval' of Catholic ritual for an over 'passionate hatred' (Allott, 1974, p. 174). The reviewer in the *Guardian* feared that in her denunciation of the same the author of *Villette* had 'degraded' all Christianity (Allott, 1974, p. 194). It is even more suggestive perhaps when the passage is read as Charlotte intended, as a testament to her own struggle with temptation. In a letter to Emily, Charlotte admitted that the confession scene written into *Villette* was indeed derived from personal experience, and whilst there is no reason to doubt her distaste at the ceremonial 'mummery' and 'idolatrous' ritual of the Catholic Mass, there is also reason to contemplate the implications of her momentary lapse (Smith, 2007, pp. 43–4; Gaskell, 1997, pp. 185–6, 196).[17] In her *Life* Gaskell later confirmed that the 'striking form and ceremonies of the Romish Church' in Brussels had 'made a deep impression' on each of the sisters (Gaskell, 1997, pp. 162–3). And it was not quite so momentary either. Charlotte, like Lucy, was to be tempted once again. Whilst visiting London in June 1851, she twice attended confirmation ceremonies conducted at the residential chapel of the Spanish ambassador by the famous – indeed the notorious – Cardinal Wiseman (Smith, 2007, p. 191; Gaskell, 1997, p. 361).[18]

As a literary genre, the testamentary novel necessarily engages familiar debates regarding the nature of author–text relations, and indeed at a further remove the relation of author, text and reader. It is perhaps true to say that these debates are rather less familiar to lawyers and legal theorists than to literary critics, but the advance of literary and hermeneutic jurisprudence has necessarily emphasised the extent to which lawyers must contemplate their unsettling implications. Whilst some, such as Ronald Dworkin or Owen Fiss, might embrace the hermeneutic insight, others cling resolutely to the formalist faith that the 'immanent' rationality of the law cannot be corrupted by considerations of authorial intent or reader reception (Dworkin, 1986, pp. 50–4, 348–9; Weinrib, 1988; Fiss, 1982). In this, the formalist shares the same anxiety that afflicted Charlotte Brontë; that of the integrity of a given text, and the extent to which an author might be able to influence or, to use Fiss's terminology, 'discipline' the audience (Fiss, 1982, p. 744). Accordingly, both are similarly concerned about the representational veracity of a text, reluctant to embrace the implications of Richard Rorty's challenge that there may anyway be no 'comprehensive' truth to be conveyed (Rorty, 1989, pp. 4–5, 50–4, 60–1). The liberation of the reader comes at a price. If a reading of a Brontë novel impresses upon the nascent lawyer nothing more than this singular and irreducible paradox it will have done much.

The 'demoniac mask'

The idea that the text might exercise a restraint over the reader has an especial resonance in the context of *Villette*. Critics have long noted the extent to which characters in Brontë novels survey and are surveyed. It is obvious, as we have already noted, in *Jane Eyre*. Coining a loaded metaphor, Nancy Armstrong concludes that Lockwood in *Wuthering Heights* 'wants nothing so much as the pornographic thrill of just looking' (Armstrong, 2003, p. 437). As, the implication runs, do Emily's readers, and Anne's and Charlotte's. But the sense is perhaps strongest of all in *Villette*, a novel that is dominated by spectacle, particularly the spectacle of the female body.[19] Everyone watches and everyone judges Lucy Snowe, Lucy above all; so much so, indeed, that it takes Charlotte's second most famous protagonist, like her first, to the edge of madness, alternating between moments of 'catalepsy', manic depression and hallucinatory hysteria, to a point where she feels the need to advise the reader as to whether at any given moment she was in her 'sane mind' or not (109, 160).[20] Of course, there is no more intense form of surveillance than the self-exposure of Catholic confession, and Madame Beck, the 'little Jesuit inquisitress' is only the most ardent of the 'strange' Romish 'schemers' who strive to keep Lucy within their constant gaze (293, 393). But surveillance in *Villette* is far from particular. A similar intensity is pervasive in the theatre, in the classroom and, it might be surmised, in the process of reading itself; for here Charlotte makes her readers complicit in precisely the same exercise in speculative intrusion.

The apparent correlation between the act of reading and the process of surveillance has long engaged critical attention, much of which has moved around Michel Foucault's idea of the disciplinary 'gaze', and the nature of the 'regulatory' state (Flint, 1993, pp. 39–41). According to Foucault, the mutation of received processes of formal legal regulation into myriad discursive networks of disciplinary control and surveillance could indeed be traced back to a critical historical 'moment' in the nineteenth century (Foucault, 1991, pp. 193, 296, 302; McNay, 1992, p. 31). Foucault, of course, made much of Jeremy Bentham's notorious panopticon; not so much as a substantive influence on later generations of law reformer than as a semiotic for an age which was ever more determined to regulate by surveillance. The panopticon, as Foucault realised, was nothing more than a 'theatre' in which could be observed the toils of the labourer, the criminal, the insane and, if he had followed Frances Power Cobbe's alignment all the way through, the women (Foucault, 1991, p. 200). These were the disciplinary processes of regulation and surveillance that would change; as we shall see shortly. In later writings Foucault himself turned to more informal processes of 'governmentality' (Goodlad, 2003, pp. 12–16; Golder and Fitzpatrick, 2009, pp. 29–33), but the overall supposition remained: that the public and private lives of nineteenth-century Englishmen and women were surveyed and regulated more closely than had ever been the case before. And the literary testament, as a mutated expression of the Christian confession, represented a peculiarly intense variant; this intensity generated precisely by the fact that it derived its authority from being the product of self-reflection and regulation, a 'technique of the self' as Foucault famously termed it (Rabinow, 1997, p. 178).

And nowhere are the techniques of surveillance more evident, as Foucault averred, than in the shaping of discourses of sexuality. In his *History of Sexuality*, Foucault identified sexuality as a prime example of the advance of disciplinary, as opposed to purely juridical, regulation (Foucault, 1990, pp. 48, 54–5). Contrary to popular historical assumption, Foucault argued, the Victorians did not seek to 'repress' sexuality through legal regulation (Foucault, 1990, pp. 8–11). Their 'policing' of sexuality was altogether more subtle, exercised through myriad prescriptive 'public discourses', each of which presents itself as an inscription on the female body, which as a 'body politic' is 'exposed' to invite judgemental surveillance (Foucault, 1990, p. 25; 1991, p. 28; McNay, 1992, pp. 15, 17–18; Golder and Fitzpatrick, 2009, pp. 13–15). Accordingly sexuality was not to 'be thought of as a natural given', but rather as a discursively shaped and re-shaped 'network in which the stimulation of bodies, the intensification of pleasures, the incitement to discourse, the formation of special knowledges, the strengthening of controls and resistance, are linked to one another in accordance with a few major strategies of knowledge and power' (Foucault, 1990, p. 104).

The writing of a distinctive bio-medical literature, of the kind we encountered in Chapter 3, represents precisely such a constitutive discourse; one, of course, of many. Another it can be argued was the romance novel, and indeed the anti-romance novel that it spawned.[21] Following Foucault, Jill Matus concludes that 'participation in literary discourse offered Victorian women an opportunity for conceptualising their own sexuality' (Matus, 1995, p. 13). Preferring a still more overtly feminist – even revolutionary – strategy, Nancy Armstrong suggests that the sisters 'call up the ghosts of the history of sexuality to represent a domain of passion that seems to well up in opposition to the contemporary conventions of courtship and kinship relations' (Armstrong, 1987, p. 204). The supposition that the literary discourse of sexuality might be distinctive, in large part because of its self-reflective impulse, is necessarily sharpened in the context of avowed testamentary novels. Foucault's suggestion that such a 'technology of the self' represented an evolved species of 'confessional science' has an especial resonance in the context of Charlotte Brontë and her novels (Foucault, 1990, p. 64).

Certainly Charlotte liked to think of herself as writing about passion, particularly female passion. She distinguished herself from Jane Austen's more 'common-place' accounts of romance on precisely these terms (Smith, 2007, p. 99).[22] But the extent to which she might have seen herself as writing about sexuality is rather different; although sexuality is an unarguable presence, particularly in her two most overtly testamentary novels, *Jane Eyre* and *Villette*. We have already encountered Jane's temptations and her agonies of resistance. The same temptations are written into *Villette*, and not just in the sexual imagery or the latent passion which pervades accounts of Lucy's relationship with M Paul.[23] It is the strategic presentation of this imagery that is so striking. Charlotte repeatedly aligns sexuality with spectacle, deploying resonant cultural imagery to impress upon her reader its subversive engagement. Thus Polly is described at the outset as a 'little Odalisque' (29).[24] Again invoking a familiar cultural trope, familiar not least from the depictions of oriental sensuality in *Jane Eyre*, Charlotte aligns Lucy's prospective seduction by M Paul with their accidental encounter in the gallery before Rubens's *Cleopatra*, the 'Venus of the Nile'. The latter is appalled that his pupil had sat 'coolly down' and looked 'at *that* picture'; a perspective that is all the more intriguing for the thought that Charlotte might have intended her readers to share the same discomfort (201, 204–5).

The most overtly sensual, and the most subversive, depiction of sensuality in *Villette* comes, however, in the shape of the 'sinister and sovereign', and again conspicuously oriental, Vashti, whose 'demoniac mask' leaves Lucy as awed and enraptured as she is appalled (257, 259; Ciolkowski, 1994, p. 225; Litvak, 1988, p. 471).[25] 'It was a marvellous sight: a mighty revelation. It was a spectacle low, horrible, immoral'; one which Lucy immediately contrasts, in terms of its human passion, with the more ornate sensuality of *Cleopatra* (258–9).

It is not just Vashti's sensuality which so intrigues Lucy. It is also the reaction to Vashti of others. She confesses to being 'amused and enlightened' when her companion Dr John strives to reassure her that he could distinguish the person of the actress from the 'artist'. It was a 'branding judgment', Lucy observed (260). And a familiar one too, commonly made by men who like to watch erotic dancers.

The depiction of Vashti was based once again on personal experience, on the performance of the renowned actress Rachel, whose dancing Charlotte witnessed during her visit to London in 1851. 'I neither love, esteem, nor admire this strange being', she confessed, 'but (if I could bear the high mental stimulus for so long) I would go every night for three months to watch and study its manifestations' (Kreilkamp, 2005, p. 143). Rachel performed to entrance and Charlotte was entranced, no less so because what she had seen was deemed by many to be little short of pornographic. The acting, she confessed 'transfixed me with wonder, enchained me with interest and thrilled me with horror', the 'worst of passions' perversely displayed by the 'gift of Genius' (Smith, 2007, p. 197; Litvak, 1988, p. 485).[26] Lucy Snowe likewise confesses to being in thrall to the 'strong magnetism' of Vashti's 'genius' (259). The idea that Rachel's or Vashti's performance is somehow liberating is tempered in the same way that all such moments of unveiling are, by the pragmatics of performativity, the capacity of the sexual subject to satisfy the ritualised expectations of her audience (Sigel, 2002, p. 13).

Regardless of the extent to which Charlotte might have thought herself to be writing about sexuality, its presence certainly troubled contemporary reviewers of *Villette*; even if the intensity was less than that experienced when contemplating the passions of *Wuthering Heights* or *Jane Eyre*. The reviewer in *Putnam's Monthly* contemplated just how the 'delicate reader' might react to the 'exuberant power' of a novel at the heart of which could be found 'sketched in the lurid gloom of the French melo-dramatic style' the wholly 'disagreeable' figure of Vashti (Allott, 1974, pp. 213–15). In an age when the broader explosion of reading created such concern, it is hardly surprising that so many ruminated on the dangers of an incendiary sexuality written into the pages of too many mid-Victorian novels (St Clair, 2007, pp. 11–13, 308–9, 330–4). By the middle of the nineteenth century literary critics broadly concurred that there was far too much sex in literature, far too many instances of adultery in particular, and that something had to be done about it; a perception that was aggravated, inevitably, by the establishment of the new Divorce Court in 1857, and the alacrity with which newspaper editors pounced on the potential of its reports for titillating their readers.[27]

The publication of *Villette* pre-dated this particular statutory enactment. But not by much, and the critical mood had already taken root. Of course, historians of sexuality commonly propose that many Victorians, particularly Victorian men, rather liked pornography (Sigel, 2002, pp. 21–8). But this did not preclude the less approving from investing considerable emotional and intellectual energy in contemplating the extent to which such material might be, or should be, regulated. The depiction of Vashti was precisely the kind of thing which appeared to confirm both the anxiety and the seeming urgency. As we have already noted, depictions of Arthur Huntingdon's violence, Jane Eyre's hallucinatory passions, and the incestuous temptations of Catherine Earnshaw, were received in similar critical vein. They do not, of course, seem pornographic today. Historical context is critical. What, as a later Lord Chief Justice observed, 'would not have been discussed in the reign of Queen Victoria' might cause little offence a century on (*Reiter*, 1954, 641). And indeed they probably did not seem obscene a century and a half ago, at least not in the main, or to that many. But they were suggestive; and as always it is what is not discussed that causes the greater agitation, the fear of what the more intemperate reader might be led to suppose lies beneath the text.

Not that the courts seemed so agitated, at least not consistently. In the case of obscenity and pornography, as in so much else, the common law in nineteenth-century England contributed little to the sharpening of perception. The authority of the Church, as judicial guardian of public morals, had been eroded during the previous two centuries, whilst the common law was again rather obviously reluctant to assume any alternative jurisdictional responsibility. During the eighteenth century the common law, in cases such as *Curll* and *Wilkes*, had begun to carve out a more consistent jurisprudence of obscene libel, based largely upon a perceived need to secure public order, rather than on anything as elusive as public morality (*Curll*, 1727; *Wilkes*, 1768; Manchester, 1991, pp. 37–44).[28] As the mood began to change, however, during the first part of the nineteenth century, in no small part due to organisations such as the Society for the Prevention of Vice, the case for tighter statutory regulation gained momentum, not least in Parliament. Arguing the case for the Obscene Publications Act in 1857, Lord Campbell advised, that a 'sale of poison more deadly than prussic acid, strychnine, or arsenic – the sale of obscene publications and indecent books – was openly going on' (Leckie, 1999, p. 36).[29]

But it was the distribution of such material that Lord Campbell's Act sought to regulate more closely, not its writing; a conclusion that chimes rather obviously with the classical Foucauldian supposition, that the preference of the law relating to sexuality in nineteenth England was to regulate rather than to judge (Manchester, 1991, pp. 47; Leckie, 1999, pp. 38–9, 67–8; Williams, 1955, pp. 640–2). Accordingly the Act eschewed the temptation to define closely what might be considered 'obscene'. Such a temptation, Lord Brougham advised, was best avoided (Leckie, 1999, pp. 40–1). A decade later, however, in the notorious *Hicklin* case, Lord Cockburn felt it necessary to try. The 'test of obscenity', he opined, 'is this, whether the tendency of the matter charged as obscenity is to deprave and corrupt those whose minds are open to such immoral influences, and into whose hands a publication of this sort might fall' (*Hicklin*, 1868, 371). Cockburn's 'test' clearly admitted that the presumed obscenity of any material is subjective, its effect calibrated by the nature of its prospective audience, rather than the result of any particular substantive essence. It was, of course, a view that accorded with the sentiments of those anxious reviewers who worried about the seeming propensity of young women to read romance novels. The perversion of any mind was a troubling thought; but particularly so if the mind was young and female (Leckie, 1999, pp. 8, 47; Williams, 1955, p. 639).[30]

Prospective audience is not, of course, the only variable. There is historical context too, as we have already noted. And then there is the argument that certain species of alleged pornography might be elevated as art, and thus removed from the purview of obscenity legislation (Manchester, 1988, p. 237; Sigel, 2002, p. 28).[31] Here again prospective audience and the nature of distribution matters. Lord Campbell indeed had striven to reassure Parliament that he never intended to seek the proscription of higher artistic forms, just the kind of stuff that might be found in 'railway stations' and other 'low thoroughfares' (Leckie, 1999, pp. 42–3; Sigel, 2002, pp. 26–7). Lord Justice Cockburn in *Hicklin* agreed. The kind of material courts should be looking to suppress, he confirmed, was the kind of material 'sold at the corners of streets' (*Hicklin*, 1868, 372).

Of course, the novels of the Brontës were not supposed to be sold in these kinds of places. Their authors were respectable, and so, it was assumed, was their audience. No one seriously contemplated regulating the distribution of their novels, no matter how appalled they were by the accounts of sexualised abuse and familial disharmony they encountered within. Here for once the familiar evasion of the law might have had something to recommend it. And anyway, there was perhaps little need. Where the formal processes of juridical regulation were absent, there were already present myriad informal networks of micro-disciplinary regulation; from the stocking of circulating libraries, to the harassment of publishers and distributors, to the presence of disapproving parents.[32] The debate itself, and the anxiety it fed, served to discipline. As history confirms, in matters of policing public morality the law is anyway a blunt instrument, rarely able to satisfy either conservative or liberal advocate, and just as rarely able to settle upon an appropriate margin of appreciation.

Hidden discourses

It is, of course, hardly surprising that the Victorians might have struggled to resolve an appropriate legal response to the perceived threat of obscenity running rampant across the pages of novels and journals distributed by unscrupulous publishers and read by undiscerning young women, and by men. Pornography has always defied consistent regulation, legal or otherwise, precisely because it is and always has been one of the more 'profoundly hidden' of discourses (Sigel, 2002, p. 6). Modern debate regarding the limits of pornography regulation tends to move around alternative liberal and feminist polarities; the former preferring as far as reasonably possible the depiction of pornography as a species of free expression, the latter countering that such an expression must admit the need for regulation where it would otherwise exacerbate gender prejudice (McGlynn and Ward, 2009, pp. 328–37). Whilst the context has necessarily evolved, there are still a number of conspicuous resonances in these modern debates; a particular concern regarding the exposure of the young – and the working classes – to pornography, and an assumption that imagery that might be termed art is somehow elevated, even commendable (Sigel, 2002, pp. 157–8). In short, depiction of the female form, particularly the sexualised female form, is just as a much a matter of critical concern as it was a century and half ago, and the merits or demerits of legal regulation just as likely to provoke fierce disagreement.[33]

Pornography regulation has emerged as something of a touchstone in modern feminist legal debate. But the same historical continuity, and the same rhetorical urgency, can be just as readily detected in other debates regarding the relation of women, gender and law: in regard to spousal abuse, the status of single mothers and child custody provisions, the role of the family and the efficacy of existing divorce and matrimonial property law. It can be discerned too in ongoing debates regarding the ability, or inability, of the law to account for gender in assessing psychological aspects of criminal responsibility. And whilst the gender implications might be less clearly drawn, few would pretend that the law does much to moderate the discrimination and disadvantage experienced by those who are described as being illegitimate or 'dark-skinned'. Indeed, it is the law that in the main part does the describing. Of course, this supposition, that the law might be complicit in the experience of prejudice and discrimination, is not controversial, still less particularly new (Munro, 2007, p. 12). The controversy lies with strategies for addressing this prejudice. Modern feminist legal debate has tended to move around a sameness/difference debate, with some arguing the case for acknowledging a fundamental difference in the female experience, and the law addressing this difference, whilst others have advised against the implications inherent in appearing to accept such differences as being somehow natural or experientially inevitable (Munro, 2007, pp. 22–8).

There is no obvious resolution to this intellectual divergence and it is in this context that some feminist jurists have looked to alternative disciplinary or cross-disciplinary approaches.[34] Here the engagement of 'law and literature' has proved to be one of the most popular, a principle attraction being the opportunities that literature, particularly testamentary literature, presents for retrieving or raising a distinctive female 'voice' (Hodges, 1988; Heilbrun and Resnick, 1990; Baron, 1999; Aristodemou, 2000; Williams, 2002, pp. 176–82). The 'strategic' case for embracing the ethical as well as pedagogical potential of literature, to a 'disproportionate' degree indeed, has been stridently argued by Robin West, not just because it provides an alternative to the masculine narratives of legal formalism, but because it corresponds to a distinctive feminist 'ethic of care' (West, 1997, pp. 207–17). Of course, such an argument cannot be detached from the same concerns regarding the fashioning of anything that might be said to be different or distinctive about the female experience or its 'voice'. But the simple fact that law has for centuries been written in a masculine voice is beyond dispute, and whilst the anxiety regarding the presentation of a distinctively female alternative should not be dismissed, so too must it be recognised that such anxieties are unavoidable in any attempt to chart a history, legal or otherwise, of an emergent female 'consciousness' (Caine, 1977, pp. 2–3; Munro, 2007, pp. 41–5; Heinzelman, 2010, pp. x, 118).

A number of feminist lawyers, literary critics and historians have noted a further resonance in the retrieval of a female 'voice'; one that invites engagement once again with Foucault. The relation of Foucault with feminism is not always comfortable, in the same way that the relation of Foucault with literature and with law is not always comfortable.[35] Foucault would have had little time for the notion that any text, let alone a fictional or testamentary one, might convey such a thing as 'truth' (Foucault, 1977, p. 206). In tones that share Charlotte's authorial anxieties, whilst also confirming their irreducibility, Foucault observed, 'There is no reason why one should write not only a book, but also lay down the law as to how it should be read.' But the 'only such law is that of all possible readings' (Kritzman, 1988, p. 52). Not surprisingly, in the light of this paradox, Foucault would have also eschewed the writing of a Whiggish narrative of female emancipation, and not just because it would be incomplete (Sawicki, 1991, p. 56; McNay, 1992, pp. 13–14). However it must be acknowledged that the congruence between his 'history' of the mutation of modern law – famously exemplified in the 'history' of sexuality – and the raising of a female 'voice' during the nineteenth century is a close one; and for this reason has proved attractive to a number of feminist legal historians and theorists (Munro, 2007, pp. 104–6).

According to Foucault, it was during the late eighteenth and nineteenth centuries that the 'ancient' jurisprudence of law, the 'juridico-discursive', founded upon the instantiated rhetoric of 'sovereignty', was superseded by a more subtle 'capillary' of micro-regulatory disciplines (Foucault, 1990, pp. 85–90, 93–4). In this way, Foucault argued, the regulatory exercise of power was both dispersed and intensified:

> Power seeps into every grain of individuals, reaches right into their bodies, permeates their gestures, their postures, what they say; how they learn to live and work with other people.
> (Sheridan, 1980, p. 217)

The exercise of power in modernity, Foucault concluded, is experienced through 'infinitesimal mechanisms' (Foucault, 1980, p. 122). Critics continue to debate the fate of the 'sovereign' conception of formal law. Some perceive its 'expulsion' (Hunt and Whickham, 1984; Golder and Fitzpatrick, 2009, p. 12). Others counter that the 'juridico-discursive' simply mutated, admitting the value of these 'infinitesimal' discursive 'mechanisms' in the pragmatics of power and control (Golder and Fitzpatrick, 2009, pp. 58, 64, 100). Either way, Foucault advanced a history of law that demanded a far more subtle perception. The 'discourse of disciplines' he suggested 'is alien to the law'. In place of the 'juridical rule derived from sovereignty' it operates through a 'code of normalization' (Foucault, 2003, p. 35). The creation of 'disciplinary' norms might still be shaped by legal statement, by statute and case law, but not only and perhaps not so much. The textual 'sovereignty' of the formal law was compromised (Golder and Fitzpatrick, 2009, pp. 24–5). And the space for alternative discourses widened.

The intimately related discourses of sexuality and medical science, as we have already noted, were nurtured in precisely this way. And there were countless others, an 'infinitesimal' number indeed, including, it can be ventured, the writing of novels that invited judgement on matters of law and gender, subterranean or otherwise. In their invitation to the reader to exercise this judgement, such literature of course imported a series of paradoxes, as Charlotte Brontë was so obviously aware. A writer might write to resist. But a reader might read to resist the writer. Literature liberated, but also constrained, offering itself as a putative site of resistance, but also as a putative site of conformity. Such tensions, between liberty and constraint, power and resistance, are just as relevant to the exercise of writing a novel as they were to the fashioning of any other regulatory discipline (Sawicki, 1991, pp. 24–5; Munro, 2007, pp. 91–2, 102–4; Golder and Fitzpatrick, 2009, pp. 74–7).

The place of the Brontë novels within this particular history of disciplinary power and resistance remains a matter of critical conjecture. There is a certain attraction in the idea that the writing of a novel such as *Jane Eyre* or *Wuthering Heights* might itself attest to a historical moment at which the formal 'sovereign' model of the 'juridico-discursive' gave way to alternative discursive disciplinary practices. One of the most consistent features of the formal law in the Brontë novels, as we have time and again noted, is its elusiveness. The law is present most strikingly in its absence. Of course, as we have also noted, the common law inscribed this absence in its embrace of the broader cultural supposition that women should inhabit a private 'sphere', away from the formal institutional gaze of the law; though not of course, the gaze of patriarchy. It is, very obviously, one of the critical factors in the prescription of a textually subterranean jurisprudence. The law appears to be evasive in the novels of the Brontës, below the surface of the text so much of the time, because it was evasive in the lives of so many mid-Victorians, particularly the 'others' of mid-Victorian England; the Gypsies and the Lascars, the criminals, idiots, minors and women.

It is moreover a very ordinary absence, an everyday juridical abrogation; experienced by all those women beaten daily by their husbands, and living in constant fear of such; by all those women confined to attics on whatever spurious basis; by all those denied legal personality, who could not obtain divorce, who had no independent economic existence. The incidental presentation emphasises this ordinariness. Perhaps this is why later critics have tended to ignore the law in the novels of the Brontës. It just seems to be there, in the background, an ordinary failure. But it matters, for the law, in its absence and its failure, as well as in its occasional presence, provides the foundations upon which the grander narratives of human relations, of violence and passion, can be constructed. It is difficult to imagine the narrative of Helen Huntingdon without the threat of spousal abuse, just as it is difficult to imagine the narrative of Heathcliff without the devastating experience of illegitimacy and exclusion. It is difficult indeed to imagine the literary triumph of the second Mrs Rochester without the tragedy of the first. Each narrative is built upon the relative failure of law.

The absence of the law appears to complement the strategic raising of alternative voices and the emergence of a nascent feminist consciousness.[36] The writing of law or more particularly the writing of its absence in the novels of the Brontës resonates with this literary and jurisprudential historiography. This does not, of course, mean that it was intended to do so; at least not necessarily. The extent to which the Brontës played a part in helping to fashion this consciousness, consciously or otherwise, remains a matter of critical debate. We can certainly note that contemporary reviewers were very often troubled by what they read, though as often by tone perhaps as by any perceived political message. Amongst those who thought that she did perceive something of political moment was Margaret Oliphant, who praised Charlotte Brontë for presenting in *Jane Eyre* a 'Rights of Women' (Jay, 1997, p. x). And, as we have already noted, some modern critics such as Adrienne Rich and Nancy Armstrong have been equally ready to applaud *Jane Eyre* as just such a manifesto. Judith Lowder Newton appraises *Villette* in comparable tones, as a novel of 'radical resistance to the ideology' of mid-Victorian patriarchy (Newton, 1985, p. 10).

Others, however, as we have also noted, have tended to be more circumspect, very often troubled by the evident conservatism of Charlotte's personal politics. Charlotte disliked politics, and politicians, all of whom she observed 'seem to be pretty much alike' (Gaskell, 1997, p. 379). As for 'convulsive revolutions', history confirms that they 'put back the world in all that is good, check civilization, bring the dregs of society to the surface' (Gaskell, 1997, p. 265). If she ever felt tempted to be 'rebellious' Charlotte preferred instead to 'resign' herself to 'every decree of God's will' (Gaskell, 1997, p. 115). This sense of resignation is evident in a letter she wrote to Gaskell shortly after the publication of *Shirley*:

> Men begin to regard the position of Women in another light than they used to do, and a few Men whose sympathies are fine and whose sense of justice is strong think and speak of it with a candour that commands my admiration. They say – however – and to a certain extent – truly – that the amelioration of our condition depends on ourselves. Certainly there are evils which our own efforts will best reach – but as certainly there are other evils – deep rooted in the foundations of the Social system which no efforts

of ours can reach – of which we cannot complain – of which it is advisable not too often to think.

(Smith, 2007, p. 173)

The situation of women must be addressed and improved; but in the greater part it will be addressed and improved by men. Women have a role to play in society. But it is not a political one, still less a revolutionary one. And it is indeed difficult to imagine a Brontë sister throwing herself under a horse at the Epsom Derby, or chaining herself to government buildings and palaces around London. The Brontës were not radical in an obvious way. But then few women were in the England of the 1840s.[37] Acutely conscious of the sensitivities that accompanied the presentation of the female person, and particularly the presentation of the female author, Charlotte would have abhorred such theatrical posturing, precisely indeed because it might have compromised her reputation as an author, and thereby the veracity of her novels. The process of authorial, particularly testamentary, unveiling was fraught enough, its writing importing a responsibility that Charlotte felt, as we have already noted, with an acute sensitivity.[38]

The writing of a literary testament did not have to be politically revolutionary. It was not simply a matter of respectability or reputation. Charlotte was not in the business of writing polemics, and neither were her sisters. The raising of a female 'voice' is not the same as the writing of a political manifesto. The absence of strong political statements, even in Charlotte's rather hesitant contribution to the 'condition of England' literary genre, is no coincidence. But what the novels of the Brontës do is reinvest tenor and tone. The same can, of course, be said of a great deal of literature; and not just that written by women. Indeed this reinvestment of a literary tenor is often championed as one of the most important 'strategies' in law and literature scholarship. Law, written in a masculine voice, is unbalanced. It neglects the necessary faculty of compassion and feeling. It neglects, in short, to account for humanity.

The tension between the alternative realms of sense and sensibility was, of course, familiar to the Brontës. It finds reflective expression in Emily's poetry as we noted at the outset of this book. Maria Aristodemou appraises *Wuthering Heights* as a definitive expression of feminist jurisprudence for the same reason (Aristodemou, 2000, pp. 106–9, 122–5). Charlotte's Lucy Snowe is just as familiar with, and just as haunted by, her inability to resolve the same essential 'struggles', between 'the actions, the conduct, that turn which Reason approves, and which Feeling, perhaps, too often opposes' (179). In the end she seeks a middle course, eschewing a more metaphysical 'Jean-Jacques sensibility' for a more appropriate Aristotelian accommodation between the two (442). It is, we might reasonably surmise, also the course that Charlotte would have us prefer. It is certainly possible to conceive her approval of Nussbaum's imputation that in the reading of novels such as *Jane Eyre* or *Villette* it becomes easier to advocate an alternative 'poetic' idea of justice, the principle concern of which is to nurture an 'imaginative' jurisprudence that 'asks us to concern ourselves with the good of other people whose lives are different from ours' (Nussbaum, 1995, p. xvi).

Of course, the claim that literature can humanise the masculine tone of the legal text is compromised by the supposition that so much of the canon has also been written in a masculine voice (Pykett, 1992, p. 3). But the compromise is not fatal, and the broader supposition that literature (regardless of the sex of the author) is well equipped to sensitise the legal mind remains anyway persuasive. As Oscar Wilde observed, 'it is much more easy to have sympathy with suffering than it is to have sympathy with thought' (Himmelfarb, 2007, p. 295). Paradoxically, literature can achieve this because in the presentation of human narrative, the literary text makes the present experience of law seem more real. The literary text humanises. The plight of Helen Huntingdon humanises the issue of spousal abuse, as the plight of Bertha Mason does the difficulties of best regulating the confinement of the insane, as do the difficulties experienced by Caroline Helstone in trying to impress upon her future husband humanise the presentation of the deeper emotional responsibilities of good governance.

The capacity of the literary text to humanise is as compelling as its capacity to chronicle; in both cases it raises those voices which, to borrow from Foucault, lie 'a little beneath history' (Sawicki, 1991, p. 28). The education of the legal mind can only benefit from both. Novels such as *The Tenant of Wildfell Hall* or *Jane Eyre* serve not just to provide accessible supplementary accounts of the operation, or more often in-operation, of contemporary laws of separation or child custody or lunatic confinement. By their very presence, in the contemporary canon and the modern, they contribute to the creation of a broader jurisprudential consciousness. In its writing, and in the history that this writing shapes, literature fashions its own reality. Of course, reconciliation to this possibility further undermines the pretence that truth can be anything other than discursively produced (Foucault, 2003, p. 25; Sawicki, 1991, p. 3, 105–6; Turkel, 1990, pp. 171–2, 175–7). But this is not something that should be regretted, still less feared. Acknowledging the contingency of truth is the necessary condition of thinking about justice (Rorty, 1998, pp. 167–85). Aligning the cause of justice with the discursive contingency of truth and the ethical responsibility to raise the voices of those diminished and excluded by law, Marianne Constable has recently affirmed that the 'call of justice today takes place in silence'. It awaits 'voice', as it always has and as it always will (Constable, 2005, p. 177). We are left to contemplate how Charlotte Brontë might have reacted to this thought, and its implications; as indeed we are left to ponder the virtual case law of *Scott v Smith Elder* or indeed *Huntingdon v Huntingdon*, or *Rochester v Rochester*, or *In re the Linton Settlement*. It is not unreasonable to speculate on the possibility that it might have struck a resonance.

Notes

Introduction: The Brontë Cases

1. In his *Autobiography*, Mill attested to the 'great affect' that reading Wordsworth's poetry had on him as he struggled with depression as a young man (Mill, 1989, pp. 120–2).
2. Charlotte was always keen to impress in correspondence 'how little actual experience I have had of life', as Gaskell, busy spinning the Brontë myth, was happy to record (Gaskell, 1997, p. 302).
3. A further and clear resonance can be heard in Allan Hutchinson's observation that the 'life of law is not logic, or experience, but a narrative way of world-making' (Hutchinson, 1988, p. 14).
4. The debate between Owen Fiss and Stanley Fish on the nature of this exercise is justly renowned (Fiss, 1982; Fish, 1990, pp. 120–40). Where Fiss clung to the hope that interpretation of legal texts could be constrained by some kind of jurisprudential morality, Fish responded with the unsettling counter that any such morality must itself be textual. Interpretation, accordingly, in law as in anything else, is ultimately irreducible. As Fish had proclaimed in his earlier *Is There a Text in this Class?*

   > Because we are never not in a situation, we are never not in the act of interpreting. Because we are never not in the act of interpreting, there is no possibility of reaching a level of meaning beyond or below interpretation... like it or not, interpretation is the only game in town.
   > (Fish, 1980, pp. 276–7)

5. A further resonance here can be found in Maria Aristodemou's observation that no jurisprudential writing 'ever takes place outside the mirroring love of, and for, others' (Aristodemou, 2000, p. 295).
6. Writing on the development of marriage law in eighteenth-century England, and the value of the literary text as a jurisprudential supplement, Rebecca Probert has recently vouched that whilst it 'is plausible that one novelist is mistaken' the possibility of 'mass delusion is unlikely'. Indeed, she concludes, in terms of 'accuracy' it is arguable that literature 'has the advantage over legal sources in recreating the past: it attempted to reflect what people did, rather than prescribing what they should do' (Probert, 2008, p. 31).
7. Observing from without the legal academy 'we know worryingly – at times shockingly – little about legal practice and legal discourse in Victorian England'.
8. James Vernon identifies a similar 'shoring up of the disciplinary walls' in the hesitant engagement of literature and history (Vernon, 2005, p. 275). So does Catherine Gallagher (2005, p. 255).

9. For fascinating jurisprudential commentaries on Austen, Browning and Melville respectively, see Treitel (1984), Schramm (2000, pp. 145–73) and Dolin (1999, pp. 122–4).
10. Despite the fact that we are, according to Lucasta Miller, writing admittedly in 2001, 'living in a golden age of Brontë scholarship' (Miller, 2001, p. 167). The same observation can be made for politics in the Brontë novels. The neglect is not quite so patent, but it remains true that the most substantive political commentary, Terry Eagleton's *Myths of Power: A Marxist Study of the Brontës* (1975), is over thirty years old. Aside from one sentence noting Jane's inheritance in *Jane Eyre*, the Brontës evade the attention of John Reed in his otherwise extensive trawl through incidences of law in the Victorian novel (Reed, 2002, pp. 155–71).
11. A woman who actually went outside the home to work, Ellis pointedly added, 'ceases to be a lady'. For broader accounts of the 'separate spheres' thesis, see Kerber (1988), Chase and Levenson (2000, pp. 72–9), and also Flint (1993, pp. 71–80) focusing more closely on its impact upon emergent 'communities' of female readers.
12. Joan Perkin refers to it as the 'gilded cage of bourgeois marriage' in mid-Victorian England (Perkin, 1989, pp. 233, 314).
13. Fitzjames Stephen was one of the leading legal scholars of his generation, author of *The History of the Criminal Law* and *Liberty, Equality, Fraternity*, in the latter of which he mounted an uncompromising defence of natural law theory, in the main as a rebuttal to the positivist utilitarianism of John Stuart Mill.
14. In like terms Lord Shaftesbury supposed that the family represented the 'deepest tradition of English life' (Shanley, 1989, pp. 4–5).
15. The point at which a nascent feminist consciousness assumed a more settled 'public' and political form remains a matter of considerable debate. Gleadle suggests that a 'protofeminist' consciousness might be discerned from around 1870 (Gleadle, 2001, pp. 31, 74–8, 163–9).
16. Concluding in the same ironic spirit, that presumably 'women run in moulds, like candles, and we can make them long-threes or short-sixes, whichever we please' (Cobbe, quoted in Newton, 1985, p. 2). George Eliot expressed a similar wariness, observing 'There is no subject on which I am more inclined to hold my peace and learn, than on the Woman Question' (Thompson, 1996, p. 12). For further discussion on the shaping of this consciousness see Drakopoulou (2007, pp. 349–55), Ingham, (1996, pp. 9–12) and also O'Brien (2009, pp. 203–10, 230–3), stressing the importance of historians of women in eighteenth and nineteenth-century England seeking to excavate the 'interior' world of female life. For a rather different, but fascinating, muse on the role that the Queen Caroline 'affair' played in catalysing this consciousness in the 1820s and 1830s, see Laqueur (1982, pp. 439–64).
17. In one of the most convincing commentaries on the literary dimension of the 'question', Constance Harsh emphasises the presentation of female protagonists as fictive drivers of the broader movement towards social reform in mid-nineteenth-century England (Harsh, 1994, pp. 15–16).

18. In his *Sign of the Times* Carlyle suggested that the root of England's present 'crisis' was a corrosive 'theological Unbelief', whilst Newman, in his *General Answer to Mr Kingsley* prophesied that a God-less world would be one of 'unspeakable distress' (Himmelfarb, 2007, pp. 45, 118).
19. Alongside, it might be added, the emergence of the woman's journal (Hamilton, 2001, pp. 437–8; Levine, 1990, pp. 294, 305).
20. See also Russell (2005) discussing the role of 'wife-stories' in mid-century female 'self-fashioning'.
21. Whilst it has become critical commonplace to note increasing literacy levels amongst women in the mid-century, more particularly and more obviously middle-class women, precise figures remain elusive and speculative (Beetham, 2001, pp. 58–61).
22. Oliphant was one of the more conservative female literary critics. In general, as we shall see in later chapters, she was inclined to approve the Brontës, recognising for example that *Jane Eyre* was 'one of the most remarkable works of modern times'. In time she would achieve notoriety as a particularly stringent critic of female sensation novelists, in particular Mary Elizabeth Braddon. She also wrote a number of short stories (Saunders, 2001, pp. 156–7).
23. Ellis chose to emphasise in particular the responsibility of mothers to provide such guidance. A 'prudent and judicious' mother would never, for example, allow a daughter to read Shakespeare unaccompanied. But it was 'possible to imagine' her reading Shakespeare to her 'family in such a manner, as to improve the taste of those around her, and to raise their estimate of what is great and good' (Flint, 1993, p. 83). In her *Book of Household Management*, published in 1861, Isabella Beeton recommended reading in like terms: 'It has often been remarked that nothing is more agreeable to the feminine members of a family than the reading aloud of some good standard work or amusing publication. A knowledge of polite literature may be thus obtained by the whole family especially if the reader is able and willing to explain the more difficult passages' (Beetham, 2001, p. 68).
24. In his *On the Preservation of Health of Women at the Critical Periods of Life*, published in 1851, E.J. Tilt expressed a similar concern for 'novels and romances' nurturing 'emotions of the same morbid description' (Flint, 1993, p. 58).
25. 'A woman and her book', Edgar Allen Poe famously remarked, 'are identical' (Shattock, 2001, p. 8).
26. In her *Literature of their Own*, Elaine Showalter for example follows G.H. Lewes who suggested in 1852, that women's writing of the period was essentially a 'literature of imitation'. A more obviously antagonistic literature of 'protest' only took distinctive shape in the final decades. (Showalter, 1977, pp. 13, 27).
27. In her recent study of Dickens and divorce law reform, Kelly Hager emphasises the extent to which Dickens can be read, and would have been read, as making a pointed intervention against the assumption that the English home was a necessarily happy home. Novels such as *Dombey*

and Son and *David Copperfield* should be read as direct interventions in broader debates regarding legal reform (Hager, 2010, pp. 43, 55–6, 96–109, 131–3).
28. For affirmation of the value of looking below the 'surface' of Victorian England in order to get a better of sense of how Victorians really lived their lives, and the particular capacity of interdisciplinary research in facilitating this, see Wolff (1964, pp. 69–70).
29. And it is a 'he'. Of course a number of women wrote about legal matters, such as Caroline Norton and Frances Power Cobbe. But the landscape of Victorian jurisprudence was mapped by men such as John Austin, Henry Maine, Fitzjames Stephen and later Frederick Maitland. And they did not find any women, perhaps because it never occurred to them to look for any. Modern jurisprudence textbooks are afflicted with the same myopia; their potted histories of Victorian jurisprudence being written, almost exclusively, as histories of what famous Victorian men thought.
30. Utility, Austin confirmed, is the 'principle' most 'suited' to the 'making' of law (Austin, 1995, pp. 58, 62–3).
31. Adding that 'all ministries and oppositions seem to be pretty much alike', and by insinuation pretty much as bad as each other.
32. The extent to which the sisters were cognisant of the higher political debates surrounding Catholic emancipation was attested by Elizabeth Gaskell in her *Life of Charlotte Bronte* (Gaskell, 1997, pp. 68–9).
33. Lord Hardwicke, under whose stewardship the Act passed through Parliament, had famously opined that clandestine marriages were 'productive of many and great evils to the nation'. It is certainly true that the 'scandal' of Fleet 'marriages' had become a subject of popular interest. Contemporary weight to the argument for statutory intervention can be found in Smollett's *History of England*, which confirmed that the 'practice of solemnizing clandestine marriages' was 'so prejudicial to the peace of families' that Parliament was obliged to act (Parker, 1987, p. 145). In his *Road to Divorce*, Lawrence Stone made much of the apparent frustrations of lawyers and judges regarding the state of matrimonial law prior to 1753 (1990, pp. 51–8, 115–28). Ginger Frost has reiterated the view that law prior to the Act was 'chaotic' (Frost, 2008, p. 9).
34. Courts for example would be inclined to take a much more liberal view of unwitting bigamy than they might conscious adultery. The intent of the parties to any unlawful affinity was critical. It is notable that the 1823 Marriage Act amended the 1753 Act so that marriages were only voided if the parties 'knowingly and wilfully' failed to comply with certain provisions (Frost, 2008, pp. 73–4, 87–91, 98–9, 231–2; Probert, 2009, pp. 288–94).
35. For detailed commentaries on the debates regarding the Act's passage and its provisions, see Parker (1987) and Lemmings (1996). One of the collateral effects of the 1753 Act was the gradual shifting of breach of promise actions into secular courts. Debate as to the efficacy of such actions continued right through the century, many women deeming it to be demeaning. The action was only finally abolished by the 1970

Law Reform Act. It should be noted that the passage of the 1836 Civil Marriage Act diluted the impact of the 1753 Act to the extent of providing a means by which dissenters could gain legal recognition of non-Anglican marriages.

36. Even where parties were unable or unwilling to conform to the stricter provisions of Anglican marriage they would, for reasons of public 'acceptability' and very often with the connivance of sympathetic clergy, go through similar ceremonies (Frost, 2008, pp. 54, 63–4, 78–82, 219, 225; Probert, 2009, p. 267; Evans, 2005, p. 71).
37. In his *Clarissa*, Samuel Richardson confirmed the impact of coverture, requiring a woman 'to give up her very name, as a mark of her becoming his absolute and dependent property' (Richardson, 1985, pp. 148–9).
38. An Act to Amend the Law Relating to Divorce and Matrimonial Causes in England 1857 20 & 21 Vict. The primary importance of the Act was jurisdictional, establishing a Divorce Court which combined the ecclesiastical jurisdiction over marital validity and separation, Chancery jurisdiction over child custody and equitable estates, common law jurisdiction over property and parliamentary jurisdiction over divorce and marital settlement. The Act further facilitated actions for divorce and separation by wives, allowing the possible granting of child custody and property rights. Prior to the Act, roughly ten Parliamentary Divorce Statutes were passed each year, only a fraction of which were at the behest of women.
39. For commentaries on Taylor Mill's essays on the subject of women and property, see Shanley (1989, p. 160) and also Hammerton (1992, pp. 57–8).
40. Intriguingly, it appears that the Brontë family lawyer wrote a separate estate into the settlement trust that accompanied Charlotte's marriage to Arthur Bell Nichols. The terms of the settlement established £1678 for her own use, and then prescribed that in the absence of children the value of the trust would revert to Patrick Brontë rather than passing to her husband. Juliet Barker surmises that Nichols was perfectly content with an arrangement which, in practice, was designed to ensure the prospective well-being of an ageing Patrick as against the potential danger that a reverted estate would be swallowed up by the collateral debts of the Irish branch of the Nichols family (Barker, 1994, p. 756).
41. The critical literature on the role of the strict settlement trust as a means of concentrating family property is considerable. Spring argues that it should accordingly have been seen as an equitable expression of the principle of primogeniture (Spring, 1988). The alternative position, that the trust was seen by Chancery as a genuine means of protecting the interests of female spouses, is taken by Amy Erickson (1990). This latter view is broadly supported in Okin (1983, pp. 130–5).
42. The 1828 Offences Against the Person Act, which permitted the trial and sentencing of abusive husbands in magistrates courts without need of a jury, had also served to reveal the extent of domestic violence, but in this case chiefly amongst the working classes.

43. Marlene Tromp makes the related point that there is an immediate correlation between the newer presence of court reports and the evolution of the 'sensation' novel in the 1860s (Tromp, 2000, pp. 10–14, 243–4).
44. So troubled was Queen Victoria that formal complaint was made to the Lord Chancellor, not with the intention of preventing domestic violence, but in the hope of addressing the ill-effects that must result from 'the present publicity of proceedings before the new Divorce Court' (Leckie, 1999, p. 93).
45. And readers of Braddon, Thackeray and Trollope, and perhaps most obviously Dickens too, as Kelly Hager has recently emphasised, identifying most obviously *Oliver Twist*, *Dombey and Son* and *Great Expectations*. By the second half of the century, as Hager also confirms, the 'failed-marriage' plot was securely embedded within the canon of nineteenth-century English literature (Hager, 2010).
46. Commenting on an article published by Mill, but written by Harriet Taylor, in 1848.
47. Though, as is now well known, life in Haworth in the 1830s and 1840s was nothing like so culturally or political bereft as Woolf chose to believe. For a commentary on the vibrancy of life in West Yorkshire at the time, including recitals by Liszt, fine art exhibitions in Leeds, and the intellectual activities of the Keighley Mechanics Institute, along with an examination of their obviously considerable breadth of reading, see Winnifrith (1988, pp. 84–109) and at a slight variant Eagleton (1975, pp. 3–7) reflecting on the probable degree of social and political awareness stimulated by radical activity in the West Yorkshire region during the period. We will revisit this context in later chapters. Certainly in her particular discussion of the context within which *Shirley* was written Gaskell attested to the extent of the sisters' awareness of local political tensions (Gaskell, 1997, pp. 77–88).
48. As they were as early as the 1890s. Ten thousand were recorded as having visited in 1895.
49. Barker opens her magisterial study of the family with the observation 'The Brontë story has always been riddled with myths' (Barker, 2001, p. xviii).
50. Contemporary reviewers noted the careful blurring of 'biography' and 'novel' in Gaskell's *Life* (Miller, 2001, pp. 62–3; Winnifrith, 1988, pp. 1–3).
51. On the emergence of a 'new' identifiably middle-class 'linguistic community' of novel readers in the middle of the century, see Armstrong (1987, pp. 160).
52. Such that, he concludes, by the end of the century there was a 'near universality' in the English reading public (St Clair, 2007, p. 433).
53. A view which resonates with Armstrong's suggestion that much 'domestic' fiction was designed to promote conformity, even passivity, as well as Leckie's supposition that critical reviews of such fiction were written to shape a form of extra-legal censorship (Armstrong, 1987, pp. 15–17; Leckie, 1999, pp. 30–2).

54. The concern was just as readily felt by authors. George Eliot famously protested against the 'mind-and-millinery species' of 'silly novels by lady novelists' (Flint, 2001, pp. 25–6).
55. Wolff confirms a pragmatic inevitability in the critical focus on a 'literate elite' (Wolff, 1964, p. 62). It does not preclude the importance of studying other sections of society. But the intrinsic value of studying an elite which, by definition, had a disproportionate influence on society is self-evident.
56. The Brontës were not alone, of course, in contributing to a genre of 'regional novels'. Regionalism was itself an increasingly popular, indeed defining, trend in mid-Victorian England (Hewitt, 2006, pp. 406–8).
57. A debate around which moves a considerable literature. For a relatively recent series of reflections on the subject see Anderson (2005), Flint (2005) and Hewitt (2006). Kaplan also notes the 'constantly shifting politics' of Victorian studies (Kaplan, 2007, p. 11).
58. 'The Victorians are still with us', A.N. Wilson rather grandly claims at the outset of his *The Victorians* (Wilson, 2002, p. 1).

1 Huntingdon v Huntingdon

1. It has been surmised that the degree of critical hostility played a significant part in Elizabeth Gaskell's determination to relegate Anne to the part of bit-player in her *Life of Charlotte Brontë* (Jay, 1997, pp. x–xi). For broad commentaries on the critical reputation of the *Tenant*, see Barker (2001, pp. 829–30), Miller (2001, pp. 156–7), Jackson (1982, p. 198) and also Winnifrith (1988, p. 4), suggesting that Anne's tendency to proselytize in her novels alienated potential readers.
2. As one critic has recently observed, in the presentation of the wholly dysfunctional Huntingdon marriage, Anne 'insists that her readers recognize the existence of failed marriages, and the shortcomings of the institution and the laws that define and govern it, just as surely as Parliament did in legalizing divorce nine years later' (Hager, 2010, p. 27).
3. The notoriety of the case was such that it became a frequent source of literary allusion, appearing in Dickens's *Pickwick Papers*, Disraeli's *Endymion* and Meredith's *Diana of the Crossways*, the latter of which was, in essence, a fictionalised 'biography' of Caroline Norton. Further literary allusions to Caroline herself could also be found in the person of Becky Sharpe in Thackeray's *Vanity Fair*. Norton's own account of the trial and her relationship with Melbourne can be found in her *English Laws for Women in the Nineteenth Century* Her alleged paramour was prime minister of a declining Whig administration. Aside from being a minor aristocrat, George Norton was also a minor Tory functionary, serving as member for Guildford between 1826 and 1830. Whether or not Caroline and Melbourne did have an affair remains uncertain. For accounts of their relationship and the trial, and Norton's reputation in literary and other circles, see Chedzoy (1992, pp. 10–22, 74–5, 108–10, 196–7, 291–2),

Acland (1948, pp. 168–78) and Craig (2009, pp. 1–5, 17–19, 41–6, 79–85, 153–66).
4. In her *Letter to the Queen* (Chedzoy, 1992, pp. 154–5).
5. The *Letter* was acknowledged by Lord Brougham to be 'as clever a thing as ever was written' and had 'produced much good' (Chedzoy, 1992, p. 251).
6. The affinity between the two has not been noted as frequently as might be expected (Gruner, 1997).
7. The granddaughter of Richard Brinsley Sheridan, Caroline counted amongst her literary friends William Makepeace Thackeray, Mary Shelley, Edward Bulmer Lytton and Edward Trelawny, as well as the actress Fanny Kemble, and various conspicuously Whig politicians, including most obviously Melbourne, but also Disraeli and the grandee Duke of Devonshire. The 'three Graces' were, of course, Caroline and her sisters Georgiana and Helen. The allusion, familiar to students of Greek mythology, was to the three daughters of Zeus and Euryoneme, namely Euphrosyne, Aglaia and Thalia.
8. For the suggestion that the novel is premised on the familiar theme of a woman who is punished for a momentary fall into sexual temptation and then forced to undergo personal redemption, see O'Toole (1999, pp. 716–17) and Eagleton (1975, pp. 122–3).
9. The fear of 'maidenhood' likewise horrifies Esther Hargrave.
10. See Doggett (1992, pp. 31–2), citing the notorious dicta from the *Holmes* case, in 1755, that such rhetorical offerings were just 'words'.
11. A phrase that was conceded, ironically, by one of the leading campaigners for reform, Lord Cranworth (Shanley, 1989, p. 40).
12. In section 27 of the Act. The House of Lords Select Committee again pointedly refused to accept that rape could be sufficient grounds. Gladstone was one of those most troubled by the prospect of women fornicating their way to marital freedom post-1858. Men, he advised his fellow parliamentarians, were only too 'apt' to be led astray, 'you know what passion dwells in an Englishman' (Holcombe, 1983, p. 103; Shanley, 1989, pp. 40–2, 159).
13. Though, as Patricia Ingham has noted, the most recent TV adaptation of the novel presumed to include scenes of actual violence; something which attracted the broad approval of critics (Ingham, 2006, pp. 246–7).
14. Norton recorded numerous instances of physical violence at the hands of her husband. The latter, evincing a peculiarly warped sense of humour, took to signing off letters to Caroline as 'Greenacre'; a reference to a recently convicted and notorious wife-murderer (Chedzoy, 1992, pp. 53–6, 90–1, 102; Craig, 2009, pp. 111–14).
15. 'Helen', the new father exclaims, on first seeing mother and child together, 'I shall positively hate that little wretch, if you worship it so madly! You are absolutely infatuated about it' (229–31).
16. Laura Berry has noted the extent to which literature depicting the lives of children emerged during the nineteenth century as one of the primary

strategies for opening up the private domestic world to public gaze (Berry, 1999, pp. 2–4, 12–16, 19–20; 1996, pp. 33–8).

17. It is notable the extent to which this displacement of the wife and mother from her natural role as governor of the domestic sphere tended to trouble courts of law in matters of marital dispute; far more so than the relative mundanity of ordinary spousal abuse (Hammerton, 1992, pp. 98–9).

18. The 'life and limb' forfeiture rule, as its name suggests, required that a father pose an immediate threat to the 'life and limb' of a child before countenancing removal (Perry, 2004, pp. 344–5; Wright, 2002, pp. 182–3, 190–2). The judge in Wollstonecraft's fictional case reaches precisely this conclusion.

19. In the words of Holdsworth, as a 'special delegation by the Crown of its prerogative rights' (O'Halloran, 1999, pp. 11–13, 24–9; Berry, 1999, pp. 97–9).

20. The case was used extensively in Caroline Norton's *The Separation of Mother and Child by the Law of Custody of Infants Considered*. If the behaviour of the father was so extreme, a court might on very rare occasions consider vesting custody in a mother. A notorious such case was *Wellesley* (1827), in which the father had fled overseas and where it was evidenced that, aside from keeping a mistress, he had also inveigled his son into various scams designed to frustrate creditors. For modern commentaries see Shanley (1989, p. 135) and Wright (2002, pp. 196–9).

21. As affirmed in *Greenhill* (1836), another case deployed repeatedly by Norton, and also *M'Clellan* (1831), where Justice Patteson admitted that whilst 'it might be better, as the child is in a delicate state of health, that it should be with the mother, we cannot make any order on that point'.

22. It was widely feared that reform might encourage many women, who would otherwise have endured domestic abuse in order to keep their children, to sue for divorce (Wright, 2002, pp. 214–15, 223).

23. See here Craig (2009, pp. 188–91) and also Wright (2002, pp. 224–5, 230–1) citing cases such as *Fynn* (1848) and *Spence* (1847) to support the argument that the common law presumption in favour of paternal custody, founded on the 'life and limb' rule, remained essentially unchanged. In *Spence* the court held that custody could only be vested in a mother where the 'misconduct' of the father was such 'as to be likely to contaminate or corrupt the morals of his children'.

24. Such contracts were expressly disproved in cases such as *Westmeath* (1826) and still later *Hope* (1857).

25. Courts repeatedly upheld this testamentary right in cases such as *Talbot* (1840).

26. The three essays, all of which appeared in short order in 1837 and 1838 were *Observations on the Natural Claims of a Mother to the Custody of her Children as affected by the Common Law Right of the Father*, *The Separation of Mother and Child by the Law of Custody of Infants* and a *Plain Letter to the Lord Chancellor*.

27. In the end, it took the death of her eldest son in a riding accident to secure for Caroline a greater degree of informal custody (Chedzoy, 1992, pp. 203–8).
28. In *Milford* the Court declared that it would look 'to see whose fault it was that led to the breaking up of the common home'. Chancery courts slowly followed suit in adopting the fault principle, enforcing it with greater regularity during the 1870s. Wright argues that the 'fault' principle represented a renewed 'ethic of traditional spousal performance' (Wright, 2002, p. 259).
29. The phrase 'manifold evils' was coined by Brougham when he presented the Law Amendment Society Petition in support of reform in 1856.
30. The phrase was articulated by Edward Kerslake in parliamentary debate in 1868 (Griffin, 2003, p. 64).
31. George was perpetually short of money, which enhanced his resentment of his wife, whom he thought should have brought a bigger marriage portion. Their separation settlement was designed to reduce the amount that he would draw from his wife's estate and settle on her each year.
32. Norton was right. It was not an uncommon experience (Chedzoy, 1992, pp. 246–7; Poovey, 1989, p. 63; Erickson, 1993, p. 151).
33. In sum, Caroline inherited £480 per annum, which was more than she received from George (Chedzoy, 1992, pp. 291–31).
34. Maine retained a suspicion of the efficacy of 'separate estates' for precisely this reason (Maine, 1906, p. 164).
35. The voice was that of Lord Campbell.
36. As Lyndhurst observed, married women's property law was 'closely connected with the law of divorce, but is not touched by the present bill' (Shanley, 1989, p. 44).
37. Dickens's *All Year Round* assumed a strongly reformist position in the debates preceding the 1870 Act (Shanley, 1989, pp. 34, 60, 68–70).
38. The words being those of Arthur Arnold (Holcombe, 1983, p. 179).
39. In the House of Commons Shaw-Lefevre observed that all women who resolved to flee an abusive marriage were necessarily impoverished by law (Griffin, 2003, pp. 65–6).
40. He seizes her diary for the same reason.
41. Though much, he also reports, seems to remain. Most of the debt is derived from Huntingdon's gambling habit. Each of his friends seems to be similarly afflicted, most obviously and most starkly perhaps Lowborough (175–8). Helen recalls her husband's 'muttered expletives' on reading certain 'business letters' (199–200).
42. In the absence of evidence to the contrary it must be assumed that Markham is right and that little Arthur has retained the tenancy in tail, rather than assumed a life tenancy. This latter assumption would be likely to occur at the moment of re-settlement in anticipation of his marriage. The alternative, altogether rarer, would have seen a re-settlement as part of Arthur senior's will, in which case little Arthur would have assumed a life tenancy on his father's death. The legal possibilities are discussed

in Spring (1993, pp. 128–31). But there is no evidence of this, probably because such material information was not necessary to the plot.
43. Markham expresses frustration on hearing that Helen is managing the Huntingdon estate, while unsure as to whether it was entailed (436). We do not know whether Helen's original marriage portion could have been, or indeed was, converted into a jointure. Similarly there is no detail as to the nature of the Huntingdon settlement trust. But it is inconceivable that one did not exist.
44. Helen's uncle suggests that the remaining part of the Huntingdon estate, that which is not yet encumbered, will need 'careful nursing' (168).
45. Markham was entitled, of course, to find the such a settlement strange. Trusts established for 'separate' use, as we have already noted, were rare (Okin, 1983, pp. 132–3). The reason for Helen's inheritance of the Staningley estate is never really explained, though it is certainly convenient; which may be reason enough. The normal course would be for the Staningley estate to have passed to the widow. But the aunt is reported as being happy to accept 'an annuity'. John Sutherland has hazarded the thought that Helen might be an illegitimate daughter. It is an ingenious thought, though whether Anne Brontë intended such an imputation must remain doubtful (Sutherland, 1996, p. 77).
46. Helen had earlier noted her dislike of Hargrave's mother, a 'hard, pretensious, worldly-minded woman'. And Hargrave himself, Helen also notes, whilst no 'spendthrift' is one who 'likes to have everything handsome about it' (219). It comes as no surprise that the Hargraves drive a hard marital bargain.
47. An opening which clearly implies that the Markham estate is also entailed (Gordon, 1984, p. 721).
48. It is quite possible that Markham was also concerned that the Huntingdon entail had not been re-settled in advance of Arthur senior's inheritance.
49. As we will see shortly, it is widely suggested that the immediate impetus for the writing of the *Tenant* lay in Branwell Brontë's disgrace and dismissal from his post as tutor to the Robinson children at Thorp Green Hall. And it is interesting, perhaps, to note that his faint hopes of marrying Lydia Robinson – with whom it was alleged that he had conducted an affair – after her husband's death, were crushed by news of a similar restriction. Mr Robinson, Branwell reported, has left his property 'in trust for the family, provided I do not see the widow; and if I do, it reverts to the executing trustees, with ruin to her' (Wise and Symington, 1932, II, p. 98; Barker, 2001, p. 493).
50. As early as 1857, W.C. Roscoe wondered why Anne Brontë abandoned her heroine to a 'truculent ill-bred young farmer' with a propensity for hitting people (Allott, 1974, p. 352). For later critical reflections, see Jacobs (1986, pp. 208–10) and Diederich, (2003, p. 37).
51. Lord Lowborough remarries in order to provide his son with a mother, and, as reward for his redemption, appears to get lucky (439–40).
52. Of the quality perhaps of Mr Metcalfe, the Brontë family lawyer, who advised Charlotte to establish a separate settlement prior to her marriage

to Arthur Bell Nicholls. In this settlement, in the event that Charlotte died childless, which was indeed the case, the entire value of her trust reverted to her father rather than passing to her husband. Barker surmises that the settlement was designed to preserve her not inconsiderable estate from the potentially ravenous hands of Nicholls's Irish relatives (Barker, 2001, p. 756).

53. The reviewer's conclusion concealed something of a compliment, however compromised. At least, he observed, it 'is not so bad a book as *Jane Eyre*'.
54. Thormahlen (1999, pp. 73–6, 83–4) argues that the deeper theology that underpins this particular passage can be read as a commentary on the doctrine of justification by faith.
55. Charlotte was so troubled by the impact that the novel would have on their enduring reputation, that she prevented its further publication for nearly a decade.
56. The relation between Anne's novel and Emily's novel was noted in contemporary reviews such as the *Athenaeum* and the *Rambler* (Allott, 1974, pp. 251, 266–7). Modern critics have explored the same relation, as we shall see in the next chapter. Resonances between Anne's novel and *Jane Eyre* have also attracted modern critical attention (Matus, 2002).
57. Something that is generally attributed to the particular influence of Aunt Branwell, herself an evangelical Methodist. Famously, when dangerously ill in 1836–37, Anne asked to see a dissenting Moravian minister, rather than an Anglican. Moravians were famed for the mystical quality of their religion, and their particular devotion to the idea of personal redemption and salvation (Winnifrith, 1988, pp. 38–9, 57–61; Thormahlen, 1999, pp. 22, 90–5, 160–1; Barker, 2001, pp. 280–2).
58. As early as 1877, TW Reid concluded that '*The Tenant of Wildfell Hall* presents us with a dreary and repulsive picture of Branwell Brontë after his fall'. Writing in the *Athenaeum* six years later, Swinburne made the same assertion (Allott, 1974, pp. 403, 440).
59. The Thorp Green Hall 'affair' was famously introduced to a shocked near-contemporary audience by Elizabeth Gaskell in her *Life*. As we shall see in the final chapter, the threat of legal action caused Gaskell to remove much of the more contentious commentary from later editions. Charlotte's correspondence confirmed the shock that Branwell's disgrace had on each member of the family, not least Branwell himself. It also implies Branwell's confession, at committing such a 'frantic folly' (Smith, 2007, p. 63).
60. Gerin prefers to ascribe much of Anne's apparent venom to her disgust at Branwell's indiscretion (Gerin, 1959, pp. 238–43).
61. Dicey deployed the Act as an example in his *Lectures* of the benefits of the common law 'tradition' of 'judicial legislation', of statutory enactment founded on judicial evolution (Dicey, 1994, pp. 362, 387–88, 394–5). For the commonly favourable reception of the 1882 Act see Holcombe (1983, pp. 201–5, 219–23) and Shanley (1989, pp. 122–8).

62. The key statutes being the 1970 Matrimonial Proceedings and Property Act and the 1973 Matrimonial Causes Act.
63. Lynn Linton received news of the judgement with the observation 'Our law lords have destroyed the old balance as completely as if a tornado had passed over a stately shrine and flung the holy image to the winds.' The principle of 'reasonable confinement' stretched back centuries. In the nineteenth century it had also arisen, not just in cases of alleged abuse, but also in cases of alleged mental instability. We shall investigate this particular species of subterranean jurisprudence in Chapter 3 in the context of *Jane Eyre*. An account of the *Jackson* case can be found in Doggett (1992, pp. 1–4, 15–18, 134–9).
64. Maitland observed that the law had merely replaced one form of paternalism with another, in the form of an 'exaggerated' juristic 'guardianship' (Doggett, 1992, pp. 63–4).

2 Heathcliff's Case

1. As G.H. Lewes noted in his review of the novel in the *Leader* in December 1850, concluding soberly 'such brutes we should all be, or most of us, were our lives as insubordinate to law; were our affections and sympathies as little cultivated, our imaginations as undirected' (Allott, 1974, p. 292). In a more recent critique, Camille Paglia has listed the 'catalog of chthonic horrors' with which *Wuthering Heights* presents its readers, the myriad instances of 'whipping, slapping, thrashing, cuffing, wrenching, pinching, scratching, hair-pulling, gouging, kicking, trampling, and the hanging of dogs' (Paglia, 1990, p. 449).
2. A Hobbesian force of 'arbitrary' violence as Eagleton put it (Eagleton, 1975, pp. 102, 110).
3. The suspicion that Heathcliff might have been modelled, at least in part, on Branwell, was insinuated by T.W. Reid in his 1877 review of the novel (Allott, 1974, p. 400). It is discussed at some length in Miller (2001, pp. 206–18), as is the possibility, popular amongst some critics at the time, that Branwell might even have been the author. The Byronic alignment is championed by Pauline Nestor (2000, p. xx) and also explored by Miller (2001, pp. 194–5) and Paglia (1990, pp. 446, 453–7). According to David Musselthwaite, who hazards the alternative possibility that Cromwell might have provided a model for Emily's protagonist, 'One of the great sports of literary criticism and scholarship must be the search for the origins of Heathcliff' (Musselthwaite, 1987, p. 97). The Byronic model has certainly proved popular amongst film directors (Ingham, 2006, pp. 228–31).
4. And so the law remained, in essence, until the 1926 Legitimacy Act which finally allowed illegitimate children to inherit in intestacy.
5. Prohibition was reinforced in *Deuteronomy* 23:2, 'No bastard shall enter the assembly of the Lord', and was further confirmed in the *Wisdom*

of Solomon 4:6, and in the New Testament in *Galations* 4:21–6. For an overview of the moral and scriptural prohibition, see Witte (2003).
6. The terms of reference explicitly referred to 'evils'. See Henriques (1967, pp. 103, 109–11), discussing the undoubted influence of Malthus on the Royal Commissioners and supporters of reform. The influence of Malthus is also explored in Cody (2000, pp. 135–6, 139–42) discussing Martineau's use of Malthusian rhetoric in her novel *Cousin Marshall*.
7. Provided there was corroborating evidence of paternal identity. Maintenance was limited to 10 shillings for the midwife, and 2 shillings and 6 pence a week until the child was 13.
8. It can be noted that evangelicals were at the forefront of campaigns to tighten bastardy provisions and, more particularly still, to place the blame squarely on mothers. Whilst Emily's religious sympathies remain a matter of critical contention, it is not inconceivable that she was, once again, fully versant with this literature. For the evangelical position see Frost (2003, p. 316).
9. It is reported in the narrative that Heathcliff takes the name of a 'son who died in childhood'. This implies that the Heathcliff name also ran in the Earnshaw family. It might also be intended to reinforce the supposition that Heathcliff is indeed Earnshaw's progeny. A patronym could be subsequently acquired 'by reputation' in common law. It did not have to be the name of the natural father. But Heathcliff, for whatever reason, possibly choice, does not acquire the Earnshaw patronym.
10. For a discussion of contemporary anxieties regarding the 'gypsy problem', a perception which, as George Eliot (cited by Behlmer) cast it, presumed that gypsies were a 'race that lives on prey as foxes do on stealthy, petty rapine', see Behlmer (1985).
11. Indian seamen were commonly known as Lascars.
12. It is interesting to note that a contemporary reviewer of *Jane Eyre* invoked the imagery of 'moral Jacobinism' in warning readers of what awaited them if they chose to read the novel (Kaplan, 2007, p. 17).
13. Especially given the close nature of their composition (Frank, 1990, pp. 228–9). Contemporary reviewers such as E.P. Whipple, assumed the two novels to be written by the one, presumably depraved and deluded, author (Allott, 1974, pp. 247–8).
14. The phrase was coined by the reviewer in *Jerrolds Weekly Newspaper* (Thompson, 1996, p. 46; Miller, 1975, p. 168; Aristodemou, 2000, pp. 112–14).
15. John Sutherland has suggested that, given the nature of Hindley's sudden demise, the reader is supposed to ponder the possibility that Heathcliff finally realised his wish (Sutherland, 1996, pp. 53–8). For a discussion of Heathcliff's 'homicidal' tendencies, imagined or otherwise, see Gilbert and Gubar (2000, pp. 296–7).
16. 'No other Victorian novel', according to Hillis Miller, 'contains such scenes of inhuman brutality' (Miller, 1975, p. 167).
17. Surridge stresses the extent to which readers of the novel would have noted the juristic undertones in this passage (Surridge, 2005, p. 86).

18. The common law bar was commonly defended in terms of public policy (Solomon, 1959, pp. 83–4; Frost, 2008, pp. 23–5). The definitive statement can be found in Halsbury's *Laws of England* (Halsbury, 1908, p. 439).
19. Sanger remarked the apparent depth of Emily's knowledge of legal technicality (Sanger, 1970, p. 12). It is certainly notable. By way of comparison 'law and literature' scholars often express admiration for the seeming depth of Dickens's knowledge of legal matters. But Dickens repeatedly testifies to a particular interest in legal debate, whilst his earlier work as a court reporter clearly enhanced his comfort with legal formality. A similar admiration is commonly articulated for Shakespeare's apparent familiarity with legal matters. In this instance, critics again tend to assume that the familiarity was bred of close personal association with the legal fraternity, most obviously the Inns of Court where a number of his plays were performed. There is no comparable interest or association evidenced in the life of Emily Brontë. We should perhaps be wary of adding a further veneer to the Brontë 'myth'. Even so, the extent to which Emily appears comfortable with legal matters of some complexity, especially in respect of property and inheritance, is genuinely striking.
20. The principle mitigated the stricter rules of redemption which operated in the common law and which required discharge and re-conveyance on a particular stipulated date (Watt, 2009, pp. 130–1; Simpson, 1985, pp. 242–3).
21. An interesting commentary on the alternative nature of such tails, in the different context of Jane Austen's novels, can be found in Treitel (1984, pp. 557–90).
22. Sanger likewise concludes that Heathcliff's 'possession' of the Linton estate appears to be de facto rather than de jure (Sanger, 1970, p. 14).
23. The text implies that Heathcliff died intestate. If so, as he had no living relatives, his personal property would escheat, and pass to the Crown; something that was confirmed in the leading case of *Brook v Brook* in 1861, and finds explicit reference in the second volume of Halsbury's *Laws* (1908, p. 439). In the ordinary course of events, the mortgagor of the Earnshaw estate would at this point be able to exercise an equity of redemption to redeem the charge. The interest in the Linton estate, having passed through to Catherine, would be undisturbed and the settlement secure.
24. The literature surrounding this particular statement and the extent to which it might be liberating, or, alternatively, submissive or sublimating, is vast. Aristodemou (2000, pp. 117–19) explores Bataille's supposition that there is a measure of erotic sublimation in the statement. Davies (1994, pp. 13–15, 26–7, 198–200), Paglia (1990, pp. 446–7, 453–7) and Miller (2001, p. 195) all explore the transgressive implications, the latter two sharing the belief that the thematic origins of the statement might be traced to Byron's *Manfred*.
25. For an influential critical commentary on the feminist implications of Foucault's theory of incest, and its role as normalising 'discourse' in

nineteenth-century Europe, see Bell (1993, pp. 15–26, 93–100, 120–1, 174–6). On the 'silence' of incest, see Giuliani (2009, pp. 923–8).

26. For a comment on the particular fear of miscegenation which attended incest debates during the nineteenth century see Corbett (2008, pp. 18–24, 129–30).

27. Heathcliff's guilt would have seemed all the greater within an inherited literary tradition in which brothers assumed a primary responsibility to protect the chastity of sisters (Perry, 2004, pp. 188–9, 376).

28. Such is the intensity that Leo Bersani famously identifies *Wuthering Heights* as a defining contribution to the theme of incest in eighteenth and nineteenth-century literature (Bersani, 1984, p. 19). The view is broadly shared by Richardson (1985, pp. 751–3).

29. It has been argued that outwith the endless debates regarding the need to repeal provisions relating to the 'deceased wife's sister' public interest in alternative species of incest and their possible genetic and moral consequences only re-emerged from around the mid-1880s (Morris, 1991, pp. 235–6, 252, 264; Bailey and Blackburn, 1979, pp. 710, 715–16).

30. Back in 1660, Jeremy Taylor admitted in his *Ductor Dubitantium* that 'questions of degrees and the matters and cases of incest are not so perfectly stated as the greatness of the matter and necessities of the world require' (Pollak, 2003, p. 28). Incest was not criminalised until the 1908 Punishment of Incest Act.

31. See for example *Watson and Watson v Farnemouth* (1881), a leading authority on the voidability of such marriages. The most common punishment in canon law was an order to separate and to do penance (Morris, 1991, p. 235).

32. The original purpose of the Act was to protect the property interests of one particular peer, the Duke of Beaufort, who had married his wife's sister and thus put his son's inheritance at risk if the marriage was subsequently declared voidable (Morris, 1991, pp. 235–7; Gruner, 1999, p. 426).

33. A Royal Commission reported that 90 per cent of unions later voided by the courts between 1835 and 1848 were between widowers and the sisters of their deceased wives (Kuper, 2009, p. 67; Corbett, 2008, pp. 10–13; Gullette, 1990, p. 144).

34. Mrs Brontë died in 1821 when Emily was just short of three and a half years old.

35. They would certainly encounter it elsewhere in their novel reading, and indeed their theatre and opera going (Corbett, 2008, pp. 57–85; Gullette, 1990, pp. 147–52). In *Iolanthe* Gilbert and Sullivan famously referred to perennial attempts in Parliament to enact reforming legislation as an 'annual blister'.

36. The scriptural argument was still pressed by many a Tory bishop, as well as the likes of Pusey, Gladstone and Matthew Arnold (Gullette, 1990, pp. 162–3; Anderson, 1982, pp. 68–74, 77, 80–4; Goetz, 1982, pp. 364–5).

37. Though a precise impression is again thwarted by the residual uncertainty regarding Heathcliff's origins (Goetz, 1982, pp. 372–3; Bersani, 1984, pp. 198–9, 206).

38. Her 'Biographical Sketch' concluded, 'This notice has been written, because I felt it a sacred duty to wipe the dust off their gravestones, and leave their dear names free from soil' (Brontë, 2009, p. 306).
39. Miller observes that the 'so-called sphinx of English literature has acquired almost supernatural status' (Miller, 2001, pp. 170–1).
40. See Plath's 'Wuthering Heights' (1985, p. 37, lines 17–18) and Hughes's 'Two Photographs of Top Withens' (2003, p. 840, line 5).
41. The reference to the 'half-savage' Catherine was made by Skelton (Allott, 1974, p. 337). Gaskell was, very obviously, one of those so troubled, balancing the 'attraction of remarkable genius' with an understanding of why such a novel 'revolted' so many readers (1997, p. 257). The same dilemma is contemplated by Davies (1994, pp. 21–2, 38–40), Frank (1990, pp. 218–20), Leavis and Leavis (1969, pp. 137–8) and Aristodemou (2000, pp. 107–9).
42. It speaks volumes that critics, long into the century, would continue to ponder the possibility that Branwell might have written the novel; it being impossible to conceive that a woman had done so (Miller, 2001, pp. 206–7, 213–16; Davies, 1994, pp. 38–9).
43. For various commentaries on Joseph, Gimmerton chapel, and the closing imagery of Cathy and Heathcliff lying together, see Thormahlen (1999, pp. 82–3, 176), Ingham (2006, pp. 193–4) and Davies (1994, pp. 148–5). The necrophilia theme is noted by Armstrong (1987, p. 1960) and also Aristodemou (2000, p. 123). For more general commentaries on the writing of theology and religion in the novel, and speculation on Emily's personal faith, or lack of it, see Hillis Miller (1975, chapter 4), suggesting that her dissent tipped over into a far more threatening atheism. Stevie Davies likewise suggests that Emily was a 'retaliatory' dissenter, determined to eschew any formal theology (Davies, 1994, pp. 19, 140). Thormahlen (1999, p. 8) however cautions that Emily's own almost pathological 'reticence' prevents any more conclusive view of her personal faith.
44. Continuing in somewhat rapturous tones at xii, 'Her ice-blue eyes beheld a world in which God was not good, civilization was a lie, humanity sordid and corrupt, male unjustly preferred to female, life to death, adult to child, father to mother, hierarchy to affinity, human to animal.'
45. In *A Room of One's Own*, Virginia Woolf famously suggested that Emily Brontë should be read as a poet first, and novelist second, and more particularly still as someone writing with an incipient feminist urgency (Woolf, 1998, pp. 87, 97). The affinity between Emily's poetry and *Wuthering Heights* is explored in Davies (1994, pp. 143–8), Miller (2001, pp. 226–8), Musselthwaite (1987, pp. 85–8), and perhaps most extensively in Chitham (2001, chapters 3 and 4).

3 The Rochester Wives

1. Charlotte pointedly rebutted 'carping critics' in the Preface to the second edition of the novel (3). For commentaries on the contemporary critical reception see Foster (1985, pp. 84–5) and Winnifrith (1996, pp. 15–16).

2. Lewes pointedly added that the incarceration of Bertha Mason was one of the significant 'defects' in the novel, a view shared by Eugene Forcade, reviewing the novel for *Revue des deux mondes* (Allott, 1974, pp. 85, 100–1).
3. Annabel Huth Jackson provides a similar testament regarding her mother's equivalent horror at finding her daughter reading *Jane Eyre* (Flint, 1993, p. 218).
4. John Austin's *The Province of Jurisprudence Determined*, published in 1832, is commonly recognised as the founding text for modern legal positivism.
5. In the circumstances, there is a further paradox in the recommendation of some psychiatrists that young women should read literature as a suitable form of treatment. The story of Ophelia was thought to be especially suitable, and sobering, and commonly prescribed.
6. Prior to the 1853 Lunacy Regulation Act, the governing statute was the 1842 Act to Alter and Amend the Practice and Course of Proceeding under Commissions in the Nature of Writs *De Lunatico Inquirendo*.
7. The term 'alienist' is slightly ambiguous, and to a degree pejorative (Scull, 1993, pp. 249–51).
8. George Mann Burrows argued that given the 'moral' dimension to lunacy, it was not just sufficient for an examination to be conducted through family members, but preferable. Burrows further argued that professional opinion when sought should not be corrupted by personal examination; a position that was famously demolished by Lord Brougham in the notorious *Davies* case, which was reported in *The Times* in 1829. When challenged in cross-examination at the commission inquiry into the lawfulness of Davies's confinement, Burrows refused to answer as to whether he had 'ever given any order of any kind for detaining a person as insane, without seeing him'. In summing up, Brougham reminded the jury of the 'alarm we feel ... when we hear refusal to answer to such a question'. The newspapers, which had followed the case closely, made much of the evasion (Suzuki, 2006, pp. 54–9, 81–4).
9. The 1889 Lunacy Acts Amendment Act would tighten the procedure for the issuing of committal orders, requiring them to be signed by magistrates who enjoyed the power to order public inquiries; a strategy which, whilst it was intended to guard against abuses, may well have simply encouraged families to conceal supposed lunatics (Suzuki, 2006, pp. 65–6, 91–2).
10. As late as 1935, in *Quarry*, Chief Justice Hewart could still articulate his frustration at medical evidence that was not just vague but very often little more than 'sentimental nonsense' (Ward, 1997, p. 336).
11. Private asylums were subject to a licensing regime from the time of the 1774 Madhouse Act, but investing the responsibility in local magistrates meant that they were rarely inspected in any formal or consistent manner. From 1828, this licensing regime was administered by the Metropolitan Commissioners in Lunacy, renamed the Commissioners in Lunacy from 1845.

12. In *Rundle's Case* in 1855 the Criminal Court of Appeal confirmed that in instances of domestic 'custody of a lunatic' the ordinary common law did not necessarily apply (*Rundle's Case*, 1855; Suzuki, 2006, pp. 128–9, 146–50 and 175). Showalter cites the contemporary writings of Furneaux Jordan, who argued that some women had a genetic propensity to encourage violence in their spouses (Showalter, 1987, p. 107). These 'congenital impulses of character, he opined, could be categorised as a form of madness. Of course, the issue of domestic violence was to come to the fore just two years later with the enactment of the Divorce Court.
13. Contemporary critics supposed that she did, though Charlotte was quick to deny the idea. Indeed a number mused on the possibility that the anonymous author of *Jane Eyre* might be the governess of the Thackeray children, even the 'keeper' of Mrs Thackeray. 'Well may it be said that Fact is often stranger than Fiction!' Charlotte observed in correspondence with her publishers, when later told of the condition of Thackeray's wife. The 'coincidence', she added, 'struck me as equally unfortunate and extraordinary' (Smith, 2007, p. 101). Thackeray, who was an avowed admirer of *Jane Eyre*, remained haunted by the assumed association, long after the identity of its author was revealed. It is recorded that when one inquisitive American admirer asked, at a dinner party in 1860, whether it was 'true, the dreadful story about you and Currer Bell', Thackeray responded 'Alas Madam, it is all too true. And the fruits of that unhallowed intimacy were six children. I slew them all with my own hand' (Small, 1996, p. 179). The evidence from correspondence otherwise suggests a genuine and deep mutual admiration. Thackeray wrote personally to thank Charlotte for receipt of an early copy of *Jane Eyre*, whilst Charlotte expressed her admiration in the prefatory dedication to the second edition of *Jane Eyre* (Allott, 1974, p. 70; Miller, 2001, p. 21; Barker, 2001, pp. 541–2; Kaye, 1995).
14. In private correspondence, referring to her earlier years at Roe Head School, Charlotte bore testimony to the 'concentrated anguish of certain insufferable moments and the heavy gloom of many long hours' from which 'the morbid nerves can know neither peace nor enjoyment – whatever touches – pierces them' (Ingham, 2006, p. 177).
15. The hyena metaphor was commonly used in literary depictions of madwomen at this time. The animalistic metaphors have attracted much critical commentary (Thomas, 1999, p. 7; Shuttleworth, 1996, pp. 165–6; Small, 1996, pp. 158–9; Sharpe, 1993, p. 43).
16. And in this intensity original too, according to Sally Shuttleworth (1996, p. 164).
17. Diary entry from 21 May 1858. In a later diary entry from 1880, Victoria confessed that she also thought it a 'wonderful book', the 'description of the mysterious maniac's nightly appearances awfully thrilling'.
18. Critics often seize upon the predominance of fairytale images in conversations between Jane and Rochester (Rowe, 1983, pp. 69–89; Moglen, 1984, pp. 108–9, 122). In his semi-jocular attempt to tempt Jane into marriage and failing that adultery, Rochester comments 'I will clasp the

bracelets on these fine wrists, and load these fairy-like fingers with rings'; a juxtaposition of images that aligns bondage with fantasy (259). In this interpretative line, the strongest resonances are perhaps with Beauty and the Beast and Cinderella (Glen, 2002, pp. 58–61, 66).
19. The allusion to Bluebeard is complemented by Jane's later condemnation of Rochester's proposed affair as the kind of thing more suited to a sultan's seraglio (269–70).
20. An altogether more brutal depiction than that which attends the death of Ulrica in Scott's *Ivanhoe*, very probably the literary progenitor of Bertha Mason's suicide (Small, 1996, pp. 157–8).
21. The observation is made by Jane, mistakenly of the situation of Grace Poole.
22. Rochester later admits that he should have intervened personally, and with greater 'cruelty', when Bertha's violent capacity became more apparent (306–9).
23. Conolly's treatise was published in 1856. Grace Poole does take the precaution of having rope always available, in order to restrain Bertha whenever necessary (293).
24. The quote is from Conolly's, *The Treatment of the Insane without Mechanical Restraints*, published in 1856. The imputation that domestic incarceration can only lead to the further deterioration of a marital or familial relationship, along very probably with the mental health of the confiner too, has found a recent echo in Carla Kaplan's suggestion that Rochester's greatest agonies lie in his, as well as Bertha's, isolation and lack of conversation (Kaplan, 1996, pp. 18–20).
25. Metaphors of 'stagnation' and decay are common in Charlotte's depiction of Thornfield (116).
26. Though, at a different place, it is attested that Grace has in general proved to be a competent keeper (309–10).
27. For commentaries on Woolf's determination to deflect simplistic assumptions that the 'rage' of Charlotte Brontë, still less that of an entire sex, might be read into the particular circumstances of either Jane Eyre or Bertha Mason, see Kaplan (2007, pp. 18–19), Small (1996, p. 160) and Miller (2001, p. 159).
28. The phenomenon of such hallucinatory voices was much debated by those interested in mesmerism and associated phenomena. The same phenomena are, of course, explored in Emily's *Wuthering Heights* (Senf, 1979, pp. 356–7; Small, 1996, pp. 171–3).
29. Or so the weight of critical commentary supposes (Kaplan, 2007, pp. 7, 15, 31; Miller, 2001, pp. 13–14; Ingham, 2006, pp. 223–5, 232–44).
30. Lucasta Miller records a striking, if slightly odd, testament to the mythic status of Bertha Mason, in Roy Jenkins's description of Margaret Thatcher as the 'great incubus of John Major's premiership, comparable with Mr Rochester's mad wife in *Jane Eyre*' (Miller, 2001, p. 164).
31. Miller (2001, pp. 72, 89) notes the apparent success of the strategy, as recorded by the daughter of the feminist critic Elizabeth Malleson, who

recalled that her mother had read her the novel as a child 'entirely omitting Rochester's mad wife, and so skilfully that we noticed nothing amiss with the plot!'
32. In fact, given that Antoinette is of mixed race it might be said that her exclusion has a fourth dimension (Gregg, 1995, pp. 85, 102; Porter, 1976, p. 543; Emery, 1990, pp. 38–9).
33. Jane's discomfort is realised by Rochester's announcement that he intends to place a 'diamond chain' around the neck of his fiancée. A similar discomfort is articulated when Jane confesses to feeling a sense of personal 'degradation' at being 'dressed like a doll' (268).
34. Sally Shuttleworth reaches the same conclusion: that Rochester, like so many of his contemporaries, has come to realise that his 'legal dominance' has been 'purchased at the cost of self-hatred' (Shuttleworth, 1996, p. 169). So too does Hearne (1990, pp. 190–1).
35. For a commentary on the parallel relation of suttee and the sacrifices required of missionary wives, sacrifices which Jane contemplates when considering St John Rivers's proposal of marriage in *Jane Eyre*, see David (1995, pp. 80–1, 90–1).
36. And always somehow 'off-stage', she later observed (Gregg, 1995, p. 82; Thorpe, 1990, p. 178).

4 The State and Shirley Keeldar

1. He would reiterate this criticism, albeit in milder form, in his review of Elizabeth Gaskell's, *Life of Charlotte Brontë*, confirming that he found *Shirley* to be possessed of a 'profound and frequently overmastering sense of intense dreariness of existence' (Allott, 1974, p. 340).
2. Charlotte took pointed exception in correspondence with Lewes to his perceived determination to 'to keep measuring me by some standard of what you deem becoming to my sex' (Gaskell, 1997, pp. 305–6).
3. 'I took great pains with Shirley', Charlotte later testified (Smith, 2007, p. 175).
4. Adding the aspersion that it rather paled in comparison with Gaskell's *Mary Barton*.
5. A view he later recanted, at least in the broader terms of his admiration for Charlotte herself. Charlotte's publishers, Smith Elder, repeatedly tried to persuade her to omit the opening passages on the bickering curates. But she refused (Barker, 2001, pp. 586–7).
6. Though William Howitt perversely concluded that depictions of the 'clerical class' were on the whole favourable, and done in a 'manner that makes you respect them' (Allott, 1974, p. 117). The *Church of England Quarterly Review* suggested that the author clearly lacked any significant knowledge in matters of theology or Church politics; a spectacular misjudgement (Allott, 1974, p. 156).
7. Heather Glen suggests that the novel is 'certainly very different' from the others that tend to be included in the genre, primarily perhaps because

of its concentration on issues of personal faith (Glen, 2002, p. 196). According to Eagleton, the fatal flaw lies in the novel's studied determination not to concern itself with the 'workers' (Eagleton, 1975, p. 50). Notably, Raymond Williams does not include *Shirley* in his discussion of the 'industrial novel' in *Culture and Society*.
8. The occasional, but persistent, tendency, as Robert Colls puts it, to endure a 'catastrophic loss of confidence' (Colls, 2002, p. 312).
9. Wellington was written into the Angrian Tales as the Duke of Zamorna. Charlotte's childhood friend Mary Taylor would later recall a fierce defence of her hero by a young Charlotte, who it was clear 'worshipped' both the man and his politics. Gaskell later confirmed that Charlotte 'worshipped' Wellington as some kind of 'demi-god' (Gaskell, 1997, pp. 70, 80; Barker, 2001, pp. 109, 117, 446; Ingham, 2006, pp. 77–80; Glen, 2002, pp. 11–14).
10. In a letter to Ellen Nussey, giving an account of various events during her visit to London in June 1850, Charlotte expressed her particular satisfaction at her 'sight' of Wellington, observing 'he is a really grand old man' (Smith, 2007, p. 165).
11. Eagleton takes a more caustic tone suggesting that the Brontës as a whole might be categorised as typical 'petty-bourgeois', anxious above all to conserve and entrench their status (Eagleton, 1975, p. 11).
12. Conor Cruise O'Brien adds a further resonance, suggesting that Burke's was a constitution of 'manners' (O'Brien, 1997, p. 317).
13. And which retains its resonance, not least in modern constitutional law textbooks. In his seminal text on the subject Ivor Jennings, for example, reduces the English constitution to nothing more than an 'attitude of mind' (Jennings, 1971, p. 205).
14. From 'You ask me why, tho' ill at ease'. The passage has been recently cited by Lord Bingham in his *The Rule of Law* (Bingham, 2010, pp. 4–5). Ackroyd suggests that Tennyson can be read as the quintessential poet of patriotic Victorian nostalgia (Ackroyd, 2002, pp. 118, 252).
15. Asa Briggs famously appraised *Shirley* as 'an important contribution to the literature of regional interpretation' (Briggs, 1958, p. 205).
16. A fragmentary 'history', written aged twelve, testifies to Charlotte's familiarity with the range of journals received, whilst further correspondence confirmed the extent of her engagement within and without her immediate family in matters of local and national politics (Greene, 1994, p. 353).
17. The supposition that Patrick Brontë instilled the same Church Tory instincts in his children is suggested by Gaskell (1997, pp. 42–3, 68). Later critics have sought to moderate his presumed influence (Barker, 2001, pp. 157–8; Ingham, 2006, p. 38; Glen, 2002, pp. 159–60). Thormahlen suggests that Haworth Parsonage 'can be viewed as a microcosmic representation' of matters of political theology in mid-nineteenth-century England (Thormahlen, 1999, p. 13).
18. In a peculiarly apposite coincidence, a generation earlier the same accounts had been read out in factories and mills across West Yorkshire as

a means of inspiring putative insurrectionists (Thompson, 1991, p. 608). According to Gaskell, in the 'days of the Luddites' Patrick Brontë 'had been for the peremptory interference of the law, at a time when no magistrate could be found to act, and all the property of the West Riding was in danger' (Gaskell, 1997, p. 43).

19. Making *Shirley*, according to Edward Thompson, a 'true expression of the middle-class myth' of the Rawfolds riot (Thompson, 1991, pp. 612–13). Thompson ventures to identify some caricatures in the novel, including Robert Moore as Cartwright and the Reverend Helstone as the notorious parson Hammond Roberson, who according to folklore hectored dying rioters into making confessions implicating friends and family. Charlotte always denied drawing caricatures in the novel (Gaskell, 1997, pp. 302, 307).

20. A few years earlier, in 1841, the Governor of the Northern Division warned his superiors in London that 'Every element of a ferocious civil war is boiling in this district' (Eagleton, 1975, p. 3). In her *Life*, Gaskell was happy to contribute to the lingering power of this myth, confirming, in her commentary on the Rawfolds mill attack, that the Luddites had assumed 'the character of an insurrectionary army' (Gaskell, 1997, p. 85).

21. According to Elizabeth Gaskell, 'in the opinion of many' the country as a whole in 1811–12 'seemed to be on the verge of a precipice', adding further that the area around Charlotte's school, Roe Head, had a particular reputation as a haven of Luddite sympathies (Gaskell, 1997, pp. 83–4). Eagleton likewise makes the point that families such as the Brontës would have felt themselves to be living in an age of political ferment (Eagleton, 1975, pp. 3–4, 8–9).

22. As the note which Robert Moore finds attached to his destroyed wagons advises 'Take this as a warning from men that are starving, and have starving wives and children to go home to when they have done this deed' (29).

23. It is suggested that Charlotte rewrote parts of the draft novel in the wake of Emily's death in order to give greater primacy to the character of Shirley Keeldar (Barker, 2001, p. 612). Miller has argued that in the creation of Shirley, Charlotte 'took on the role of Emily's first mythographer' (Miller, 2001, pp. 174–5).

24. The reviewer in the *Atlas* certainly did (Allott, 1974, p. 121).

25. As did the reviewer in *Fraser's Magazine* (Allott, 1974, p. 153).

26. The core of constitutional establishment lies in the fact that the monarch must be a member of the Church of England, and that any successor to the throne must admit a consonant affinity. The latter aspect is still required by the terms of the Act of Settlement. The ceremonial aspect remains prominent, of course, not least during coronations and services of national commemoration. Informative modern commentaries on the continuing constitutional status of the Church of England can be found in Harte (1996) and Oliva (2010).

27. According to Chadwick, evangelicalism propelled by an identifiable evangelical 'party' within the established Church was the 'strongest religious force in British life' during the middle decades of the nineteenth century (Chadwick, 1977, pp. 5, 62–4, 441–9).
28. The first of these abolished livings held *in commendam* with sees. The second limited the number of benefices held by one person to two. The third of the statutes suppressed all non-resident prebends, all sinecure rectories and resident canonries above the number of four to each cathedral, with one or two particular exceptions.
29. For a discussion of the purpose of the Discipline Act, as a measure designed to counter the perceived Catholicism in the Ritualist movement, see Moorman (1973, pp. 380–1).
30. A position the bishop maintained despite the judgement of the committee. In the end the Dean of Arches was obliged to provide the testimonial and confirm the appointment having first obtained the *fiat* of the Archbishop of Canterbury.
31. Finding perhaps its loudest and most notorious expression in the writings of Richard Hurrell Froude (Nockles, 1994, pp. 79–82, 86–8).
32. Chadwick notes for example that the number of non-resident curates dropped from 3078 to 955 between 1838 and 1864 (Chadwick, 1977, p. 127).
33. Charlotte was a strong admirer of Arnold.
34. According to Constance Harsh, far more so than any other 'condition of England' novel (Harsh, 1994, pp. 131–2). Gilbert and Gubar suggest that the novel was written 'very consciously' as 'an attack on the religion of the patriarchs' (Gilbert and Gubar, 2000, p. 392).
35. A Babel that was becoming ever louder in the environs of Haworth (Gaskell, 1997, pp. 142–3; Glen, 2002, p. 145; Barker, 2001, pp. 257–8).
36. The same sentiment was expressed by Elizabeth Gaskell who, in private correspondence, confirmed that the first responsibility of writing lay 'in advancing the kingdom of God' (Jay, 1997, p. xii). Bunyan was a central figure in Victorian Evangelicalism, of either Church or dissenting variety, as was Milton. And both were favourites in the Brontë household (Thormahlen, 1999, p. 165).
37. Gaskell emphasised Charlotte's distaste for Pusey (Gaskell, 1997, p. 143). The fact that she later married a Puseyite, albeit a relatively moderate one, might seem ironic. But clear demarcations, in terms of political as well as intellectual sympathies within the Church, were elusive (Nockles, 1994, pp. 25–6, 35–7). It is commonly suggested that Charlotte preferred rather lower Church evangelical inclinations, in line perhaps with those of her friend Ellen Nussey, as well of course with those of her father (Thormahlen, 1999, pp. 13–23, Winnifrith, 1988, pp. 31, 35–8, 40–1). Sister Anne's evangelical affinities are, of course, well chronicled (Ingham, 2006, p. 199).
38. Hall is described as gazing down on Caroline with 'the aspect of a smiling Melancthon'; a simile that, according to Thormahlen, attests

to Charlotte's 'deference to the ideal of right-minded toleration'. Thormahlen further suggests that Hall comes about as close as any to an ideal clerical characterisation in Charlotte's novels (Thormahlen, 1999, pp. 41, 201–3).
39. Certainly resonant with the kind of congregation that might be expected in a Moravian chapel. Anne's flirtation with the Moravian church is well documented (Thormahlen, 1999, pp. 7–8).
40. As she confirmed in private correspondence, whilst she certainly did not 'regard' its ministers as 'infallible personages', she remained 'sincerely attached' to the Church of England (Thormahlen, 1999, p. 203; Lawson, 1980, pp. 729–30, 744).
41. Appraising G.H. Lewes for noting in his review the 'wanting' of 'all unity' in narrative clerical voices, Glen suggests that the bickering 'cacophony' of curates was intended to depict a potentially debilitating divisiveness (Glen, 2002, pp. 149–52). Thormahlen, however, who suggests that the depictions of Donne and Malone in particular can be traced to curates who passed through the parsonage at Haworth, prefers to see Charlotte engaging her bickering curates with an 'easygoing humour' (Thormahlen, 1999, pp. 194–6).
42. The kind of cleric Robert Moore suggests who defends 'the divine right of kings, which you often stickle for in your sermons' (35).
43. There is an obvious significance in Caroline's choice of play, the tragedy of a man 'faulty as well as great' (117). Armstrong suggests that it represents a 'paradigm for the power of reading' (Armstrong, 1987, pp. 214–15).
44. Making her, in the words of Terry Eagleton, a curious 'hybrid of progressive capitalist and traditional landowner' (Eagleton, 1975, p. 51).
45. The inflection is deployed repeatedly by male characters in the novel too. In chapter nineteen, Helstone advises the 'captain of the house' to locate her sword and pistols, as rumours of further Luddite attacks have spread throughout the community (280–1).
46. Gaskell famously concentrated on the 'gentle', unassuming nature of her heroine, noting on one occasion that Charlotte was quick to distance herself from any 'democrat' tendencies (Gaskell, 1997, pp. 30–1, 377–9). There was, according to Lucasta Miller, an 'enormous gulf' between Charlotte and Elizabeth Gaskell in their 'approaches to art, femininity and sexuality' (Miller, 2001, p. 46).
47. Patricia Ingham suggests that *Shirley* represents one of the most concerted attempts in mid-Victorian fiction to examine what she terms the 'English woman question' (Ingham, 2006, p. 133).
48. The gender of Currer Bell was then unknown. Others were convinced it must be a man. In his notorious review, Lewes suggested that a 'more masculine book, in the sense of vigour, was never written' (Allott, 1974, pp. 161–3). Whilst she took exception to much of Lewes's review, Charlotte did later concede that parts of the novel might have seemed 'unfeminine' in tone (Miller, 2001, p. 19). It was Virginia Woolf who was

to later make the most renowned assertion, that whilst Emily wrote like a woman, Charlotte wrote like a man (Woolf, 1998, pp. 97, 100).
49. Dismissed by Eagleton as 'embarrassing feminist mysticism' (Eagleton, 1975, p. 58). For a discussion of the passage as evidence of Charlotte's flirtation with a naturalistic Christianity, see Lawson (1980, pp. 737–8). For a broader discussion of the passage as representative of a critique of Milton levelled by a number of incipient feminist writers of the period see Gilbert and Gubar (2000, pp. 193–5).
50. Both Barker and Gilbert and Gubar argue that the novel, being focused on the woman 'question', is necessarily political (Barker, 2001, p. 603: Gilbert and Gubar, 2000, pp. 371, 374). Constance Harsh takes a sceptical view suggesting that the novel ultimately confirms a 'failure of female power', and concluding that at 'best feminism in *Shirley* is a fragmentary affair' (Harsh, 1994, pp. 17, 142).
51. A view Shirley reiterates later, commenting, in oblique conversation with Robert Moore that 'Miss Helstone, though gentle, tractable, and candid enough, is still perfectly capable of defying even Mr Moore's penetration' (305).
52. The same sentiment can be read in Caroline's attempt to dissuade Robert from the pursuit of formal justice against suspected machine-breakers, 'Because it will set all the neighbourhood against you more than ever' (105).
53. A view further confirmed by Mrs Pryor, as a solitary and 'constrained' life (316). It was, indeed, a view commonly presented in Victorian fiction. Geraldine Jewsbury has her governess protagonist in *Marian Withers* declare 'I feel as if I were buried alive' (Ingham, 2006, pp. 35, 102–3).
54. As, of course, to a degree at least, was Charlotte herself, rejecting three proposals before agreeing to marry Bell Nichols.
55. Eagleton suggests that Shirley's relationship with her putative husband is 'strongly sadomasochistic' (Eagleton, 1975, p. 57).
56. Bodenheimer likewise muses on the willingness of Shirley and Caroline to seek refuge in 'fantasies of domestic paternalism' (Bodenheimer, 1988, pp. 51–3). A similar tone can be detected in Moglen's regret, at the fate of a pair who, at the conclusion of the novel, simply fade away, 'deprived of energy and vitality' (Moglen, 1984, pp. 188–9). And again in Harsh's conclusion, that it is 'difficult to believe that' the Shirley who submits so eagerly to Louis Moore, is 'the same woman who started a relief program for the poor, made politics her habitual study, and arranged a loan to Robert Moore' (Harsh, 1994, p. 141).

Conclusion: The Trials of Lucy Snowe

1. Newby was loathed by both Gaskell and the Brontës for his unscrupulous attempt to pass off the novels of Anne and Emily as being written by the author of *Jane Eyre*. Lady Eastlake had written a peculiarly caustic review

of the latter novel in the *Quarterly* implying that it had been written by a woman of doubtful reputation. She was not to be forgiven either.
2. Elizabeth Gaskell was in Rome at the time of publication. The letter signed by Newton and Robinson, which accompanied the retraction, confirmed that Gaskell had written in good faith, but that her sources had been subsequently discovered 'not to be trustworthy' (Uglow, 1999, p. 247).
3. As of course was true of the aspersions directed towards Newby and Lady Eastlake. The former blustered, the latter made no comment. The family of William Carus Wilson, head of the school at Cowan Bridge which Charlotte so hated, also threatened legal action but in the end were seemingly mollified by the promise of rewriting in any subsequent edition. Gaskell also received, amongst a broadly supportive series of reviews, letters from Lewes and Arthur Bell Nichols requesting removal or rewriting of certain passages in any subsequent edition (Uglow, 1999, pp. 431–5).
4. Penalties, which could include penance, recantation and retraction, were generally performed in the vestry of the local parish church.
5. The 1832 Ecclesiastical Courts Commission had recommended abolition of canon jurisdiction in cases of sexual defamation.
6. Waddams notes that ecclesiastical courts, in comparison with civil courts, at least recognised the independent legal personality of the wife, thus providing her with the right to pursue an action on her own behalf (Waddams, 2000, pp. 179–86). Very often such actions were pursued against husbands, as a precursor to secondary matrimonial actions, such as applications for separation decrees.
7. Gaskell found the writing of Charlotte's biography unexpectedly frustrating, commenting to George Smith, 'Oh! If once I have finished this biography, catch me writing another!' (Jay, 1997, p. xiv; Uglow, 1999, p. 397). Her relationship with Patrick Brontë was oddly ambivalent. Rather fanciful accounts of his fearsome temper and unpredictable habits which Gaskell wrote into her *Life* coloured his reputation for many years (Gaskell, 1997, pp. 42–3, 68). It is often suggested that the character of the stern and unbending John Thornton in *North and South* is also based, at least in part, on Patrick Brontë. Patrick, however, seemingly sensing the strategic merit in the endeavour, preferred to accept martyrdom to his daughter's better remembrance and declined to take offence. He and Gaskell remained on cordial terms, the latter accepting subsequent invitations to visit Haworth.
8. The 'last work by Charlotte Brontë', according to Joanne Shattock (2001, p. 19).
9. The array of 'grim and terrible criminals' imagined in *Wuthering Heights* is ascribed to a peculiarly untutored metaphysical genius, whilst the contrasting spirituality of Anne is sanctified in Gaskell's embellished account of her death (Gaskell, 1997, pp. 257, 288–93).
10. Oliphant was more immediately troubled here with the 'sensation' novels of Mary Elizabeth Braddon and Ellen Wood.

11. 'It is Currer Bell speaking to you', Lewes advised readers of the *Leader* (Allott, 1974, p. 185). Anne Mozley in the *Christian Remembrancer* noted the autobiographical style as did an anonymous reviewer in the *Literary Gazette* who likewise suggested that *Villette* should be read as a testamentary companion to *Jane Eyre* (Allott, 1974, pp. 179, 204).
12. In comparison, she admitted to Gaskell, with the latter's *Ruth* which had 'a goodness, a philanthropic purpose, a social use' (Gaskell, 1997, p. 398).
13. Brenda Silver notes the implication of Lucy's aligned 'public silence and private dialogue' (Silver, 1983, p. 102). According to Gillian Beer, Charlotte Brontë 'was the most introspective of all Victorian novelists' (Beer, 1977, p. 185). Commentaries suggesting the political import of Lucy Snowe's peculiarly introspective testament can be found in Kreilkamp (2005, pp. 142–3, 147–52) and Newsom (1991, pp. 79–80).
14. Something that undoubtedly fired George Eliot's conspicuous enthusiasm for a novel of 'preternatural power', one which 'we, at least, would rather read for a third time than most new novels for the first' (Gilbert and Gubar, 2000, p. 408).
15. Musing, 'I know not how it would have ended' (163).
16. The conclusion, which recounts M Paul's death at sea, is notorious, not simply because it seemed inappropriate to so many reviewers, but because Charlotte wrote alternatives and was clearly herself exercised as to which was the most suitable.
17. And perhaps a little embarrassed too. Charlotte urged Emily not to tell 'papa'. In correspondence with Ellen Nussey in 1842, Charlotte had observed 'I consider Methodism, Quakerism & the extremes of high & low Churchism foolish but Roman Catholicism beats them all' (Smith, 2007, p. 38).
18. Wiseman's public statements accompanying the creation of Catholic dioceses in England in October 1850 had made him something of a focus for anti-Popery media campaigns.
19. The depiction of the 'female body' in the nineteenth-century novel, according to Nancy Armstrong, 'comprised a grammar of subjectivity capable of regulating desire, pleasure, the ordinary care of the body' and the 'dynamic of family relationships' (Armstrong, 1987, p. 95). For the dominance of this theme in *Villette*, see Gilbert and Gubar (2000, pp. 408–9).
20. Unsurprisingly, much critical commentary here moves around the passage towards the end of the novel in which Lucy appears to hallucinate (Hodge, 2005; Hughes, 2000, pp. 714, 717–22; Newsom, 1991, pp. 60–4). Elizabeth Gaskell was so bemused by the passage that she enquired of Charlotte whether she had written from a personal experience of opium.
21. Amongst the most pointed and most renowned of the latter can be placed the likes of Mary Hays's *Victim of Prejudice* and Mary Wollstonecraft's *Mary* (Caine, 1977, pp. 13, 17–18, 37–9; Ward, 2009).

22. The principle defect in Austen, she later reiterated, is that she 'ignores' human passion (Smith, 2007, pp. 161–2). Charlotte otherwise confessed her admiration for Austen, a writer of 'clear commonsense and subtle shrewdness' (Smith, 2007, p. 100).
23. So pervasive indeed that Charlotte's first biographer, Thomas Wemyss Reid, editor of the *Leeds Mercury*, was led to suppose that his subject must have committed adultery with Constantin Heger whilst at his academy; a possibility which, so tempting and so titillating, was perpetuated in a number of later studies of Charlotte and her writings (Miller, 2001, pp. 114–18).
24. A description very obviously intended to resonate with familiar images of harem slaves and concubines (Matus, 1995, p. 141).
25. The name Vashti was intended to resonate with the queen of the same name who, in the Old Testament *Book of Esther*, defied her husband King Ahasuerus when he demanded that she should display her beauty at his behest. As a result of her refusal Ahasuerus passed a law which formally decreed the sovereignty of men in all households in his kingdom.
26. Charlotte was not the only Victorian writer to be entranced by Rachel. So were George Eliot and G.H. Lewes, the latter confessing himself to be infatuated with the 'beautiful devil'. Such was her power of literary seduction that she became herself something of a 'creature of myth' (Stokes, 1984, pp. 774–5).
27. Barbara Leckie suggests that the court operated as a kind of 'legal confession'; a metaphor which again imports, for our purposes, a particular pertinence (Leckie, 1999, p. 67).
28. The distinguishing feature of the criminal offence of obscene libel, in comparison with civil libel, being the absence of a need to identify a maligned subject.
29. The reference to poison was intended to resonate with legislation which had just passed through Parliament for the better regulation of the sale of noxious substances. A comprehensive discussion of the background to the 1857 Act can be found in Manchester (1988, pp. 224–9).
30. The same prejudice finds expression in modern obscenity jurisprudence (Manchester, 1991, pp. 49–50).
31. The case for courts intervening to proscribe the publication of certain pieces of literature which might be deemed obscene has always been a matter of contention. The difficulties found famous, if rather overblown expression, in the words of Justice Stable in *Secker and Warburg*, who advised the jury that their verdict would be of 'great importance in relation to the future of the novel in the civilized world' (*Secker and Warburg*, 1954, p. 1138).
32. George Smith recalled in his memoirs Lady Herschel's horror that a novel such as *Jane Eyre* might be left lying around a drawing room, where anyone might pick it up (Miller, 2001, p. 22). Such liberality was evidently not the custom in the Herschel household.
33. And it is not just the critical debate. The legal proscription of pornography is still, in large part, defined by the terms of the 1959 Obscene

Publications Act. Its definition of pornography as material which is likely to 'deprave or corrupt' the consumer is derived from that originally enunciated by Lord Cockburn in *Hicklin* (Edwards, 1998, p. 849; McGlynn and Ward, 2009, p. 329).
34. Nicola Lacey urges the need for contemporary feminist lawyers to reject 'attractively simple, monolithic theories in which everything is reduced to one explanatory concept' (Lacey, 1998, p. 31).
35. The critical literature here is, unsurprisingly, considerable. For acknowledgement of the tensions that Foucault can generate across disciplines and attempts to resolve some kind of accommodation with associated aspects of feminist politics, literary criticism and jurisprudence, and law and politics more broadly conceived, see respectively Sawicki (1991, pp. 34–5, 49) and McNay (1992, pp. 1–10), Tromp (2000, p. 7) and Munro (2007, pp. 88–9), and then Turkel (1990) and Golder and Fitzpatrick (2009, pp. 3–4, 53) and Fraser (1981, 1985).
36. This is not to suggest that it was an original moment. There are of course earlier voices. Chaucer's Wife of Bath is an obvious one (Heinzelman, 2010, pp. 11–14, 17–22).
37. As Barbara Caine has shown there were no properly organised women's political campaigns until the later 1850s. The formation of the Langham Place 'group' under the direction of Barbara Leigh Smith and Bessie Raynor Parkes can be traced to early publications in 1854, but only took on a readily identifiable form as a putatively feminist 'organisation' in 1859. Incipient suffrage campaigns were another decade away (Caine, 1977, pp. 88–94, 117–23). Until that time writing novels and essays, and reading them, was pretty much the only strategy available to the nascent feminist.
38. In the rather different context of modernist literature, more especially that of Virginia Woolf and Hannah Arendt, Ravit Reichman has explored the burden of ethical responsibility experienced by writers who strive to present testamentary narratives (Reichman, 2009).

Bibliography

Ackroyd, P. (2002) *Albion: The Origins of the English Imagination*, London: Chatto and Windus.
Acland, A. (1948) *Caroline Norton*, London: Constable.
Allen, A. (1992) 'The Jurisprudence of *Jane Eyre*', *Harvard Women's Law Journal*, 15, 173–238.
Allott, M. (1974) *The Brontës: The Critical Heritage*, London: Routledge.
Anderson, A. (2005) 'Victorian Studies and the Two Modernities', *Victorian Studies*, 47, 195–203.
Anderson, N. (1982) 'The Marriage with a Deceased Wife's Sister Bill Controversy: Incest Anxiety and the Defense of Family Purity in Victorian England', *Journal of British Studies*, 21, 67–86.
Angel, M. (2003) 'Teaching Susan Glaspell's *A Jury of Her Peers* and *Trifles*', *Journal of Legal Education*, 53, 548–63.
Argyle, G. (1995) 'Gender and Generic Mixing in Charlotte Brontë's *Shirley*', *Studies in English Literature*, 35, 741–56.
Aristodemou, M. (1993) 'Studies in Law and Literature: Directions and Concerns', *Anglo-American Law Review*, 22, 157–93.
Aristodemou, M. (2000) *Law and Literature: Journeys from Her to Eternity*, Oxford: Oxford University Press.
Armstrong, N. (1987) *Desire and Domestic Fiction: A Political History of the Novel*, Oxford: Oxford University Press.
Armstrong, N. (2001) 'Gender and the Victorian Novel', in D. David (ed.), *The Cambridge Companion to the Victorian Novel*, Cambridge: Cambridge University Press.
Armstrong, N. (2003) 'Imperialist Nostalgia and *Wuthering Heights*', in L. Peterson (ed.), *Wuthering Heights: Case Studies in Contemporary Literature*, New York: St Martins Press.
Austin, J. (1995) *The Province of Jurisprudence Determined*, Cambridge: Cambridge University Press.
Baer, E. (1983) 'The Sisterhood of Jane Eyre and Antoinette Cosway', in E. Abel, M. Hirsch and E. Langland (eds), *The Voyage In: Fictions of Female Development*, Dartmouth: University Press of New England.
Bagehot, W. (2001) *The English Constitution*, Cambridge: Cambridge University Press.
Bailey, V. and S. Blackburn (1979) 'The Punishment of Incest Act 1908: A Case Study of Law Creation', *Criminal Law Review*, 708–18.
Barker, J. (2001) *The Brontës*, London: Phoenix.
Baron, J. (1999) 'Law, Literature, and the Problems of Interdisciplinarity', *Yale Law Journal*, 108, 1059–85.
Bartlett, P. (2001) 'Legal Madness in the Nineteenth Century', *Social History of Madness*, 14, 107–31.

Bataille, G. (1990) *Literature and Evil*, London: Marion Boyars.
Beer, G. (1977) 'Coming Wonders: Uses of Theatre in the Victorian Novel', in M. Axon and R. Williams (eds), *English Drama: Forms and Development*, Cambridge: Cambridge University Press.
Beetham, M. (2001) 'Women and the Consumption of Print', in J. Shattock (ed.), *Women and Literature in Britain 1800–1900*, Cambridge: Cambridge University Press.
Behlmer, G. (1985) 'The Gypsy Problem in Victorian England', *Victorian Studies*, 28, 231–53.
Bell, V. (1993) *Interrogating Incest: Feminism, Foucault and the Law*, London: Routledge.
Berry, L. (1996) 'Acts of Custody and Incarceration in *Wuthering Heights* and *The Tenant of Wildfell Hall*', *Novel*, 30, 32–55.
Berry, L. (1999) *The Child, the State and the Victorian Novel*, Charlottesville: University Press of Virginia.
Bersani, L. (1984) *A Future for Astynax: Character and Desire in Literature*, New York: Columbia University Press.
Best, G. (1958) 'The Protestant Constitution and its Supporters 1800–1829', *Transactions of the Royal Historical Society*, 5 ser. 8, 105–27.
Best, G. (1970) 'Evangelicalism and the Victorians', in A. Symondson (ed.), *The Victorian Crisis of Faith*, London: SPCK.
Bingham, T. (2010) *The Rule of Law*, Harmondsworth: Penguin.
Blackstone, W. (1828) *Commentaries on the Laws of England*, volume 1, London: William Walker.
Blakemore, S. (1988) *Burke and the Fall of Language*, Dartmouth: University Press of New England.
Bodenheimer, R. (1988) *The Politics of Story in Victorian Social Fiction*, Ithaca: Cornell University Press.
Briggs, A. (1958) 'Public and Private Themes in *Shirley*', *Brontë Society Transactions*, 13, 203–19.
Brontë, A. (1993) *The Tenant of Wildfell Hall*, Oxford: Oxford University Press.
Brontë, C. (2000) *Jane Eyre*, Oxford: Oxford University Press.
Brontë, C. (2000) *Villette*, Oxford: Oxford University Press.
Brontë, C. (2007) *Shirley*, Oxford: Oxford University Press.
Brontë, E. (1992) *The Complete Poems*, Harmondsworth: Penguin.
Brontë, E. (2009) *Wuthering Heights*, Oxford: Oxford University Press.
Burke, E. (1986) *Reflections on the Revolution in France*, Harmondsworth: Penguin.
Burke, E. (1990) *A Philosophical Enquiry*, Oxford: Oxford University Press.
Caine, B. (1977) *English Feminism 1780–1980*, Oxford: Oxford University Press.
Camus, A. (1979) *Collected Essays and Notebooks*, Harmondsworth: Penguin.
Carnell, R. (1998) 'Feminism and the Public Sphere in Anne Brontë's *The Tenant of Wildfell Hall*', *Nineteenth Century Literature*, 53, 1998, 1–24.
Chadwick, O. (1970) 'The Established Church under Attack', in A. Symondson (ed.), *The Victorian Crisis of Faith*, London: SPCK.

Chadwick, O. (1977) *The Victorian Church, pt. 1, 1829–1859*, London: SCM Press.
Chandler, J. (1998) *England in 1819: The Politics of Literary Culture and the Case of Romantic Historicism*, Chicago: University of Chicago Press.
Chaplin, S. (2007) *The Gothic and the Rule of Law*, Basingstoke: Palgrave.
Chase, K. and M. Levenson (2000) *The Spectacle of Intimacy: A Public Life for the Victorian Family*, Princeton: Princeton University Press.
Chedzoy, A. (1992) *A Scandalous Woman*, London: Allison and Busby.
Chitham, E. (1986) *The Brontës' Irish Background*, London: Macmillan.
Chitham, E. (2001) *The Birth of Wuthering Heights*, Basingstoke: Palgrave.
Christ, C. (1979) 'Imaginative Constraint, Feminist Duty, and the Form of Charlotte Brontë's Fiction', *Women's Studies*, 6, 287–96.
Ciolkowski, L. (1994) 'Charlotte Brontë's *Villette*: Forgeries of Sex and Self', *Studies in the Novel*, 26, 218–34.
Clarke, P. (1999) *Hope and Glory: Britain 1900–1990*, Harmondsworth: Penguin.
Cody, L. (2000) 'The Politics of Illegitimacy in an Age of Reform: Women, Reproduction, and Political Economy in England's New Poor Law of 1834', *Journal of Women's History*, 11, 131–56.
Colls, R. (2002) *Identity of England*, Oxford: Oxford University Press.
Constable, M. (2005) *Just Silences: The Limits and Possibilities of Modern Law*, Princeton: Princeton University Press.
Corbett, M. (2008) *Family Likeness: Sex, Marriage, and Incest from Jane Austen to Virginia Woolf*, Ithaca: Cornell University Press.
Cousins, E. and S. Ross (1989) *The Law of Mortgages*, London: Sweet and Maxwell.
Cover, R. (1983) 'Nomos and Narrative', *Harvard Law Review*, 97, 4–68.
Craig, R. (2009) *The Narratives of Caroline Norton*, Basingstoke: Palgrave.
Crenshaw, K. (1988) 'Race, Reform and Retrenchment: Transformation and Legitimation in Antidiscrimination Law', *Harvard Law Review*, 101, 1331–87.
David, D. (1995) *Rule Britannia: Women, Empire and Victorian Writing*, Ithaca: Cornell University Press.
Davies, S. (1994) *Emily Brontë: Heretic*, London: Women's Press.
Dicey, A. (1994) *Lectures on the Relation between Law and Popular Opinion in England during the Nineteenth Century*, London: Macmillan.
Dickens, C. (2002) *Dombey and Son*, Harmondsworth: Penguin.
Diederich, N. (2003) 'The Art of Comparison: Remarriage in Anne Brontë's *The Tenant of Wildfell Hall*', *Rocky Mountain Review of Language and Literature*, 57, 25–41.
Doggett, M. (1992) *Marriage, Wife-Beating and the Law in Victorian England*, London: Weidenfeld and Nicolson.
Dolin, K. (1999) *Fiction and the Law: Legal Discourse in Victorian and Modern Literature*, Cambridge: Cambridge University Press.
Dolin, K. (2007) *A Critical Introduction to Law and Literature*, Cambridge: Cambridge University Press.

Douzinas, C. (2000) *The End of Human Rights: Critical Legal Thought at the Turn of the Century*, Oxford: Hart.

Drakopoulou, M. (2007) 'Feminism and the Siren Call of Law', *Law and Critique*, 18, 331–60.

Dunlop, C. (1991) 'Literature Studies in Law Schools', *Cardozo Studies in Law and Literature*, 3, 63–109.

Dworkin, R. (1986) *Law's Empire*, Cambridge, MA: Belknap Press.

Eagleton, T. (1975) *Myths of Power: A Marxist Study of the Brontës*, London: Macmillan.

Eagleton, T. (1995) *Heathcliff and the Great Hunger: Studies in Irish Culture*, London: Verso.

Edwards, S. (1998) 'On the Contemporary Application of the Obscene Publications Act 1959', *Criminal Law Review*, 843–53.

Eliot, G. (2008) *Adam Bede*, Oxford: Oxford University Press.

Emery, M. (1990) *Jean Rhys at 'World's End': Novels of Colonial and Sexual Excess*, Austin: University of Texas Press.

Erickson, A. (1990) 'Common Law versus Common Practice: The Use of Marriage Settlements in Early Modern England', *Economic History Review*, 43, 21–39.

Erickson, A. (1993) *Women and Property in Early Modern England*, London: Routledge.

Ermarth, E. (1997) *The English Novel in History 1840–1895*, London; Routledge.

Evans, T. (2005) '"Blooming Virgins All Beware": Love, Courtship, and Illegitimacy in Eighteenth Century British Popular Literature', in A. Levene, T. Nutt and S. Williams (eds), *Illegitimacy in Britain 1700–1920*, Basingstoke: Palgrave.

Fanon, F. (2001) *The Wretched of the Earth*, Harmondsworth: Penguin.

Finn, M. (2002) 'Victorian Law, Literature and History: Three Ships Passing in the Night', *Journal of Victorian Culture*, 7, 134–46.

Fish, S. (1980) *Is There a Text in This Class? The Authority of Interpretive Communities*, Cambridge, MA: Harvard University Press.

Fish, S. (1990) *Doing What Comes Naturally: Change, Rhetoric and the Practice of Theory in Literary and Legal Studies*, Oxford: Oxford University Press.

Fiss, O. (1982) 'Objectivity and Interpretation', *Stanford Law Review*, 34, 739–63.

Flint, K. (1993) *The Woman Reader 1837–1914*, Oxford: Oxford University Press.

Flint, K. (2001) 'The Victorian Novel and its Readers', in D. David (ed.), *The Cambridge Companion to the Victorian Novel*, Cambridge: Cambridge University Press.

Flint, K. (2005) 'Why "Victorian"?: Response', *Victorian Studies*, 47, 230–9.

Foster, S. (1985) *Women's Fiction: Marriage, Freedom and the Individual*, London: Croom Helm.

Foucault, M. (1977) 'Intellectuals and Power: a Conversation between Michel Foucault and Gilles Deleuze', in D. Bouchard (ed.), *Language,*

Counter-Memory, Practice: Selected Essays and Interviews by Michel Foucault, Ithaca: Cornell University Press.
Foucault, M. (1980) *Introduction to Herculine Barbin: Being the Recently Discovered Memoirs of a 19th Century French Hermaphrodite*, New York: Pantheon.
Foucault, M. (1990) *A History of Sexuality*, vol. 1, Harmondsworth: Penguin.
Foucault, M. (1991) *Discipline and Punish: The Birth of the Modern Prison*, Harmondsworth: Penguin.
Foucault, M. (2003) *Society must be Defended: Lectures at the College de France 1975–76*, London: Allen Lane.
Frank, K. (1990) *Emily Brontë: A Chainless Soul*, London: Hamish Hamilton.
Fraser, N. (1981) 'Foucault on Modern Power: Empirical Insights and Normative Confusions', *Praxis International*, 1, 272–87.
Fraser, N. (1985) 'Michel Foucault: A Young Conservative?' *Ethics*, 96, 165–84.
Frost, G. (1995) *Promises Broken: Courtship, Class, and Gender in Victorian England*, Charlottesville: University Press of Virginia.
Frost, G. (2003) 'The Black Lamb of the Black Sheep: Illegitimacy in the English Working Class 1850–1939', *Journal of Social History*, 37, 293–322.
Frost, G. (2008) *Living in Sin: Cohabiting as Husband and Wife in Nineteenth Century England*, Manchester: Manchester University Press.
Furniss, T. (1993) *Edmund Burke's Aesthetic Ideology: Language, Gender and Political Economy in Revolution*, Cambridge: Cambridge University Press.
Gallagher, C. (1985) *The Industrial Reformation of English Fiction: Social Discourse and Narrative Form 1832–1867*, Chicago: University of Chicago Press.
Gallagher, C. (2005) 'Theoretical Answers to Interdisciplinary Questions or Interdisciplinary Answers to Theoretical Questions?' *Victorian Studies*, 47, 253–9.
Gargano, E. (2004) 'The Education of Brontë's New *Nouvelle Heloise* in *Shirley*', *Studies in English Literature*, 44, 799–803.
Gaskell, E. (1997), *The Life of Charlotte Brontë*, Harmondsworth: Penguin.
Gemmette, E. (1989) 'Law and Literature: An Unnecessarily Suspect Class in the Liberal Arts Component of the Law School Classroom', *Valparaiso Law Review*, 23, 267–302.
Gerin, W. (1959) *Anne Brontë*, London: Thomas Nelson.
Gilbert, S. and S. Gubar (2000) *The Madwoman in the Attic: The Woman Writer and the Nineteenth Century Literary Imagination*, New Haven: Yale University Press.
Gilmour, R. (1993) *The Victorian Period: The Intellectual and Cultural Context of English Literature*, London: Longman.
Giuliani, F. (2009) 'Monsters in the Village? Incest in Nineteenth Century France', *Journal of Social History*, 42, 919–32.
Gleadle, K. (2001) *British Women in the Nineteenth Century*, Basingstoke: Palgrave.
Glen, H. (2002) *Charlotte Brontë: The Imagination in History*, Oxford: Oxford University Press.
Goetz, W. (1982) 'Genealogy and Incest in *Wuthering Heights*', *Studies in the Novel*, 14, 359–76.

Golden, C. (2003) *Images of the Woman Reader in Victorian British and American Fiction*, Gainesville: University of Florida Press.
Golder, B. and P. Fitzpatrick (2009) *Foucault's Law*, London: Routledge.
Goodlad, L. (2003) *Victorian Literature and the Victorian State: Character and Governance in a Liberal Society*, Baltimore: Johns Hopkins University Press.
Gordon, E. and G. Nair (2003) *Public Lives: Women, Family and Society in Victorian Britain*, New Haven: Yale University Press.
Gordon, J. (1984) 'Gossip, Diary, Letter, Text: Anne Brontë's Narrative *Tenant* and the Problematic of the Gothic Sequel', *ELH*, 51, 719–45.
Green, L. (2001) *Educating Women: Cultural Conflict and Victorian Literature*, Athens: Ohio University Press.
Greenblatt, S. (1988) *Shakespearean Negotiations*, Oxford: Oxford University Press.
Greene, S. (1994) 'Apocalypse When? *Shirley*'s Vision and the Politics of Reading', *Studies in the Novel*, 26, 350–71.
Gregg, V. (1995) *Jean Rhys's Imagination: Reading and Writing the Creole*, Chapel Hill: University of North Carolina Press.
Griffin, B. (2003) 'Class, Gender, and Liberalism in Parliament 1868–1882: The Case of the Married Women's Property Acts', *Historical Journal*, 46, 59–87.
Grudin, P. (1977) 'Jane and the Other Mrs Rochester: Excess and Restraint in *Jane Eyre*', *Novel*, 10, 145–58.
Gruner, E. (1997) 'Plotting the Mother: Caroline Norton, Helen Huntingdon, and Isabel Vane', *Tulsa Studies in Women's Literature*, 16, 303–25.
Gruner, E. (1999) 'Born and Made: Sisters, Brothers, and the Deceased Wife's Sister Bill', *Signs*, 24, 423–47.
Gullette, M. (1990) 'The Puzzling Case of the Deceased Wife's Sister: Nineteenth Century England deals with a Second-Chance Plot', *Representations*, 31, 132–66.
Hager, K. (2010) *Dickens and the Rise of Divorce: The Failed-Marriage Plot and the Novel Tradition*, Farnham: Ashgate.
Halsbury, Lord (1908) *The Laws of England*, London: Butterworths.
Hamilton, S. (1995) *Criminals, Idiots, Women, and Minors: Victorian Writing by Women on Women*, London: Broadview Press.
Hamilton, S. (2001) 'Making History with Frances Power Cobbe: Victorian Feminism, Domestic Violence, and the Language of Imperialism', *Victorian Studies*, 43, 437–60.
Hammerton, J. (1990) 'Victorian Marriage and the Law of Matrimonial Cruelty', *Victorian Studies*, 33, 269–92.
Hammerton, J. (1992) *Cruelty and Companionship: Conflict in Nineteenth Century Married Life*, London: Routledge.
Harsh, C. (1994) *Subversive Heroines: Feminist Resolutions of Social Crisis in the Condition of England Novels*, Ann Arbor: Michigan University Press.
Harte, J. (1996) 'Constitutional Aspects of the English Monarchy and the Church of England', *Comparative Law and Culture*, 4, 51–109.
Hearne, J. (1990) 'The Wide Sargasso Sea: A West Indian Reflection', in P. Frickey (ed.), *Critical Perspectives on Jean Rhys*, New York: Three Continents Press.

Heilbrun, C. and J. Resnick (1990) 'Convergences: Law, Literature and Feminism', *Yale Law Journal*, 99, 1913–53.
Heinzelman, S. (2010) *Riding the Black Ram: Law, Literature, and Gender*, Stanford: Stanford University Press.
Henriques, U. (1967) 'Bastardy and the New Poor Law', *Past and Present*, 37, 103–29.
Hewitt, M. (2006) 'Why the Notion of Victorian Britain Does Make Sense', *Victorian Studies*, 48, 395–438.
Heywood, C. (1987) 'Yorkshire Slavery in *Wuthering Heights*', *Review of English Studies*, ns. 38, 184–98.
Hill, B. (1974) 'Fox and Burke: the Whig Party and the Question of Principles 1784–1789', *English Historical Review*, 89, 1–24.
Himmelfarb. G. (2006) *The Moral Imagination: From Edmund Burke to Lionel Trilling*, New York: Ivan Dee.
Himmelfarb, G. (2007) *The Spirit of the Age: Victorian Essays*, New Haven: Yale University Press.
Hodge, J. (2005) '*Villette*'s Compulsory Education', *Studies in English Literature*, 45, 899–916.
Hodges, E. (1988) 'Writing in a Different Voice', *Texas Law Review*, 66, 629–40.
Holcombe, L. (1983) *Wives and Property: Reform of the Married Women's Property Law in Nineteenth Century England*, Toronto: University of Toronto Press.
Homans, M. (1998) *Royal Representations: Queen Victoria and British Culture 1837–76*, Chicago: University of Chicago Press.
Hughes, J. (2000) 'The Affective World of Charlotte Brontë's *Villette*', *Studies in English Literature*, 40, 711–26.
Hughes, T. (2003) *Collected Poems*, London: Faber and Faber.
Hunt, A. and G. Whickham (1994) *Foucault and Law: Towards a Sociology of Law as Governance*, London: Pluto.
Hutchinson, A. (1988) *Dwelling on the Threshold: Critical Essays in Modern Legal Thought*, Toronto: Carswell.
Ingham, P. (1996) *The Language of Gender and Class: Transformation in the Victorian Novel*, London: Routledge.
Ingham, P. (2006) *The Brontës*, Oxford: Oxford University Press.
Irigaray, L. (1977) *The Sex Which is Not One*, Ithaca: Cornell University Press.
Jackson, A. (1982) 'The Question of Credibility in Anne Brontë's *The Tenant of Wildfell Hall*', *English Studies*, 63, 198–206.
Jacobs, N. (1986) 'Gender and Layered Narrative in *Wuthering Heights* and *The Tenant of Wildfell Hall*', *Journal of Narrative Technique*, 16, 204–19.
Jay, E. (1997) 'Introduction' to E. Gaskell, *The Life of Charlotte Brontë*, Harmondsworth: Penguin.
Jennings, I. (1971) *The British Constitution*, Cambridge: Cambridge University Press.
Jordan, A. (1998) '*Gorham v Bishop of Exeter*: A Case of Anglican Anxieties', *Ecclesiastical Law Journal*, 5, 104–11.
Kaplan, C. (1986) *Sea Changes: Essays on Culture and Feminism*, London: Verso.

Kaplan, C. (1996) 'Girl Talk: *Jane Eyre* and the Romance of Women's Narration', *Novel*, 30, 5–31.

Kaplan, C. (2007) *Victoriana: Histories, Fictions, Criticism*, Edinburgh: Edinburgh University Press.

Kaye, R. (1995) 'A Good Woman on Five Thousand Pounds: *Jane Eyre, Vanity Fair* and Literary Rivalry', *Studies in English Literature*, 35, 723–39.

Kerber, L. (1988) 'Separate Spheres, Female Worlds, Woman's Place: The Rhetoric of Women's History', *Journal of American History*, 75, 9–39.

Kermode, F. (1975) *The Classic*, London: Faber and Faber.

Kloepper, D. (1989) *The Unspeakable Mother: Forbidden Discourse in Jean Rhys and HD*, Ithaca: Cornell University Press.

Kramnick, I. (1977) *The Rage of Edmund Burke: Portrait of an Ambivalent Conservative*, New York: Basic Books.

Kreilkamp, I. (2005) *Voice and the Victorian Storyteller*, Cambridge: Cambridge University Press.

Kritzman, L. (1988) *Politics, Philosophy, Culture: Interviews and Other Writings 1977–1984*, London: Routledge.

Kuper, A. (2009) *Incest and Influence: The Private Life of Bourgeois England*, Cambridge, MA: Harvard University Press.

Lacey, N. (1998) *Unspeakable Subjects: Feminist Essays on Legal and Social Theory*, Oxford: Hart.

Langland, E. (1989) *Anne Brontë: The Other One*, London: Macmillan.

Laqueur, T. (1982) 'The Queen Caroline Affair: Politics as Art in the Reign of George IV', *Journal of Modern History*, 54, 417–66.

Lawson, K. (1980) 'The Dissenting Voice: *Shirley*'s Vision of Women and Christianity', *Studies in English Literature*, 29, 729–43.

Le Gallez, P. (1990) *The Rhys Woman*, London: Macmillan.

Leavis, F. and Q. Leavis (1969) *Lectures in America*, London: Chatto and Windus.

Leckie, B. (1999) *Culture and Adultery: The Novel, the Newspaper, and the Law 1857–1914*, Philadelphia: University of Pennsylvania Press.

Leff, A. (1978) 'Law And', *Yale Law Journal*, 87, 989–1011.

Lemmings, D. (1996) 'Marriage and the Law in the Eighteenth Century: Hardwicke's Marriage Act of 1753', *Historical Journal*, 39, 339–60.

Levine, P. (1990) 'The Humanising Influences of Five o'Clock Tea: Victorian Feminist Periodicals', *Victorian Studies*, 33, 293–306.

Litvak, J. (1988) 'Charlotte Brontë and the Scene of Instruction: Authority and Subversion in *Villette*', *Nineteenth Century Studies*, 42, 467–89.

Lovell-Smith, R. (1994) 'Childhood and Adoption in Scott and the Writing of *Wuthering Heights*', *Scottish Literary Journal*, 21, 24–31.

Macfarlane, A. (1980) 'Illegitimacy and Illegitimates in English History', in P. Laslett, K. Oosterveen and M. Smith (eds), *Bastardy and its Comparative History*, London: Arnold.

Maine, H. (1906) *Ancient Law*, New York: Holt.

Manchester, C. (1988) 'Lord Campbell's Act: England's First Obscenity Statute', *Journal of Legal History*, 9, 223–41.

Manchester, C. (1991) 'A History of the Crime of Obscene Libel', *Journal of Legal History*, 12, 36–57.
Matus, J. (1995) *Unstable Bodies: Victorian Representations of Sexuality and Maternity*, Manchester: Manchester University Press.
Matus, J. (2002) 'Strong Family Likeness: *Jane Eyre* and *The Tenant of Wildfell Hall*', in H. Glen (ed.), *The Cambridge Companion to the Brontës*, Cambridge: Cambridge University Press.
McCandless, P. (1981) 'Liberty and Lunacy: The Victorians and Wrongful Confinement', in A. Scull (ed.), *Madhouses, Mad-Doctors and Madmen: A Social History of Psychiatry in the Victorian Era*, Philadelphia: University of Pennsylvania Press.
McCandless, P. (1983) 'Dangerous to Themselves and Others: the Victorian Debate over the Prevention of Wrongful Confinement', *Journal of British Studies*, 23, 84–104.
McGlynn, C. and I. Ward (2009) 'Pornography, Pragmatism and Proscription', *Journal of Law and Society*, 36, 327–51.
McKelvey, W. (2007) *The English Cult of Literature: Devoted Readers 1774–1880*, Charlottesville: University Press of Virginia.
McMaster, J. (1982) 'Imbecile Laughter and Desperate Earnest in *The Tenant of Wildfell Hall*', *Modern Language Quarterly*, 43, 352–68.
McNay, L. (1992) *Foucault and Feminism*, London: Polity Press.
Meyer, S. (1990) 'Colonialism and the Figurative Strategy of *Jane Eyre*', *Victorian Studies*, 33, 247–68.
Meyer, S. (1996) *Imperialism at Home: Race and Victorian Women's Fiction*, Ithaca: Cornell University Press.
Michie, E. (1992) 'From Simianized Irish to Oriental Despots: Heathcliff, Rochester and Racial Difference', *Novel*, 25, 125–40.
Mill, J. (1955) *On Liberty*, Chicago: Chicago University Press.
Mill, J. (1987) *Utilitarianism and Other Essays*, Harmondsworth, Penguin.
Mill, J. (1988) *The Subjection of Women*, Indianapolis: Hackett.
Mill, J. (1989) *Autobiography*, Harmondsworth: Penguin.
Miller, J. (1975) *The Disappearance of God: Five Nineteenth Century Novels*, Evanston: University of Illinois Press.
Miller, L. (2001) *The Brontë Myth*, London, Jonathan Cape.
Moglen, H. (1984) *Charlotte Brontë: The Self-Conceived*, Madison: University of Wisconsin Press.
Montrose, L. (1989) 'Professing the Renaissance: The Poetics and Politics of Culture', in A. Veeser (ed.), *The New Historicism*, London: Routledge.
Moorman, J. (1973) *A History of the Church in England*, London: A. and C. Black.
Morris, P. (1991) 'Incest or Survival Strategy? Plebeian Marriage within the Prohibited Degrees in Somerset 1730–1835', *Journal of the History of Sexuality*, 2, 235–65.
Morse, D. (2001) 'I Speak of Those I do Know: Witnessing as Radical Gesture in *The Tenant of Wildfell Hall*', in J. Nash and B. Suess (eds), *New Approaches to the Literary Art of Anne Brontë*, Aldershot: Ashgate.

Munro, V. (2007) *Law and Politics at the Perimeter: Re-Evaluating Key Debates in Feminist Theory*, Oxford: Hart.

Musselthwaite, D. (1987) *Partings Welded Together: Politics and Desire in the Nineteenth Century Novel*, London: Methuen.

Nestor, P. (2000) 'Introduction' to E. Brontë, *Wuthering Heights*, Harmondsworth: Penguin.

Newsom, R. (1991) '*Villette* and *Bleak House*: Authorizing Women', *Nineteenth Century Literature*, 46, 54–81.

Newsome, D. (1998) *The Victorian World Picture*, London: Harper Collins.

Newton, J. (1985) *Women, Power and Subversion: Social Strategies in British Fiction 1778–1860*, London: Methuen.

Nixon, C. (2007) *Family Ties in Victorian England*, New Haven: Yale University Press.

Nockles, P. (1994) *The Oxford Movement in Context: Anglican High Churchmanship 1760–1857*, Cambridge: Cambridge University Press.

Nussbaum, M. (1995) *Poetic Justice*, New York: Beacon Press.

O'Brien, C. (1997) *Edmund Burke*, London: Random House.

O'Brien, K. (2009) *Women and Enlightenment in Eighteenth Century Britain*, Cambridge: Cambridge University Press.

O'Halloran, K. (1999) *The Welfare of the Child: The Principle and the Law*, Aldershot: Ashgate.

O'Toole, T. (1999) 'Siblings and Suitors in the Narrative Architecture of *The Tenant of Wildfell Hall*', *Studies in English Literature*, 39, 715–31.

Oates, J. (1985) 'Romance and Anti-Romance: From Brontë's *Jane Eyre* to Rhys's *Wide Sargasso Sea*', *Virginia Quarterly Review*, 61, 44–58.

Okin, S. (1983) 'Patriarchy and Married Women's Property in England: Questions on Some Current Views', *Eighteenth Century Studies*, 17, 121–38.

Oliva, J. (2010) 'Church, State and Establishment in the United Kingdom in the 21st Century: Anachronism or Idiosyncracy?' *Public Law*, 482–504.

Orwell, G. (1984) *The Essays of George Orwell*, Harmondsworth: Penguin.

Paglia, C. (1990) *Sexual Personae: Art and Decadence from Nefertiti to Emily Dickinson*, New Haven: Yale University Press.

Paine, T. (1985) *The Rights of Man*, Harmondsworth: Penguin.

Parker, S. (1987) 'The Marriage Act 1753: A Case Study in Family Law-Making', *International Journal of Law and the Family*, 1, 133–54.

Perkin, J. (1989) *Women and Marriage in Nineteenth Century England*, London: Routledge.

Perry, R. (2004) *Novel Relations: The Transformation of Kinship in English Literature and Culture 1748–1818*, Cambridge: Cambridge University Press.

Petch, S. (2007) 'Law, Literature, and Victorian Studies', *Victorian Literature and Culture*, 35, 361–84.

Peters, J. (2005) 'Law, Literature, and the Vanishing Real: On the Future of an Interdisciplinary Illusion', *Proceedings of the Modern Language Association of America*, 120, 442–53.

Plath, S. (1985) *Selected Poems*, London: Faber and Faber.

Pollak, E. (2003) *Incest and the English Novel 1684–1814*, Baltimore: Johns Hopkins University Press.
Poovey, M. (1989) *Uneven Developments: The Ideology of Gender in Mid Victorian England*, London: Virago.
Porter, D. (1976) 'Of Heroines and Victims: Jean Rhys and *Jane Eyre*', *Massachusetts Review*, 17, 540–52.
Probert, R. (2008) 'Examining Law through the Lens of Literature: The Formation of Marriage in Eighteenth Century England', *Law and Humanities*, 2, 29–48.
Probert, R. (2009) *Marriage Law and Practice in the Long Eighteenth Century*, Cambridge: Cambridge University Press.
Pykett, L. (1992) *The Improper Feminine: The Women's Sensation Novel and the New Woman Writing*, London: Routledge.
Qualls, B. (1982) *The Secular Pilgrims of Victorian Fiction*, Cambridge: Cambridge University Press.
Rabinow, P. (1997) *Essential Works of Foucault 1954–1984: Ethics, Subjectivity and Truth*, Harmondsworth: Penguin.
Reed, J. (2002) 'Laws, the Legal World, and Politics', in P. Brantlinger and W. Thesing (eds), *A Companion to the Victorian Novel*, Oxford: Blackwell.
Reichman, R. (2009) *The Affective Life of Law: Legal Modernism and the Literary Imagination*, Stanford: Stanford University Press.
Rhys, J. (2000) *The Wide Sargasso Sea*, Harmondsworth: Penguin.
Rich, A. (1979) *On Lies, Secrets and Silence: Selected Prose 1966–1978*, New York: Norton.
Richardson, A. (1985) 'The Dangers of Sympathy: Sibling Incest in English Romantic Poetry', *Studies in English Literature*, 25, 737–54.
Richardson, S. (1985) *Clarissa*, Harmondsworth: Penguin.
Rogers, P. (2003) 'Tory Brontë: *Shirley* and the Man', *Nineteenth Century Literature*, 58, 141–75.
Rorty, R. (1989) *Contingency, Irony, and Solidarity*, Cambridge: Cambridge University Press.
Rorty, R. (1998) *Truth and Progress: Philosophical Papers, Volume 3*, Cambridge: Cambridge University Press.
Rorty, R. (1999) *Philosophy and Social Hope*, Harmondsworth: Penguin.
Rorty, R. (2007) *Philosophy as Cultural Politics*, Cambridge: Cambridge University Press.
Rowe, K. (1983) 'Fairy-Born and Human-Bred: Jane Eyre's Education in Romance', in E. Abel, M. Hirsch and E. Langland (eds), *The Voyage In: Fictions of Female Development*, Dartmouth: University Press of New England.
Russell, P. (2005) 'Wife-Stories: Narrating Marriage and Self in the Life of Jane Franklin', *Victorian Studies*, 48, 36–57.
Sacks, J. (1993) *From Jacobite to Conservative: Reaction and Orthodoxy in England 1688–1832*, Cambridge: Cambridge University Press,
Said, E. (1994) *Culture and Imperialism*, London: Vintage.
Said, E. (2003) *Orientalism*, Harmondsworth: Penguin.
Sanger, C. (1970) 'The Structure of *Wuthering Heights*', in I. Gregor (ed.), *The Brontës: A Collection of Critical Essays*, Englewood Cliffs: Prentice-Hall.

Saunders, V. (2001) 'Women, Fiction and the Marketplace', in J. Shattock (ed.), *Women and Literature in Britain 1800–1900*, Cambridge: Cambridge University Press.
Sawicki, J. (1991) *Disciplining Foucault: Feminism, Power, and the Body*, London: Routledge.
Schramm, J. (2000) *Testimony and Advocacy in Victorian Law, Literature, and Theology*, Cambridge: Cambridge University Press.
Scull, A. (1981) 'The Social History of Psychiatry in the Victorian Era', in A. Scull (ed.), *Madhouses, Mad-Doctors and Madmen: The Social History of Psychiatry in the Victorian Era*, Philadelphia: University of Pennsylvania Press.
Scull, A. (1993) *The Most Solitary of Afflictions: Madness and Society in Britain 1700–1900*, Newhaven: Yale University Press.
Seaton, J. (1999) 'Law and Literature: Works, Criticism, and Theory', *Yale Journal of Law and Humanities*, 11, 479–507.
Senf, C. (1979) '*Jane Eyre*: The Prison-house of Victorian Marriage', *Journal of Women's Studies in Literature*, 1, 353–9.
Shanley, M. (1989) *Feminism, Marriage and the Law: Victorian England 1850–1895*, Princeton: Princeton University Press.
Shapiro, A. (1968) 'Public Themes and Private Lives: Social Criticism in *Shirley*', *Papers on Literature and Language*, 4, 74–84.
Sharpe, J. (1993) *Allegories of Empire: The Figure of Woman in the Colonial Text*, Minneapolis: University of Minnesota Press.
Shattock, J. (2001) 'The Construction of the Woman Writer', in J. Shattock (ed.), *Women and Literature in Britain 1800–1900*, Cambridge: Cambridge University Press.
Sheridan, A. (1980) *Michel Foucault – the Will to Truth*, London: Tavistock.
Showalter, E. (1975) 'Review Essay', *Signs*, 1, 234–7.
Showalter, E. (1977) *A Literature of their Own: British Women Novelists from Brontë to Lessing*, Princeton: Princeton University Press.
Showalter, E. (1987) *The Female Malady: Women, Madness and English Culture 1830–1980*, London: Virago.
Shuttleworth, S. (1996) *Charlotte Brontë and Modern Psychology*, Cambridge: Cambridge University Press.
Sigel, L. (2002) *Governing Pleasures: Pornography and Social Change in England 1815–1914*, New Brunswick: Rutgers University Press.
Silver, B. (1983) 'The Reflecting Reader in *Villette*', in E. Abel, M. Hirsch and E. Langland (eds), *The Voyage In: Fictions of Female Development*, Dartmouth: University Press of New England.
Simpson, A. (1985) *A History of the Land Law*, Oxford: Oxford University Press.
Small, H. (1996) *Love's Madness: Medicine, the Novel and Female Insanity 1800–1865*, Oxford: Oxford University Press.
Smith, E. (2007) *Selected Letters of Charlotte Brontë*, Oxford: Oxford University Press.
Solomon, E. (1959) 'The Incest Theme in *Wuthering Heights*', *Nineteenth Century Fiction*, 14, 80–3.

Spacks, P. (1975) *The Female Imagination*, New York: Knopf.
Spivak, G. (1985) 'Three Women's Texts and a Critique of Imperialism', *Critical Inquiry*, 12, 243–61.
Spring, E. (1988) The Strict Settlement: Its Role in Family History', *Economic History Review*, 41, 454–60.
Spring, E. (1993) *Law, Land, and Family: Aristocratic Inheritance in England 1300–1800*, Chapel Hill: University of North Carolina Press.
St Clair, W. (2007) *The Reading Nation in the Romantic Period*, Cambridge: Cambridge University Press.
Stokes, J. (1984) 'Rachel's "Terrible Beauty": An Actress among the Novelists', *ELH*, 51, 771–93.
Stone, L. (1990) *Road to Divorce*, Oxford: Oxford University Press.
Surridge, L. (2005) *Bleak Houses: Marital Violence in Victorian Fiction*, Athens: Ohio University Press.
Sutherland, J. (1996) *Is Heathcliff a Murderer?* Oxford: Oxford University Press.
Sutherland, J. (2006) *Victorian Literature: Writers, Publishers, Readers*, Basingstoke: Palgrave.
Suzuki, A. (2006) *Madness at Home: The Psychiatrist, the Patient and the Family in England 1820–1860*, Berkeley: University of California Press.
Talley, L. (2001) 'Anne Brontë's Method of Social Protest in *The Tenant of Wildfell Hall*', in J. Nash and B. Seuss (eds), *New Approaches to the Literary Art of Ann Brontë*, Aldershot: Ashgate.
Thomas, S. (1999) 'The Tropical Extravagance of Bertha Mason', *Victorian Literature and Culture*, 27, 1–17.
Thompson, E. (1991) *The Making of the English Working Class*, Harmondsworth: Penguin.
Thompson, N. (1996) *Reviewing Sex: Gender and the Reception of Victorian Novels*, London: Macmillan.
Thormahlen, M. (1999) *The Brontës and Religion*, Cambridge: Cambridge University Press.
Thormahlen, M. (2001) 'Aspects of Love in *The Tenant of Wildfell Hall*', in J. Nash and B. Seuss (eds), *New Approaches to the Literary Art of Anne Brontë*, Aldershot: Ashgate.
Thorpe, M. (1990) 'The Other Side: *Wide Sargasso Sea* and *Jane Eyre*', in P. Frickey (ed.), *Critical Perspectives on Jean Rhys*, New York: Three Continents Press.
Tomes, N. (1999) 'Devils in the Heart: A Nineteenth Century Perspective on Women and Depression', *Transactions and Studies of the College of Physicians of Philadelphia*, 5 ser. 13, 363–86.
Tosh, J. (1999) *A Man's Place: Masculinity and the Middle-Class Home in Victorian England*, Newhaven: Yale University Press.
Treitel, G. (1984) 'Jane Austen and the Law', *Law Quarterly Review*, 100, 549–86.
Tromp, M. (2000) *The Private Rod: Marital Violence, Sensation and the Law in Victorian Britain*, Charlottesville: University Press of Virginia.

Turkel, G. (1990) 'Michel Foucault: Law, Power, and Knowledge', *Journal of Law and Society*, 17, 170–93.
Turner, J, (1995) 'Teaching Law through Literature', *University of Queensland Law Journal*, 14, 61–9.
Uglow, J. (1999) *Elizabeth Gaskell*, London: Faber and Faber.
Vernon, J. (2005) 'Historians and the Victorian Studies Question: Response', *Victorian Studies*, 47, 272–9.
Vickery, A. (2003) *The Gentleman's Daugher: Women's Lives in Georgian England*, New Haven: Yale University Press.
Waddams, S (2000) *Sexual Slander in Nineteenth Century England: Defamation in the Ecclesiastical Courts 1815–1855*, Toronto: University of Toronto Press.
Ward, I. (1993) 'The Educative Ambition of Law and Literature', *Legal Studies*, 13, 323–31.
Ward, I. (2004) *The English Constitution: Myths and Realities*, Oxford: Hart.
Ward, I. (2009) 'The Prejudices of Mary Hays', *International Journal of Law in Context*, 5, 131–46.
Ward, I. (2010) 'The Perversions of History: Constitutionalism and Revolution in Burke's *Reflections*', *Liverpool Law Review*, 10, 207–32.
Ward, T. (1997) 'Law, Common Sense and the Authority of Science: Expert Witnesses and Criminal Insanity in England c. 1840–1940', *Social and Legal Studies*, 6, 343–62.
Watt, G. (2009) *Equity Stirring: The Story of Justice beyond the Law*, Oxford: Hart.
Weinrib, E. (1988) 'Legal Formalism: On the Immanent Rationality of Law', *Yale Law Journal*, 97, 949–1016.
Weisberg, R. (1992) *Poethics and Other Strategies of Law and Literature*, New York: Columbia University Press.
West, R. (1997) *Caring for Justice*, New York: New York University Press.
Westcott, A. (2001) 'A Matter of Strong Prejudice: Gilbert Markham's Self Portrait', in J. Nash and B. Seuss (eds), *New Approaches to the Literary Art of Anne Brontë*, Aldershot: Ashgate.
Wiener, M. (2004) *Men of Blood: Violence, Manliness and Criminal Justice in Victorian England*, Cambridge: Cambridge University Press.
Williams, J. (1955) 'Obscenity in Modern English Law', *Law and Contemporary Problems*, 20, 630–47.
Williams, M. (2002) *Empty Justice: One Hundred Years of Law, Literature and Philosophy*, London: Cavendish.
Williams, M. (2005) *Secrets and Laws: Collected Essays in Law, Lives and Literature*, London: UCL Press.
Williams, P. (1991) *The Alchemy of Race and Rights*, Cambridge, MA: Harvard University Press.
Williams, R. (1963) *Culture and Society 1780–1950*, Harmondsworth: Penguin.
Wilkes, J. (2001) 'Remaking the Canon', in J. Shattock (ed.), *Women and Literature in Britain 1800–1900*, Cambridge: Cambridge University Press.
Wilson, A. (1999) *God's Funeral*, London: John Murray.

Wilson, A. (2002) *The Victorians*, London: Hutchinson.
Wilt, J. (2002) '*Shirley*: Reflections on Marrying Moores', *Victorian Literature and Culture*, 30, 1–17.
Winnifrith, T. (1988) *The Brontës and their Background: Romance and Reality*, London: Macmillan.
Winnifrith, T. (1996) 'Charlotte and Emily Brontë: A Study in the Rise and Fall of Literary Reputations', *Yearbook of English Studies*, 26, 14–24.
Wise, T. and J. Symington (eds) (1932) *The Brontës: Their Lives, Friendships and Correspondence*, 2 vols, London: Shakespeare Head Brontë.
Witte, J. (2003) 'Ishmael's band: The Sin And Crime of Illegitimacy Reconsidered', *Punishment and Society*, 5, 327–45.
Wolff, M. (1964) 'Victorian Study: An Interdisciplinary Essay', *Victorian Studies*, 8, 59–70.
Woolf, V. (1998) *A Room of One's Own and Three Guineas*, Oxford: Oxford University Press.
Wright, D. (2002) 'The Crisis of Child Custody: A History of the Birth of Family Law in England', *Columbia Journal of Gender and Law*, 11, 175–270.
Wright, D. (2004) 'Well-Behaved Women Don't Make History: Rethinking English Family, Law, and History', *Wisconsin Women's Law Journal*, 19, 211–318.
Yaeger, P. (1988) 'Violence in the Sitting Room: *Wuthering Heights* and the Woman's Novel', *Genre*, 21, 203–29.
Zedner, L. (1991) *Women, Crime and Custody in Victorian England*, Oxford: Oxford University Press.
Zlotnik, S. (1991) 'Luddism, Medievalism and Women's History in *Shirley*: Charlotte Bronte's Revisionist Tracts', *Novel*, 24, 282–95.
Zonana, J. (1993) 'The Sultan and the Slave: Feminist Orientalism and the Structure of *Jane Eyre*', *Signs*, 18, 592–617.
Zunshine, L. (2005) *Bastards and Foundlings: Illegitimacy in Eighteenth Century England*, Columbus: Ohio State University Press.

Cases

Ball v Ball 2 Sim. 35 (1827)
Blisset's Case 98 Eng. Rep. 899 (1767)
Cranmer (ex p) 12 Ves, Jun. 445 (1806)
Curll 2 Str. 788 (1727)
Delavel (R v) 97 Eng. Rep. 913 (1763)
De Manneville v De Manneville 32 Eng. Rep. 762 (Ch. 1804)
Dysart v Dysart 163 Eng. Rep. 992 (1847)
Evans v Evans 161 Eng. Rep. 467 (1790)
Eyre v Countess of Shaftesbury 24 Eng. Rep. 659 (Ch. 1722)
Fynn (in re) 63 Eng. Rep. 205 (1848)
Gorham v Bishop of Exeter 2 Rob. Eccl. 1 (1849)
Gosling v Veley 12 QB 328 (1850)

Greenhill v Greenhill 163 Eng. Rep. 162 (1836)
Hicklin LR 3 QBD 371 (1868)
Hope v Hope 44 Eng. Rep. 572 (1857)
Jackson (R v) 1 QB 671 (1891)
Lavallee v the Queen [1990] SCR 852.
Lord Donegal's Case 2 Ves. Sen. 407 (1751)
Martin v Martin 29 LR–Ch. 106 (1860)
Milford v Milford 38 LR–Ch. 63 (1869)
M'Clellan (ex p) 33 Eng. Rep. 45 (1831)
Nottidge, The Times Law Reports 27 June 1849.
Reiter (R v) 2 WLR 638 [1954]
Ridgeway v Darwin 8 Ves. 65 (1802)
Rundle's Case Eng. Rep. Deras. 482 (1855)
Secker and Warburg (R v) 1 WLR 1138 [1954]
Spence (re) 41 Eng. Rep. 939 (Ch. 1847)
Talbot v Earl of Shrewsbury 41 Eng. Rep. 259 (Ch. 1840)
Watson and Watson v Farnemouth, 53 Ann. Reg. 136 (1881)
Wellesley v Duke of Beaufort 27 Ann. Reg. 297 (1827)
Westmeath v Westmeath 162 Eng. Rep. 992 (1826)
Wilkes 4 Burr. 2527 (1768)

Index

Ackroyd, Peter 98
Act of Settlement (1700) 109
Alleged Lunatics Friend Society 74
Allen, Anita 72
Aristodemou, Maria 68–9, 95, 142
Arnold, Thomas 112
Armstrong, Nancy 10, 12, 68, 84, 130–2, 141
Athenaeum, The 43, 85
Atlas, The 71, 97
Austen, Jane 7, 65–6
   Mansfield Park 66
   Northanger Abbey 83
   Sense and Sensibility 83
Austin, John 14, 72
   Province of Jurisprudence Determined 14

Bagehot, Walter 103
   The English Constitution 103
Baldwin, Stanley 99
Ball (1827) 35
Bataille, Georges 66
Bede, the Venerable 98
Bentham, Jeremy 1–2, 4, 14
   Principles of Morals and Legislation 14
Best, Geoffrey 100
Blackstone, Sir William 16, 30, 52, 101
   Commentaries 16, 52
Blake, William 98
Blisset (1767) 35
Bodichon, Barbara Leigh Smith 27, 39
Bolingbroke, Oliver St John, Viscount 64
Bonaparte, Napoleon 99
Book of Common Prayer 111

Braddon, Mary Elizabeth 80
   Lady Audley's Secret 80
Bright, John 65
Britannia, The 49
Brontë, Anne 12, 24–5, 28, 33, 35–6, 44–6, 49, 55, 67, 71, 108, 113, 124, 126, 130
   The Tenant of Wildfell Hall 12, 18–19, 22–3, 25–34, 36, 40–7, 49–51, 55, 61, 67, 71, 97–8, 125–6, 143
Brontë, Branwell 45–6, 51, 81, 122–3
Brontë, Charlotte 8, 9, 14, 20–1, 24, 45, 48, 51, 55, 66, 71–3, 81–5, 87, 89, 93, 96, 98–101, 103–9, 112–15, 117, 119, 121, 124–30, 132–3, 139, 141–4
   Jane Eyre 3, 10, 16, 21, 23, 71–4, 79, 81–91, 93, 96–8, 125–7, 130, 132–3, 140–1, 143
   Shirley 9–10, 12, 16, 24, 51, 90, 96–7, 99, 101–8, 112–21, 125–6, 140
   The Professor 127
   Villette 22, 24, 121, 124–30, 132–4, 143
Brontë, Emily 3, 24, 45, 48–51, 53–6, 62, 66–9, 71, 82, 108, 124, 128, 130
   'The Butterfly' 70
   'To Imagination' 2
   'The Old Stoic' 69
   'The Philosophy' 69
   Wuthering Heights 19, 21–4, 48–69, 71, 90, 97–8, 108, 125, 133, 140, 142
Brontë, Patrick 64, 104, 110, 124
Brougham, Henry Lord 13, 17, 77, 135

Browning, Elizabeth Barrett 65
Browning, Robert 7
Buckle, Henry 100
Bucknill, John 79
Burke, Edmund 55, 99–103, 105, 112
  A Philosophical Inquiry 105
  Reflections on the Revolution in France 100–3, 105, 112
Butler, Josephine 27, 38, 80
Byron, Lord 51

Caird, Mona 16, 18, 67, 80
Campbell, John Lord 22, 135
Camus, Albert 67
Carlyle, Thomas 9, 115
  Sign of the Times 115
Catholic Emancipation Act (1829) 14, 111
Chadwick, Owen 110
Chandler, James 6
Chartism 105, 117
Cheyne, John 80
Chorley, Henry Fothergill 85
Christian Remembrancer, The 44, 57
Church Discipline Act (1840) 111
Clandestine Marriage Act (1753) 15
Cobbe, Frances Power 8–9, 16, 18–19, 25, 80, 130
  Criminals, Idiots, Women and Minors 18, 80
Cockburn, Henry Lord 135
Coleridge, John, Lord Chief Justice 17
Coleridge, Hartley 100
Coleridge, Samuel Taylor 1–2, 4
Collins, Wilkie 80
  The Woman in White 80
Colls, Robert 98
Conolly, John 75, 77, 86
  Enquiry Concerning the Indication of Lunacy 75
  Treatment of the Insane without Medical Restraint 86
Constable, Marianne 144
Cover, Robert 5

Cowper, William 108, 113
Cox, Joseph Mason 73
Cranmer (1806) 76
Cranworth, Robert Lord 38
Croly, George 100
Curll (1727) 134

Daily News 96, 108
Dallas, Eneas Sweetland 11
Darwin, Charles 110
  On the Origin of Species 110
Davies, Stevie 68
De Manneville (1804) 34
Dean and Chapter Act (1840) 111
Delaval (1763) 35
Derrida, Jacques 92
Deuteronomy 64
Dickens, Charles 7, 13, 78
  Bleak House 4
  Dombey and Son 13
  Hard Times 104
  Pickwick Papers 4
Divorce Court 17, 19, 25, 32, 74, 134
Dobell, Sidney 62
Dolin, Kieran 5, 7
Dworkin, Ronald 129

Eagleton, Terry 55, 101, 105, 107
Ecclesiastical Commission (1835) 110–11
Eldon, John Scott, Lord 75
Eliot, George 6, 10–11, 26, 74
  Adam Bede 26
Ellis, Sarah Stickney 7–9, 24, 29, 43, 102
  Women of England 7–8, 102
  The Young Lady's Reader 8, 10–11
Elmy, Elizabeth Wolstenholme 46
Engels, Friedrich 9
English Matron, The 102
Ermarth, Elizabeth Deeds 22
Established Church Act (1836) 111
Examiner, The 29, 50–1
Eyre (1722) 34

Fanon, Frantz   70
  The Wretched of the Earth   70
Finn, Margot   7
Fiss, Owen   129
Flint, Kate   10
Fonblanque, Albert   97
Forcade, Eugene   117, 120
Foucault, Michel   62, 130–1, 138–9, 143
  History of Sexuality   131

Gaskell, Elizabeth   11, 21, 49, 65–6, 89, 104, 108, 117, 122–5, 129, 141
  Life of Charlotte Brontë   21, 104, 117, 122–4, 129
  Mary Barton   6, 104
Gaskell, William   123
Genesis, Book of   52
George IV, King   111
Glen, Heather   72, 117
Gilbert, Sandra   10, 12, 23
Gorham (1849)   112
Gosling (1850)   111
Graham's Magazine   49
Greenblatt, Stephen   6
Greg, William Rathbone   10
Guardian, The   128
Gubar, Susan   10, 12, 23
Guardianship of Infants Act (1886)   46
Guardianship of Infants Act (1925)   46

Hale, Sir Matthew   101
  History of the Common Law of England   101
Hardwicke, Philip Yorke, Lord   15
Harsh, Constance   12
Haworth Parsonage   21, 45, 114
Hays, Mary   9, 81
  Victim of Prejudice   81
Hicklin (1868)   135–6
Hooker, Richard   101–2, 112
  Laws of Ecclesiastical Polity   101–2
Howells, William Dean   43

Howitt, William   97
Hughes, Ted   66

Infant Custody Act (1839)   19, 35
Infant Custody Act (1873)   37
Infant Custody Act (1886)   38
Ingham, Patricia   12, 121
Irigaray, Luce   87

Jackson (1891)   46
Jefferson, William   18
Jerrold's Weekly Newspaper   49
Johnson, Samuel   52, 101
Judicature Act   37, 40

Kames, Henry Home, Lord   119
Kaplan, Cora   7, 72
Keighley Mechanics Institute   104
Kingsley, Charles   43, 96

Lancet, The   75
Law Amendment Society   13, 39
Leavis, Frank Raymond   57
Leckie, Barbara   19
Leeds Mercury   104, 107–8
LeFanu, Sheridan   80–1
  The Rose and the Key   81
Leviticus   63–5
Lewes, George Henry   3, 21, 49, 71, 96, 104, 126
Lewis, Sarah   8–9
  Women's Mission   8
Literary World, The   43
London and Westminster Review   1
Lord Donegal's Case (1751)   75
Luddite riots   104
Lunacy Commissions   74–7, 79
Lyndhurst, John Copley, Lord   15, 63
Lytton, Henry Bulwer   80
  Lucretia   80

Mackay, Angus   66
Major, John   99
Mansfield, William Murray, Lord Chief Justice   35

Marriage Act (1835)   15, 63–4
Married Women's Property Act
   (1870)   40
Married Women's Property Act
   (1882)   46
Martin (1860)   37
Martineau, Harriet   45, 128
Matrimonial Causes Act (1857)   17, 31, 37, 39
Matrimonial Causes Act (1878)   32
Matus, Jill   131
Maudsley, Henry   80
Mayhew, Sir Henry   104
   The London Poor   104
McKelvey, William   112
Medical Critic   10
Melbourne, William Lamb, Lord   27
Melville, Herman   7
Milford (1869)   37
Mill, Harriet Taylor   18, 38
Mill, John Stuart   1–3, 14, 16, 39, 78
   'Bentham'   1
   'Coleridge'   1
   On Liberty   14, 78
   The Subjection of Women   16
Miller, Hillis   79
Miller, Lucasta   72
Milton, John   67, 99, 118
Moglen, Helene   121
Monro, Henry   75
Montegut, Emile   56
Montrose, Louis   6
Morison, Alexander   79
   Outlines of Lectures on Mental Diseases   79
Mudie's Circulating Library   22
Municipal Corporations Act
   (1835)   14, 111

Newman, John Henry, Cardinal   9
Newton, Judith Lowder   141
North American Review, The   44, 49–50
Northern Star, The   105
Norton, Caroline   19, 28, 31, 33, 36–9

   English Laws for Women   28
   A Letter to the Queen   28
   Separation of Mother and Child   36
Norton, George   27, 37–8
Norton Conyers   81
Nottidge, 1849   76
Nussbaum, Martha   5, 143
Nussey, Ellen   48, 81, 114

Oastler, Richard   107
   Yorkshire Slavery   107
Obscene Publications Act
   (1857)   22, 135
Oliphant, Margaret   10, 12, 15, 21, 72, 89, 103, 117, 125, 141
Orwell, George   99

Paine, Tom   103
Paley, William   65
Patmore, Coventry   8, 24
   'The Angel in the House'   8
Peck, George Wilbur   49
Peel, Sir Robert   77, 110–11
Perry, Ruth   11
Petch, Stephen   7
Plath, Sylvia   66
Pluralities Act (1838)   111
Poor Law (1733)   52
Poor Law (1834)   14, 52, 111
Poor Law (1844)   53
Poovey, Mary   12, 23
Potter, Beatrix   65
Prichard, James   75, 79
   Treatise on Insanity   75
Probert, Rebecca   15
Pusey, Edward   112
Putnam's Monthly   133

Quarterly Review, The   71

Rambler, The   44
Rawfolds Mill   104
Reade, Charles   80
   Hard Cash   80
Reform Act (1832)   14, 110
Registration Act (1836)   111

Regulation of Proceedings under Commissions of Lunacy Act (1853) 75
Rhys, Jean 89–94
  Wide Sargasso Sea 89–94
Rich, Adrienne 72, 82, 141
Richardson, Samuel 45
Ridgway (1802) 75
Rigby, Elizabeth 71
Robinson, Lydia *see* Scott, Lady Lydia
Rorty, Richard 69, 129
Roscoe, William Caldwell 62
Rossetti, Dante Gabriel 67
Rubens, Peter Paul 132
  Cleopatra 132
Ruskin, John 8–9

Said, Edward 55, 70
Sartre, Jean-Paul 70
Scott, Lady Lydia 45, 122–4
Scott, Sir Edward 123–4
Scott, Sir Walter 45
Scott, Sir William 32
Scull, Andrew 78
Seymour, Edward 73
Shakespeare, William 99
  Coriolanus 116
Shanley, Mary 47
Sharpe's London Magazine 44
Shelley, Percy Bysshe 6
  'England in 1819' 6
Showalter, Elaine 12, 73, 80
Skelton, John 62
Small, Helen 88
Smith, George 71, 122
Smith Elder 83, 122–3
Society for the Prevention of Vice 135
Southey, Robert 125
Spacks, Patricia Meyer 12
Spectator, The 44, 48, 71
Spenser, Edmund 98

Spivak, Giyatri 89–90
Standard of Freedom, The 97
Stephen, James Fitzjames 9, 14
Surridge, Lisa 6, 12
Suzuki, Akihito 76
Swinburne, Walter 66
Sutherland, John 12, 23

Talfourd, Sergeant 37
Tennyson, Alfred Lord 99, 103
Thackeray, William Makepeace 65, 77, 81
Thorp Green Hall 45, 122
Times, The 97
Tithe Commutation Act (1836) 111
Trollope, Anthony 65

University College London 110

Victoria, Queen 15, 84

Ward, Mary 101
Weisberg, Richard 5
Wellington, Arthur Wellesley, Duke of 99
West, Robin 138
Westminster Review 96
Wilde, Oscar 143
Williams, Patricia 94
  The Alchemy of Race and Rights 94
Williams, Raymond 9
Wilson, Justice Bertha 47
Whipple, Edwin Percy 49–50
Wilkes (1768) 134
Winslow, Forbes 76
Wiseman, Nicholas, Cardinal 129
Wolff, Michael 23
Wollstonecraft, Mary 9, 27, 34, 81
  Maria 34, 81
  Mary 81
Woolf, Virginia 20, 87, 104
Wordsworth, William 99
Wright, Danaya 17